Language and Linguistics in a Complex World

Diskursmuster
Discourse Patterns

Edited by
Beatrix Busse and Ingo H. Warnke

Volume 32

Language and Linguistics in a Complex World

Edited by
Beatrix Busse, Nina Dumrukcic, and Ingo Kleiber

DE GRUYTER

Free access to the e-book version of this publication was made possible by the 40 academic libraries and initiatives that supported the open access transformation project in German Linguistics.

ISBN 978-3-11-162814-1
e-ISBN (PDF) 978-3-11-101743-3
e-ISBN (EPUB) 978-3-11-101789-1
ISSN 2701-0260
https://doi.org/10.1515/9783111017433

Library of Congress Control Number: 2022948172

Bibliographic information published by the Deutsche Nationalbibliothek
The Deutsche Nationalbibliothek lists this publication in the Deutsche Nationalbibliografie; detailed bibliographic data are available on the internet at http://dnb.dnb.de.

Typesetting: Integra Software Services Pvt. Ltd.

www.degruyter.com

Open-Access-Transformation in Linguistics

Open Access for excellent academic publications in the field of German Linguistics: Thanks to the support of 40 academic libraries and initiatives, 9 frontlist publications from 2023 can be published as gold open access, without any costs to the authors.

The following institutions and initiatives have contributed to the funding and thus promote the open access transformation in German linguistics and ensure free availability for everyone:

Dachinitiative „Hochschule.digital Niedersachsen" des Landes Niedersachsen
Universitätsbibliothek Augsburg
Freie Universität Berlin
Staatsbibliothek zu Berlin Preußischer Kulturbesitz
Technische Universität Berlin / Universitätsbibliothek
Universitätsbibliothek der Humboldt-Universität zu Berlin
Universität Bern
Universitätsbibliothek Bielefeld
Universitätsbibliothek Bochum
Universitäts- und Landesbibliothek Bonn
Staats- und Universitätsbibliothek Bremen
Universitäts- und Landesbibliothek Darmstadt
Sächsische Landesbibliothek Staats- und Universitätsbibliothek Dresden
Universitätsbibliothek Duisburg-Essen
Universitäts- und Landesbibliothek Düsseldorf
Universitätsbibliothek Eichstätt-Ingolstadt
Universitätsbibliothek Johann Christian Senckenberg, Frankfurt a. M.
Albert-Ludwigs-Universität Freiburg – Universitätsbibliothek
Niedersächsische Staats- und Universitätsbibliothek Göttingen
Fernuniversität Hagen, Universitätsbibliothek
Gottfried Wilhelm Leibniz Bibliothek Niedersächsische Landesbibliothek, Hannover
Technische Informationsbibliothek (TIB) Hannover
Universitätsbibliothek Hildesheim
Universitätsbibliothek Kassel Landesbibliothek und Murhardsche Bibliothek der Stadt Kassel
Universitäts- und Stadtbibliothek Köln
Université de Lausanne
Zentral- und Hochschulbibliothek Luzern
Bibliothek des Leibniz-Instituts für Deutsche Sprache, Mannheim
Universitätsbibliothek Marburg
Universitätsbibliothek der Ludwig-Maximilians-Universität München
Universitäts- und Landesbibliothek Münster
Bibliotheks- und Informationssystem (BIS) der Carl von Ossietzky Universität Oldenburg
Universitätsbibliothek Osnabrück
Universität Potsdam
Universitätsbibliothek Trier

Universitätsbibliothek Vechta
Herzog August Bibliothek Wolfenbüttel
Universitätsbibliothek Wuppertal
ZHAW Zürcher Hochschule für Angewandte Wissenschaften, Hochschulbibliothek
Zentralbibliothek Zürich

Contents

Beatrix Busse, Nina Dumrukcic, Ingo Kleiber

Introduction

Abstract: In the wake of the COVID-19 pandemic, ICAME41, somewhat prophetically titled *Language and Linguistics in a Complex World*, was shifted from a physical to a virtual conference. In light of a rapidly changing world, ICAME41 aimed
at challenging the future of (corpus) linguistics, its approaches, questions of
transfer, and the intersection between various fields and areas of expertise. By exploring new formats of presenting, sharing, and discussing research, the conference also provided a glimpse into one of many possible futures for the field and
academia as a whole. While this introduction is devoted to these questions, the
articles in this volume focus on the complexity and diversity of language and on
analyzing it with increasingly sophisticated methods and ever-larger datasets.

1 Questions and Concepts

The articles in this volume *Language and Linguistics in a Complex World* evolved
from presentations at the 41st Conference of the *International Computer Archive of
Modern and Medieval English* (ICAME41). This conference was initially planned to
be held on-site at Heidelberg University in May 2020. However, it was then one
of the first linguistics conferences which were realized online because of the
COVID-19 pandemic. But let's not get ahead of ourselves and first outline the
theme of both the conference and this volume. It will illustrate why – at least to
some extent – the topic of the conference was chosen somewhat prophetically,
especially given the deep crisis and massive changes affecting all of our human
existence due to the COVID-19 pandemic, and that we write this introductory
chapter with the experience of the last two years of being in a pandemic and now
even with an atrocious war by the Russian aggressor against Ukraine. Our world
has massively changed, and it is not easy to focus on the topics of the conference
alone. However, we are fully convinced of the fact that the work we do, education and generating new research, have never been more important for this and
the next generation, our society, and the planet – hence, for a peaceful, democratic, and sustainable world.

Next to discussing cutting edge research in, for example, the field of English
(historical) corpus linguistics, the conference *Language and Linguistics in a Complex World: Data, Interdisciplinarity, Transfer, and the Next Generation* aimed to

take (corpus) linguistics out of its comfort zone and discuss its (inter-)disciplinary and transfer potential in detail.

It aimed to determine the intersections between (corpus) linguistics and other academic fields such as sociology and psychology as well as marketing, law, politics, education, and art.

As a result of (hyper)globalization, digitization, gaining access to more and more information, and technological developments, we are faced with growing global and local complexity and interdependence of matter, lives, people, and things, which also includes language. Language continues to be the link between cultures, fields of study, and people. Furthermore, the means of analyzing, producing, and comprehending language is rapidly evolving through machine learning, artificial intelligence, and big data research, yet it remains at the core of the humanities.

We have not even begun to understand how all of these issues and concepts will interact (humanely, sensibly, peacefully, and sustainably) under the new circumstances of rapid change – nor have we yet considered what role linguistics and corpus linguistics may have to play in the solution of global challenges, a new world order, and how education and teaching will consequently have to be transformed. People communicate with one another and use language every day, yet a large section of the population is not familiar with the types of questions that are addressed in (corpus) linguistics. For example, how do scientists in this field look for patterns, and what can that tell us about human behaviour? Moreover, our aim was to scrutinize how contemporary, as well as upcoming methods and techniques which we have developed, might impact these questions in the future.

As corpus linguistics developed as a sub-branch of linguistics, a wealth of qualitative and quantitative research has been accumulated over the years, and highly innovative and ground-breaking tools have become accessible to linguists. We find that it is necessary to also share this knowledge with the public to be used for other purposes and to bridge the gap between academia and industry more than ever before. It is also of crucial importance to acknowledge software development and data itself as research outputs in their own right. This also extends to the way we present and publish findings, reviews, and analyses. While peer-reviewed journals, edited volumes, and monographs continue to add credibility and maintain a level of quality assurance, many scholars are also extending their outreach to include preprints, blogs, podcasts, video tutorials, code and data repositories such as GitHub, using forums to discuss important issues, and utilizing social media.

This has also been acknowledged and pointed out in the past. For example, in 2015, Mónica I. Feliú-Mójer wrote a blog post on the importance of effective communication, and how the more clearcut and comprehensible the message is, "science thrives." Wu (2017) questions the use of complex terminology and jargon as well as compromising the ability to be an effective communicator when thinking of the general public as "other." Making linguistic research accessible, Wagner et al. (2015) describe establishing a *Language Sciences Research Lab* within a science museum, that combines formal instruction with outreach and integration with the general public.

By transferring the methods and insights of (corpus) linguistics to society, we are not only increasing our impact as researchers, but also gaining further knowledge and input directly from stakeholders about their needs, which, given the current geopolitical circumstances, will become even more important. Furthermore, it has become essential to examine the issue of increasingly complex data and whether researchers have to acquire novel skills in areas outside of their current expertise. This also opens up the question of whether this needs to happen on an individual level or if there should be a more comprehensive collaboration between experts from various disciplines. Corpus linguistics is at a crossroads, and the time has come to evaluate and consider what the field will look like in the forthcoming years and how it will be shaped by young and emerging scholars as well as people from outside the traditional academic sphere.

The transition from workshops and conferences in physical presence to digital and hybrid spaces also means that participants from all over the world, who might otherwise be prevented from attending due to, for example, travel expenses and time constraints, are able to contribute to, and learn from, participating in discussions with their peers. The virtual conference format has resulted in a number of sociodemographic changes such as greater attendance by women, members of historically under-represented institutions, as well as graduate students and postdoctoral associates (Skiles et al. 2021). Equity and inclusivity on this scale are unprecedented, and although establishing the schedules sometimes is challenging due to various time zones, nonetheless, academics are able to partake in networking with fellow researchers wherever they happen to be in the world. Moreover, Skiles et al. (2021) show in their study, which compares remote and in-person conferences, that the former has positive environmental factors because the participants' travel-related carbon footprint is greatly decreased. All these observations raise the question of what conferences will and should look like in the future.

2 Digital Conferences

The decision to host ICAME41 in digital space instead of physically at Heidelberg University due to the COVID-19 pandemic was not made lightly. This shift challenged all of the previously well-established and familiar methods of organizing and executing academic conferences. The lockdown that ensued was an unprecedented way of working for most, where we embraced the technology that we had at our disposal to make the best of the situation. As an important international corpus linguistics conference that has been taking place since 1979, the *International Computer Archive of Modern and Medieval* English (ICAME) conferences have been inextricably linked to a multitude of traditions, social events, and culture – many of which are closely tied to the spaces ICAME has been happening in and at. Hence, one of the biggest challenges was to recreate the sense of community and establish a platform and fitting formats for discussing and sharing innovative ideas in the digital space.

Aside from the effort that usually goes into organizing large events, there was a myriad of questions about how high-quality content and social interactions can be brought into the digital space. The original blueprint for the conference and ideas that the organizing committee deliberated had to be radically modified. In early 2020, society was engulfed in fear and doubt as the COVID-19 pandemic swept across the globe. Yet, this was also an opportunity for creative thinking and opened the door to questioning the previously well-established way of organizing and attending conferences. While virtual conferences and events existed prior to the COVID-19 pandemic, the number of conferences offered in virtual and hybrid formats has since skyrocketed. Our team took this challenge as an opportunity to brainstorm and think about not just how to recreate the familiar experience in the digital space, but what new and exciting prospects this could bring. Therefore, next to the established formats, ICAME41 featured, for example, a design thinking workshop with industry experts as well as a publicly streamed plenary discussion. Regarding the core academic program, the organizing committee combined synchronous and asynchronous contributions to balance the excitement of attending live plenaries while minimizing technical difficulties and stress by asking participants to upload pre-recorded talks and poster presentations. The keynote speakers and participants embraced these novelties and co-creatively, together with the organizers and other participants, created meaningful and interesting content. The process of moving ICAME41 into the digital space is discussed in further detail in Busse/Kleiber (2020), and the purpose of the paper is to share our experiences and best practices that serve as guidelines for future event organizers.

One of the pillars of contemporary academic research ought to be sharing knowledge and ideas with others. Closely related to this, we are seeing that more and more linguists are embracing open science and open education. We see an unprecedented amount of code, data, and (learning) resources being developed and made available publicly, collaboratively, and openly. By providing people both within and outside the academic community with the opportunity to be able to learn about research currently conducted at higher education institutions, not only is the information available to more people, but they are able to make their own contributions and replicate and verify the research being conducted by others. This process ensures that there is less discrimination towards people and institutions who may not have the resources to conduct similar studies but nonetheless have the intellect and creative thinking that we as a society would very much all benefit from.

3 Articles in this Volume

Upon successful completion of the conference, scholars who were interested in publishing their papers in these proceedings were invited to submit their work. This is a more in-depth look at some of the papers which were outlined in a more concise manner in the published Extended Book of Abstracts (Busse/Dumrukcic/Möhlig-Falke 2021). The papers underwent a double peer-review process by experienced and qualified experts in the field who kindly provided feedback to the contributors. The general trend we noticed over the course of the conference, and by reading the contributions was that there is a wide and inclusive perspective on language(s). Moreover, there is a continuation of the tendency to use increasingly sophisticated quantitative and qualitative methods. The adoption of more complex and sophisticated technology and methodology is also enhancing research as corpus linguists are finding new as well as faster, and more efficient ways of looking for language patterns in ever-increasing amounts of linguistic data.

In his paper on World Englishes, Axel Bohmann uses the Contrastive Usage Profiling (CUP) method in order to quantify relations among different varieties of English based on lexical co-occurrence. This method relies on word embeddings to represent word usage using online discourse data from the Corpus of Global Web-based English (GloWbE, Davies 2013). The author considers the profiles of individual words (i.e., 'English', 'holy', 'chop', 'yard', 'football', 'boot') in 20 varieties of English such as New Zealand, Irish, the United States, Canadian etc., and introduces a word embedding model that is constructed for each national sub-corpus of GloWbe (Davies 2013). This procedure uncovers relationships among varieties, both in regard to individual words and in an aggregate view. The results show differentiation between countries in phase five according to Schneider (2007) and formerly colonized countries that are still in the process of postcolonial linguistic emancipation. Furthermore, most other varieties differ from British English and American English rather than being more drawn to either of them.

Axel Bohmann, Julia Müller, Mirka Honkanen, and Miriam Neuhausen present the findings of a large-scale, multivariate study of how passive alternation developed in 19th- and 20th-century American English. There has been an increase in the use of GET to form passive sentences in American English, and a decrease in frequency of the BE-passive construction. A Python script was written to extract all instances of lemma BE and GET + past participle from the Corpus of Historical American English (COHA, Davies 2010), totalling 2,318,251 tokens. Intervening adverbs and negators were also included. Diachronic change, informality, subject responsibility, adversativity, and non-neutrality were assessed in relation to the GET-passive along with a range of syntactic predictors. One of the strongest predictors in the logistic mixed-effects model was the publication year of the text. There was a general rise in GET both in absolute numbers and as a competitor to BE throughout the observed time period (1830–2000), confirming the informality hypothesis that it is more likely to be used in informal contexts. Other constraints such as subject responsibility have weakened over time. Findings for adversativity/non-neutrality were less conclusive, but there was no strong evidence for the significance of these suggested semantic characteristics of the GET-passive. The semantic group of the passivized verb shows a particularly strong effect size. The article concludes that there is strong lexical-semantic conditioning of the passive alternation.

Gavin Brookes examines discourses around social class in British press coverage of obesity and how language has the power to shape societal perspectives on health and illness. The author uses a broadly social constructionist view of discourse, and a corpus-based approach is used to conduct a critical discourse analysis (CDA). The data is taken from a 36-million-word corpus of obesity-related newspaper articles published between 2008 and 2017 (Brookes/Baker 2021). Normalized frequency analysis of the phrase *social class* as a sub-sample of the newspapers mentioning obesity showed that left-leaning broadsheets have a tendency to frame obesity and poor diet as consequences of social class with social inequalities construed as the cause not only of obesity but also of health inequalities more widely. On the other hand, the right-leaning newspapers, including both tabloids and broadsheets, offered discourses that mitigated the influence of social class on obesity, claiming that obesity affects people at all class levels and that lifestyle choices are more influential in the development of obesity.

Steven Coats examines corpora compiled from YouTube automatic speech recognition (ASR) transcripts from channels in the United States, Canada, and the British Isles to study regional language variation in spoken English. The method of data collection relies on web scraping and open-source software for the automatic identification and downloading of suitable channel content as well as dealing with the rate-limiting issues that arise thereby. Word frequency statistics are used to assess the accuracy of the downloaded transcripts. The ASR transcripts (approximately 500,000 words) are compared to manual transcripts of city council meetings in Philadelphia to determine word error rates. Moreover, word embeddings are used to create a language model from a subset of the corpus. A transcript classification task is undertaken using vector-based distributed representations of transcript content. Furthermore, the article concludes that although there is a certain degree of error, utilizing ASR transcripts in corpus linguistic research is useful for the study of regional language variation.

The following article is by María-Isabel González-Cruz, who explores the pragmatic roles and effects that Anglicisms seem to play in a corpus of headings taken from the Spanish regional digital newspaper *Canarias 7*. The corpus includes a total of 1,618 headings with Anglicisms collected between 2019 and 2020. Using a qualitative approach, the author differentiates between three categories of Anglicisms: 1) new Anglicisms – those which have not been registered yet in the *Diccionario de la Lengua Española* (DLE), the official dictionary published online by the Royal Academy of the Spanish Language; 2) registered Anglicisms and 3) proper nouns. The proper nouns are further divided into categories such as titles, names, toponyms, and acronyms. The author concludes that Anglicisms tend to be used for their brevity and precision, to indicate certain attitudes, such as giving a humorous touch (through word-play or by resorting to familiar phrases), to provide connotations of modernity as well as perform a euphemistic role.

Yoko Iyeiri and Mariko Fukunaga compiled the ABCFM Hawaii Corpus by assembling selected writing from the Hawaiian Mission Children's Society Library (HMCS Library) in Honolulu which holds a large collection of 19th-century journals, letters, and an autobiography written by members of the American Board of Commissioners for Foreign Missions (ABCFM) (cf. Forbes et al. 2018). The Hawaii Corpus, which encompasses approximately 653,100 words, represents the state of 19th-century American English, while at the same time providing material suitable for historical sociolinguistic analyses, showing the variability of English among different authors. The eight authors in the corpus were well-educated, and all belonged to the same community with shared missionary aims. Therefore, any individual deviations from the norm tend to be rather subtle. The style of one person showed a relatively informal trend when compared to other members. Although other authors also employed some features of negation, this particular person's deviation was always marked and consistent. The paper explores some variable aspects of negation in the data, with a focus on the use of the auxiliary do in negation. After considering the frequency of negation, findings show that while negative constructions are relatively stable in the 19th century, the use of 'do' in negation was not yet consistent.

Gerold Schneider uses context-aware language models to compare the reading performance of L1 to L2 language users. The main research questions addressed which features correlate to and predict reading time, variation between L1 and L2 readers, whether reading time can be predicted in L2 as well as for L1 readers, and if longer reading time shows which constructions are particularly difficult for L2 readers. Data from the Ghent Eye tracking Corpus (GECO, Cop et al. 2017) was used and restricted to only L1 English readers whose dataset was complete, and L2 readers who had less than 50% daily exposure to English. Key points of analysis include surprisal, recency in the discourse, word length, and punctuation to predict reading times in psycholinguistic experiments obtained by measuring eye tracking since research shows that frequency and expectation can affect what is easier to process (e.g., Conklin/Pellicer-Sánchez/Carrol 2018). The study showed strong correlations between reading times and surprisal, although considerably less for L2 readers.

This collection of papers demonstrates how research can thrive even in times of great unpredictability and concern. As Mahlberg/Brookes (2021: 442) mention in their recently published article on corpus linguistics and the COVID-19 pandemic, this is a "testament to the applied nature of corpus linguistics, as well as to the innovativeness of our research community to respond rapidly and creatively to the most urgent global challenges of our time." While ICAME41 was in some ways a deviation from the traditional conference experience, it nonetheless provided insight into new ways of carrying out, presenting, and sharing research with the ICAME community and beyond.

References

Brookes, Gavin/Baker, Paul (2021): *Obesity in the News: Language and Representation in the Press*. Cambridge: Cambridge University Press.
Busse, Beatrix/Kleiber, Ingo (2020): "Realizing an online conference: Organization, management, tools, communication, and co-creation." In: *International Journal of Corpus Linguistics* 25, 322–346.
Busse, Beatrix/Dumrukcic, Nina/Möhlig-Falke, Ruth (Eds.) (2021) *Language and Linguistics in a Complex World Data, Interdisciplinarity, Transfer, and the Next Generation. ICAME41 Extended*

Book of Abstracts. The International Computer Archive of Modern and Medieval English Annual Conference, May 20–23, 2020, Heidelberg University and University of Cologne, Germany.

Conklin, Kathy/Pellicer-Sánchez, Ana/Carrol, Gareth (2018): *Eye–Tracking. A Guide for Applied Linguistics Research*. Cambridge: Cambridge University Press.

Cop, Uschi/Dirix, Nicolas/Drieghe, Denis/Duyck, Wouter (2017): "Presenting GECO: An eye tracking corpus of monolingual and bilingual sentence reading." In: *Behavior Research Methods 49*, 602–615.

Davies, Mark (2010-): *The Corpus of Historical American English (COHA). 400 million words, 1810–2009*. Online at: http://corpus.byu.edu/coha/ <14 April, 2022>.

Davies, Mark (2013): *GloWbE. Global Web-based English*. Online at: https://www.english-corpora.org/glowbe/ <14 April, 2022>.

Feliú-Mójer, Mónica I. (2015): *Effective Communication, Better Science*. Online at: https://blogs.scientificamerican.com/guest-blog/effective-communication-better-science/ <14 April, 2022>.

Forbes, David W./Kam, Ralph Thomas/Woods, Thomas A. (2018): *A Biographical Encyclopedia of American Protestant Missionaries in Hawaii and their Hawaiian and Tahitian Colleagues, 1820–1900*. Honolulu: Hawaiian Mission Children's Society.

Mahlberg, Michaela/Brookes, Gavin (2021): "Language and Covid-19: Corpus linguistics and the social reality of the pandemic." In: *International Journal of Corpus Linguistics 26*, 441–443.

Schneider, Edgar W. (2007): *Postcolonial English. Varieties Around the World*. Cambridge: Cambridge University Press.

Skiles, Matthew/Yang, Euijin/Reshef, Orad/Muñoz1, Diego Robalino/Cintron, Diana/ Lind, Mary Laura/Rush, Alexander/Calleja, Patricia Perez/Nerenberg, Robert/Armani, Andrea/ Faust, Kasey M./Kumar, Manish (2021): Conference demographics and footprint changed by virtual platforms. *Nature Sustaianability*.

Wagner, Laura/Speer, Shari R./Moore, Leslie C./ McCullough, Elizabeth A./Ito, Kiwako/ Clopper, Cynthia G./Campbell-Kibler, Kathryn (2015): "Linguistics in a science museum: Integrating research, teaching, and outreach at the language sciences research lab." In: *Language & Linguistics Compass 9*, 420–431.

Wu, Katherine (2017): *Why can't scientists talk like regular humans*. Scientific American. Online at: https://blogs.scientificamerican.com/observations/why-cant-scientists-talk-like-regular-humans/ <14 April, 2022>.

Axel Bohmann

Contrastive Usage Profiling: A Word Vector Perspective on World Englishes

Abstract: This paper introduces Contrastive Usage Profiling (CUP), a method for quantifying relationships among varieties of English based on lexical co-occurrence patterns in large corpora. The approach is situated in relation to similar research and illustrated with a case study from the context of World Englishes. Based on the national sub-corpora of the Corpus of Global Web-based English (GloWbE, Davies/Fuchs 2015), varietal profiles are constructed for twenty varieties of English. Patterns for individual words as well as aggregate patterns for varietal differentiation based on many words are shown to yield theoretically plausible results and to remain robust across different parameter settings of the method. Model interpretability is identified as an important area for future research.

1 Introduction

In this paper, I outline steps towards contrastive usage profiling (CUP), a method for quantifying relationships among varieties of English based on lexical co-occurrence patterns in large corpora. Measuring similarities and differences among varieties in robust, statistically elaborate terms has become a recent focus in both dialectological (Grieve 2016; Szmrecsanyi 2013) and World Englishes research (Bohmann 2019; Szmrecsanyi/Grafmiller/Rosseel 2019). The present paper concentrates on the latter using online discourse from the 20 countries represented in the Corpus of Global Web-based English (GloWbE, Davies/Fuchs 2015) as a case study. However, the method can be extended to any comparison of varieties, whether these be dialects, text types, diachronic snapshots, etc., provided the respective corpora are sufficiently large to allow for the construction of robust word-vector representations.

The procedure I introduce here relies on word embeddings (also known as word vector models or distributional models) to represent word usage. Such models describe individual words by means of their co-occurrence profiles with other words. A separate word embedding model is constructed for each national sub-corpus of GloWbE. Differences between these models, i.e., between the varieties they represent, are then measured by aggregating over differences in the profiles of the most frequent individual words in the corpus on the whole. The resulting inter-varietal distance pattern remains relatively stable even after consideration of only the 100 most frequent words. The picture of differentiation in English worldwide is theoretically plausible and shows traces of both developmental status (according to Schneider 2007) and areal groupings of varieties.

A problem that remains is to identify what factors drive the output of the CUP procedure. Capitalizing on a large number of words, and representing each by its co-occurrence patterns with other words, means the results cannot easily be traced to a single, unified explanation. In the Discussion, I outline some steps to enhance the interpretability of the results, but recognize that these are largely objectives of future research. In its present form, CUP, as detailed below, is a flexible and robust method for comparing large corpora of text and can be adapted by other researchers with relative ease.

2 Quantitative Relations among Varieties: Methodological Approaches

Measuring relationships among varieties has been central to several subfields of linguistics for much of the discipline's history. In traditional dialectology, linguistic atlases are constructed based on the degree of similarity different regions show in relation to individual – lexical, morpho-syntactic, or phonological – features. Where several isoglosses, i.e., geographical boundaries of feature distribution, overlap, borders between dialect areas are drawn. Similarly, in historical linguistics the comparative method (Hoenigswald 1960) uses feature correspondences among varieties at one synchronic stage to reconstruct common ancestor languages. Typological research proceeds along similar lines, but focuses on synchronic comparison and the discovery of pervasive relationships.

Both traditional dialectology and historical linguistics rely on categorical observations about the presence or absence of features. Recently, however, these have been complemented by approaches that employ more sophisticated methods of quantification in probabilistic rather than categorical terms. The quantitative dialectological methods developed in Salzburg (e.g., Goebl 2006) and Groningen (e.g., Heeringa/Nerbonne 2013; Nerbonne 2006) are early examples of this development, which has been more fully realized in recent studies such as Szmrecsanyi (2013) and Grieve (2016). In this perspective, covariance among large sets of linguistic features in different places is used to establish dialect areas statistically.

The comparative method from historical linguistics, likewise, has found application in quantitative terms, as prominently elaborated by Poplack/Tagliamonte (2001). In their comparative sociolinguistic approach, rather than relating varieties as to the presence or absence of a feature, the full set of constraints conditioning individual linguistic variables is considered. The three lines of evidence in this perspective are the statistical significance of constraints, their relative strength, and the rank ordering of their importance in different varieties or communities. An extension to this approach, which directly quantifies the lines of evidence, is the "variation-based distance and similarity modeling" (VADIS) paradigm developed by (Szmrecsanyi/Grafmiller/Rosseel 2019).

In research on World Englishes, the use case under discussion here, such aggregate quantitative methods are still in the minority. Detailed investigation of isolated features based on comparable corpora remains the dominant paradigm. Such studies have much to offer in relation to the specific variables they consider; however, extrapolating from their findings to general relationships among varieties can be problematic. The assumption that the behaviour of one isolated feature is indicative of difference or similarity among varieties on the whole is often unjustified (Bohmann 2021; Hundt 2009).

A recent contribution towards grounding the description of inter-varietal relations in World Englishes in more robust aggregate terms is Bohmann's (2019) multidimensional analysis. Following the procedures pioneered by Biber (1988), and using ten corpora from the International Corpus of English (ICE) project (Greenbaum/Nelson 1996) representing educated standard English from various countries, this study extracts frequency information about 236 linguistic features for each corpus text. On the basis of this data, dimensions of variation are established that give structure to the range of varieties and registers represented in ICE. Without going into detail about the interpretation of any of these dimensions, the dominant finding is that register – whether a corpus text is a piece of fiction writing, a broadcast interview, etc. – significantly outperforms the country a text is from in structuring variation along these dimensions.

Lexical variation has received comparably sparse attention in the context of World Englishes. Most frequent are attempts to quantify the normative orientation of varieties towards British and/or American English. Gonçalves et al. (2018), for instance, demonstrate overwhelming "Americanization" on a global scale based on a large corpus of Twitter messages. They calculate the proportion of British and American words from a closed set of clearly marked alternants, e.g., *eggplant* and *aubergine*, on "a grid of cells of 0.25 ° × 0.25 ° spanning the globe" (Gonçalves et al. 2018: 4). This approach is well-suited for the specific question it is aimed at addressing, but reducing varieties of English to their relative dependence on British or American norms arguably does not do justice to the full range of differentiation to be found in World Englishes.

Another choice in the literature has been to focus on "cultural keywords," i.e., "words that are revealing of a culture's beliefs or values" (Rocci/Wariss

Monteiro 2009: 66). Mukherjee/Bernaisch (2015) adopt this perspective in an analysis of three South Asian varieties. They establish a set of words that are generally more frequent in South Asian Englishes compared to a reference corpus of British English and narrow this list down to relevant keywords through "a socio-culturally motivated selection" (Mukherjee/Bernaisch 2015: 420). For each keyword established in this way, they contrast collocates in the three varieties under discussion.

To a certain extent, the cultural keyword perspective can be seen as complementary to the one taken in Gonçalves et al. (2018). Whereas the latter subsumes the status of New Englishes under their relative adherence to British/American norms, Mukherjee and Bernaisch's (2015) perspective is firmly focused on nativization, linguistic acculturation, and locally specific usage. Their method, however, pre-selects the most distinctive items and focuses heavily on denotationally rich content words. Yet, the innovation that results from structural nativization is not limited to this level. Nativization can often be seen in collocational preferences, e.g., between verbs and prepositions and other constructional peculiarities (Schneider 2003). The more general collocational analysis presented below is based on common words in general without further pre-selection of relevant items. This choice was motivated by the fact that local innovations may be found not only in the frequency of "big" content words, but in the subtleties of how relatively common function words enter into collocation patterns.

In general, CUP is not proposed as a competitor to the approaches discussed above, each of which achieves a level of sophistication that cannot be matched by simply considering word co-occurrence profiles. Instead, the method should be seen as a complementary view achieved by zooming out from individual items of interest to a bird's eye view of varietal differentiation. The utility of CUP will depend largely on the extent to which it can plausibly be tied back to more particular, fully contextualized analyses.

3 Methodological Procedure

In the present analysis, a similar focus on pervasive patterns beyond individual variables as in Bohmann (2019) is employed. However, whereas that study draws on a catalogue of features that are attested to play a role in register and/or variety differentiation, the selection of relevant features presented here is both more comprehensive and more agnostic in regards to prior expectations. Specifically, the usage profiles of the most frequent 28,341 words in GloWbE are considered (all words that occur in all sub-corpora and with a total frequency of 1000 or more).

The profile for a given word in a given variety is encoded based on its co-occurrence behaviour with other words in that variety (see below for details). This has often been framed in terms of distributional semantics (see Erk 2012 for an overview), but in fact encompasses other aspects of word use as well, "including syntactic, semantic, and pragmatic aspects" (Hovy/Purschke 2018: 4383).

At the heart of contrastive usage profiling are word vector models, also known as word embeddings or distributional word models. These represent individual words as vectors in an N-dimensional space. The dimensions are derived from properties of large amounts of naturally occurring text, usually in the form of co-occurrence profiles. An established approach is to count for each possible pair of unique word types in a corpus how often its two members occur within close proximity to each other, e.g., within a 5-word window. The information derived from this procedure is then used to construct a vector space in which words that show similar co-occurrence behaviours are located close to each other. The mathematical details are beyond the scope of the present paper (see Erk 2012 for more details).

In the resulting vector space, proximity between words is taken to express commonalities. These commonalities can be along semantic dimensions, such as when the equation *king – man + woman* leads to a point in the vector space whose closest word is *queen*. Likewise, grammatical properties are encoded, allowing for similar calculations as the above in the form of *sitting – sit + walk* finding the word vector for *walking*. These relationships are usually developed from the patterning of surface forms without recourse to semantic or syntactic knowledge. As such, the method is not predisposed to express a particular kind of linguistic knowledge, whether grammatical, semantic, stylistic, etc.

CUP uses word vector models constructed with the word2vec algorithm (Mikolov et al. 2013) as implemented in the Gensim Python library (Řehůřek/Sojka 2010). Word2vec has seen wide application in computational linguistics due to its computational efficiency and competitive performance. Unlike approaches based on simple co-occurrence frequencies as described above, word2vec works on a predictive basis. This approach has been shown to outperform more traditional, count-based methods (Baroni/Dinu/Kruszewski 2014). Word2vec's objective is to find word vector representations that, given a training sentence, maximize the probability of encountering the sentence's words close to each other. There are, in fact, two separate training algorithms to achieve word vector representations in word2vec: continuous bag-of-words (CBOW) and skip-gram. CBOW is trained by optimizing predictions of words given a set of surrounding context words, whereas the latter attempts to predict context words from an individual target word (see Mikolov et al. 2013 for more detail). CBOW is faster and tends to achieve robust results even with smaller data sets, whereas skip-gram is able to construct more nuanced word vectors based on very large data. CUP draws on the CBOW algorithm by default; however, choosing skip-gram instead is an option that should be considered depending on the nature of the data.

In the analysis of linguistic variation, word embeddings have not been widely utilized to date. Two notable exceptions are the studies by Hovy/Purschke (2018) and Rosenfeld (2019), both of which use an extension of word2vec, the doc2vec algorithm (Le/Mikolov 2014). Hovy/Purschke reconstruct dialect continua in the German-speaking area (Austria, Germany, and Switzerland). Training their model from a corpus of social media data and employing post-hoc geographic smoothing, the authors are able to reproduce results from established dialect atlases with high accuracy. An advantage of their method is that the results can be scaled to the desired level of granularity, e.g., in terms of how many distinct dialect areas to construct. Rosenfeld (2019), in addition to performing diachronic analyses of word usage, employs similar methods with a different geographic smoothing procedure to establish Texas English dialect regions based on Twitter messages. His research includes discussion of demographic difference as a mediator of linguistic differences.

CUP differs from these two examples, both of which draw on the doc2vec algorithm, in important ways. The latter represents document labels – such as city or district identifiers in the examples cited above – as vectors in the same space in which words are embedded. Consequently, individual words are more or less closely associated with individual cities or geographic regions. The method therefore answers questions about how the frequencies of individual words are associated with varieties. CUP instead quantifies the similarities and differences between varieties in relation to the usage profiles of individual words. It does not ask whether a given word is more or less frequent in a given variety, but whether it tends to enter into the same collocational patterns in one variety compared to another. In order to achieve such a comparison, a separate word2vec model is constructed for each variety.

In the case study below, the varieties considered are the 20 national components of GloWbE (Davies/Fuchs 2015). Comprising a total of about 1.9 billion word tokens sampled from blogs and general web sites in the different countries, there is significant variance in the corpus size for individual countries, ranging from over 380 million words (for the USA and Great Britain) down to 35 million for Tanzania. The median size of national sub-corpora is 44,169,602 words. The choice of GloWbE is opportunistic, as large amounts of data are required to construct word embeddings. This does not mean, however, that it should be seen uncritically. Loureiro-Porto (2017) identifies some important issues in GloWbE's composition, the most relevant for the present context being a tendency to under-represent genuinely local usage and to over-represent Americanisms. A degree of levelling is therefore expected in the corpus that will make it more difficult to find local differences.

The goal of CUP is to achieve comparability of word usage in the 20 varieties at a general level. While this makes it desirable to include as many individual words as possible, several factors impose restrictions in this regard. Most importantly, words that occur only in a sub-set of the corpora pose problems, since their vector representations cannot be learned for all varieties. This motivates the exclusion of all such items, which are generally low-frequency and often locally specific. In order to keep computational complexity manageable, the additional restriction is imposed that a word has to occur with a total frequency of at least 1,000 (amounting to a normalized frequency of about 0.5 pmw). This threshold is fundamentally arbitrary and subject to further modification, depending on how much or little data CUP requires to arrive at stable inter-varietal distance profiles. After these exclusions, a total of 28,341 unique surface forms are retained for further analysis.

Next is the problem that word embeddings are abstract spaces that are not directly comparable. The vector for a given word in the vector model for Jamaican English cannot immediately be related to that for the same word in New Zealand English, etc., because neither the origins of the coordinate systems for each variety nor the individual dimensions of each vector space are in themselves meaningful. What is comparable across models, however, is the distance between individual words. For instance, if the word *biscuit* is found to be closer in vector space to *tea* in British English than in American English, but closer to *gravy* in the latter, this fact expresses a meaningful aspect of lexical variation. Drawing on this property, CUP represents each word under analysis, for each variety, as the vector of its distances to all other words (according to the selection criteria outlined above) in that variety. For each pair of varieties, then, the cosine distance of the two word-distance vectors for a given word can be calculated. Doing this for each pairing of varieties, a distance matrix can be constructed representing the (dis)similarity of varieties to each other. Tab. 1, for the word *language*, is an example of such a matrix, abbreviated to the alphabetically first nine varieties in GloWbE.

The steps detailed above create separate distance profiles for individual words. These can be visually inspected for qualitative interpretation and utilized for proof-of-concept. However, the profile for any one word retains only isolated information. To arrive at an aggregate view, the general tendency behind many words needs to be quantified. This is achieved by simply summing distance matrices. One question in this regard is how to treat words with different overall frequencies. It is apparent that the profiles of highly frequent words should contribute

Tab. 1: Sample CUP distance matrix for the word *language*.

	AU	BD	CA	GB	GH	HK	IE	IN	JA
AU	0	0.21	0.11	0.09	0.24	0.20	0.12	0.14	0.19
BD	0.21	0	0.21	0.21	0.27	0.24	0.21	0.19	0.24
CA	0.11	0.21	0	0.08	0.24	0.18	0.11	0.14	0.17
GB	0.09	0.21	0.08	0	0.23	0.19	0.09	0.12	0.17
GH	0.24	0.27	0.24	0.23	0	0.28	0.25	0.23	0.24
HK	0.20	0.24	0.18	0.19	0.28	0	0.18	0.19	0.23
IE	0.12	0.21	0.11	0.09	0.25	0.18	0	0.14	0.17
IN	0.14	0.19	0.14	0.12	0.23	0.19	0.14	0	0.19
JA	0.19	0.24	0.17	0.17	0.24	0.23	0.17	0.19	0

more strongly to the aggregate measure of inter-varietal distances than infrequent ones. However, word occurrences generally follow a power-law distribution in which the most common items are so much more frequent than all others that scaling distance matrices by raw frequency amounts to disregarding the majority of words entirely. Instead, as is common practice (e.g., van Heuven et al. 2014), the contribution of individual words is scaled by the natural logarithm of their frequency of occurrence.

The outcome of this analysis is a matrix containing pairwise distances generalized over all of the 28,341 words. These can then be used in hierarchical clustering to represent the relationships among individual varieties. Compared to other clustering solutions, hierarchical clustering has the benefit of not requiring a set number of clusters. Instead, the entirety of the data is represented in a tree diagram (dendrogram) where each branching node corresponds to a subdivision creating an additional cluster. Inspection of such trees can reveal the most basic splits in the data as well as the immediate relationships of individual items to each other. Specifically, CUP, as presented below, uses hierarchical agglomerative clustering with Ward's (1963) minimum variance as a linkage method.

4 Individual Word Usage Profiles

Before discussing the end result of the CUP procedure, i.e., the aggregate picture of cross-variety distance, it is useful to consider the profiles of individual words. Doing so illustrates the results below in more concrete terms and helps to test the plausibility of the method in relation to specific terms. As such, Fig. 1 shows the profiles for six selected words. For illustration purposes, the optimal number of clusters is calculated by means of the dynamicTreeCut (Langfelder/Zhang/Horvath 2016) package in R (R Core Team 2020), and individual varieties' cluster membership represented by different font colours. Since the colour-coding is illustrative rather than essential for interpretation, and since the procedure for finding the optimal number of clusters would require a lengthier explanation, the reader is referred to Langfelder/Zhang/Horvath (2009).

The top two panels in Fig. 1 show items chosen for their cultural distinctiveness. To the left, *english* shows a first split that may be interpreted in relation to the linguistic situation in each country. The left branch, in red, comprises countries in which English is clearly the dominant language. This is obvious in the case of New Zealand, Great Britain, Australia, Canada, and the United States. The remaining two countries, Ireland and Jamaica, require qualification. The official language of Ireland is Irish, with English constitutionally "recognized as a second official language" (Constitution of Ireland, Article VIII, § 2).

However, despite language policy efforts, Irish continues to have a small native speaker base while English dominates in everyday communication. In Jamaica, Jamaican Creole is more widely spoken than English. However, the distinction between the two languages, descriptively accurate as it may be, is not normally made in everyday discourse. The countries in the right branch all feature more intense levels of societal multilingualism, and in most, the majority of inhabitants are not native speakers of English. The second split in the tree, further differentiating these countries into a Southeast-Asian and an African-South-Asian group, is less relevant here.

In the top right of Fig. 1, *holy* was chosen for its obvious religious meaning. The first split, separating Pakistan from all other countries, requires explanation in terms of a peculiarity of GloWbE. The word *holy* is significantly over-represented in the Pakistan sub-corpus compared to all other parts of GloWbE, with a per-million-word frequency of 545, i.e., 7.5 times the global average and almost four times as high as the next most frequent country (Philippines).

More interesting is the second split, creating an almost perfect distinction between countries in which Christianity is and those where it is not the dominant religion. Nigeria is an in-between case, with Islam being slightly more widespread than Christianity. However, the material in GloWbE-Nigeria appears to contain more Christian than Muslim references: the search term "god" is about 20 times more frequent than "allah" (60,344 and 3,152 respectively), and "bible" (7,097) occurs about seven times as often as the sum of "quran" (914) and "koran" (205). The only consistently puzzling country remaining is South Africa. The difficulty in relation to this country is not limited to the word *holy*. In all plots below, South Africa and Sri Lanka are the two countries that form the tightest minimal cluster (in other words, the last split to occur is always the one

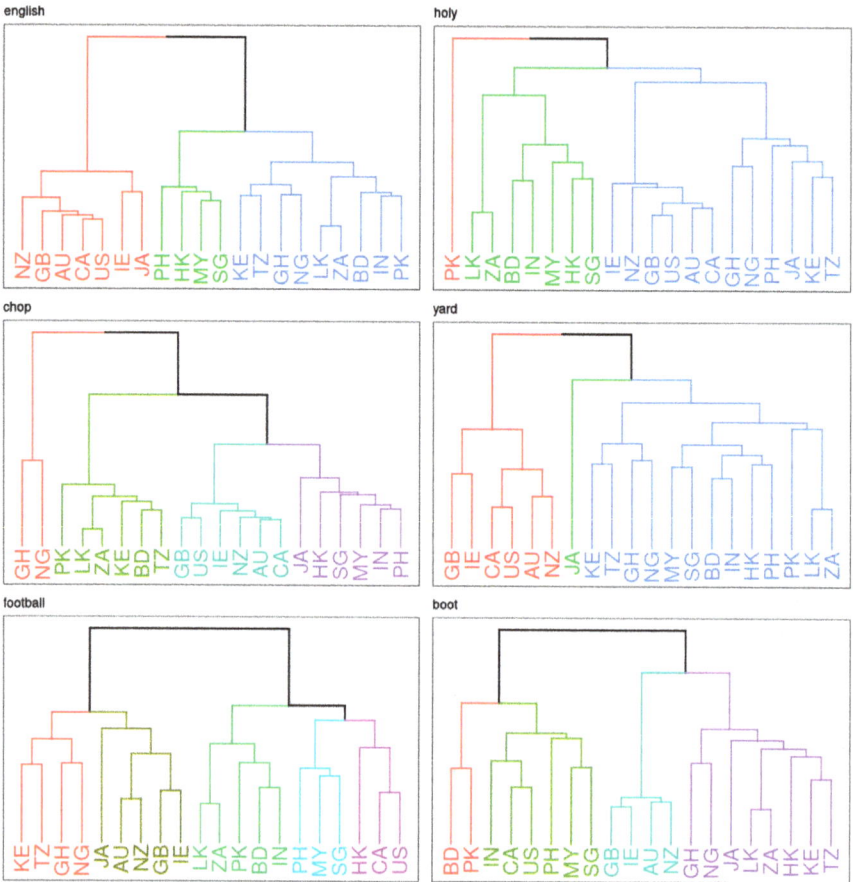

Fig. 1: CUP profiles for six selected content words in 20 varieties of English.

separating these two), often leading to implausible group membership for the former. The reasons are unclear at present and require further analysis.[1]

Moving on to the middle row of Fig. 1, the dendrograms for *chop* and *yard* were chosen because both items represent innovative uses in particular varieties.

---

[1] At the time the article is going into publication, I have been able to identify the reason for this unexpected behavior. The offline version of GloWbE, which has to be purchased from english-corpora.org, contains a file each for South Africa and Sri Lanka, comprising over 3 million words, with completely identical content. This is, then, an obvious problem of corpus compilation, not of the CUP method. Scholars interested in working with the offline version of GloWbE should be aware of this fact and consider whether the issue persists in the version of the corpus they have available.

In West African Englishes, *chop* refers to eating, whereas in Jamaica, the word *yard* has generalized into the meaning of 'home'. Both these local idiosyncrasies are clearly reflected in the CUP dendrograms. An anonymous reviewer points out that *chop* also has an idiosyncratic meaning in Hong Kong, where it means "to stamp a document," and that this should also be reflected in the dendrogram. This point is well taken. Qualitative consideration of the 253 instances of *chop* in GloWbE-HK shows that indeed 53 of them are used with this meaning. The fact that Hong Kong is not clearly shown as separate from other varieties, however, may be explained by the fact that the "stamp" use of *chop* exists in other sub-corpora as well. For instance, example 1) is from GloWbE-SG and example 2) from GloWbE-MY.

1) The stamp chop of your company must be affixed (GloWbE-SG)
2) The use of company stamp, chop and personal seal shall be discontinued (GloWbE-MY)

Nonetheless, this example points to several limitations of the CUP method. First, it does not include an option for disambiguating between homographs or polyse-mous items. It may be that the locally specific usage in GloWbE-HK, despite mak-ing up about 20% of all cases of *chop*, gets suppressed by the predominant general usage. Second, once a split (or lack thereof) in the dendrogram is noted, it is possible to look for explanations by considering examples from the corpus data. Yet the precise mathematical link between the structure of the dendrogram and specific kinds of usage cannot easily be established. Developing procedures to make this link more tangible is a major desideratum for future work.

The bottom row of Fig. 1 shows two words that clearly show different usage in British and American English. Whereas *football* refers to two different sports, *boot* in British English refers to the part of a car that would be called *trunk* in American English. The left panel indicates a first split that creates two groups, the left of which contains countries in which football in the British English sense is widely played. The countries in the right branch all feature popular sports other than football. In relation to *boot*, the difference between an Ameri-can and a British sphere of influence is even clearer in the first split. The British group, to the right, is further divided in a second split, into the core settler vari-eties and the formerly colonized countries. The American group contains a cou-ple of questionable candidates, notably the South Asian varieties. As with the close link between South Africa and Sri Lanka, more work would need to be done to shed light on this pattern.

These six examples, selected on the basis of theoretical expectations, show that CUP is able to produce plausible results at the level of individual words. Im-portant issues remain in regards to homography/polysemy, and the precise structure of a given dendrogram cannot easily be attributed to specific explanations. These limitations notwithstanding, the method's strength, discussed in the next section, is its ability to average over many individual words' usage profiles.

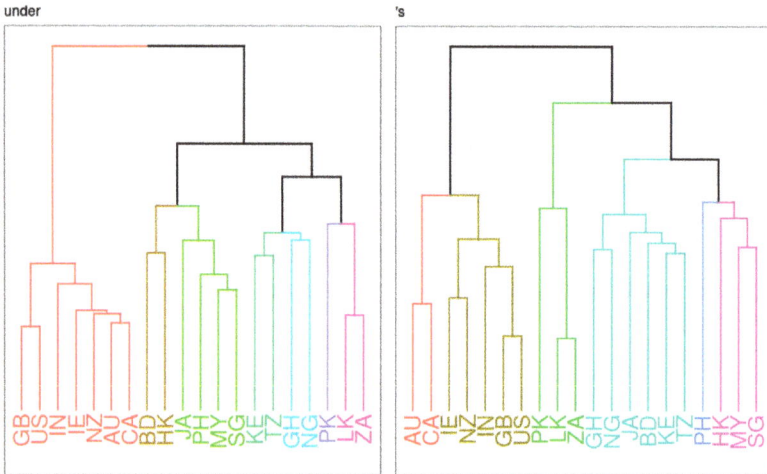

Fig. 2: CUP profiles for the function words "under" and "'s" in 20 varieties of English.

Before moving on to the aggregate picture, Fig. 2 illustrates a different aspect of CUP, once again on the basis of individual items. The two surface forms chosen here, the word *under* and the sequence *'s*, do not come with clear expectations as to the cross-varietal differentiation they create. As a basic function word, *under* is clearly part of the core vocabulary of English everywhere. The *'s* sequence is interesting because it may represent genitive case marking or enclitic versions of *is* and *has*. As such, some register sensitivity may be expected, but not strong cross-varietal differentiation. Yet, Fig. 2 shows that both these items, in fact, create more fine-grained groupings of countries than the content words discussed above. In Fig. 1, the number of clusters identified as optimal ranged between three and five. With seven and six clusters respectively, *under* and *'s* produce more nuanced profiles. This fact underlines two aspects of CUP: first, that the underlying word vector model not only captures semantics, but more general aspects of word usage; and second, that differences between varieties of English should not only be ascribed to lexical words, as cultural keyword analysis tends to do. Instead, the collocational preferences of high-frequency function words like prepositions are a rich area of structural nativization and should be considered alongside denotationally "heavy" items.

5 Aggregating Usage Profiles of Many Words

With these exploratory remarks established, it is now time to consider the big-picture view of cross-varietal differentiation suggested by a CUP for the varieties of English covered in GloWbE. Fig. 3 shows the clustering solutions produced on the basis of combined distance matrices for the most common 100, 1,000, and 10,000 words in the corpus, as well as the final diagram based on all words that meet the inclusion criteria specified in section 3. The number of groups in each tree was kept constant at 4 in order to facilitate the discussion of similarities and differences.

The general impression is one of relative stability. In all four diagrams, there is an important first split, followed at quite a distance in height by two further, almost co-occurring splits. The four groups of countries created in this way appear consistent on the whole, with a few varieties showing inconsistent group membership across the four diagrams.

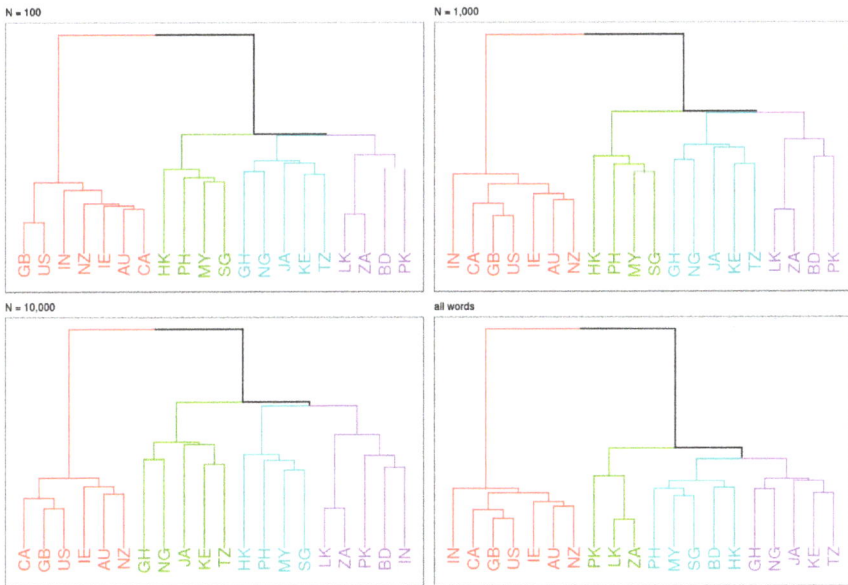

Fig. 3: Aggregate CUP profiles after the most frequent 100, 1,000 and 10,000 words as well as all words in GloWbE.

The first split constitutes a relatively clear division between British English and former settlement colonies to the left and formerly colonized nations to the right. In Schneider's (2007) evolutionary model, the countries to the left are those that have progressed furthest along the trajectory of postcolonial linguistic independence, having entered the fifth and final stage of the evolutionary process, 'differentiation.' Only one variety troubles this view: India, featuring in the left branch in three out of the four dendrograms. Situated somewhere between the third and fourth stage in Schneider's model and sharing a history of forceful colonization with most countries in the right branch, the inclusion of India among the phase five group is not immediately plausible. One explanation might be that Indian English continues to follow a British normative model closely, but in this case, one would expect India to be closer to Great Britain throughout.

The formerly colonized countries in the right branch are further sub-divided into areal clusters. The order in which these appear in each tree is an effect of how the second and third split separate the data. Given that these two splits occur at almost the same height, differences in the order of the three areal groups across dendrograms are of little consequence. The most robust group shows up consistently in all four clustering solutions and comprises Nigeria, Ghana, Kenya, Tanzania, and Jamaica, showing a clear African profile with Jamaica as the odd variety out. However, with reference to the African ancestry shared by the majority of Jamaicans, including substrate influence from African languages, the patterning of Jamaica among African varieties is not entirely implausible.

Similarly robust is the (South-) East Asian cluster, containing Singapore, the Philippines, Malaysia, and Hong Kong. These countries pattern together in all four dendrograms, being joined by Bangladesh only in the bottom right panel based on the largest number of words.

The least consistent group are the South Asian countries India, Pakistan, Bangladesh, and Sri Lanka. While all four dendrograms show a group that might be interpreted as representing this area, none of these groups is internally pure or consistent. It has already been noted above that South Africa shows up as closely related to Sri Lanka throughout the CUP analysis. This leads to the inclusion of South Africa among the tentatively labelled South Asian clusters in all cases. Similarly, India only makes a brief appearance in the areal cluster at N=10,000, whereas it patterns with the phase five countries in all other panels. Bangladesh and Pakistan appear consistent in their participation in the South Asian cluster with the exception of the dendrogram based on all words, which sees Bangladesh switch groups and join the (South-) East Asian cluster. As a country on the borderline between these two regions, this behaviour is not altogether surprising.

Approaching the dendrograms from the opposite perspective, i.e., looking at the most immediate connections between countries, similarly plausible pairs emerge, with the exception of South Africa and Sri Lanka. Australia and New Zealand, Kenya and Tanzania, as well as Nigeria and Ghana are among the lowest-level clusters, indicating sensitivity to smaller-scale areal patterns than the ones discussed above. The fact that Great Britain and the United States also form a tight micro-cluster speaks to their shared history as well as their position as globally dominant varieties in the world system of Englishes (Mair 2013). This view also underlines the limited theoretical purchase of attempts to treat other varieties of English as normatively dependent on either British or American English. For the most part, CUP shows other Englishes to be different from both British and American English.

Finally, a brief remark is in order in relation to the parameter settings chosen for the CUP reported here. There are considerable levels of choice in regards to at least the following variables: the frequency cut-off to include words in the analysis, the metric to represent the distance between varieties in their word usage, the question of what kind of item to focus on (surface forms vs. pre-processed data containing lemma and part-of-speech information), and the relative weighting of words by their frequency of occurrence. Space limitations prevent a detailed discussion of each of these choices; yet, it is obvious that a CUP method is preferable that does not produce vastly divergent results depending on how each parameter is set.

In order to explore this aspect of CUP, solutions were run with variations to the parameters mentioned above: once with no frequency cut-off, i.e., including all words that occurred at least once in each national sub-corpus of GloWbE, once with a Euclidean distance measure instead of cosine distances, once with (part-of-speech-tagged) lemmas instead of surface forms, and once with individual word profiles scaled by their raw rather than log frequency. Aggregate distance matrices for each of these were calculated for the first 10, 100, 1,000, and 10,000 most frequent words. A Mantel test for the correlation between the solutions presented in Fig. 3 above and each of the new variations was performed at each of these four steps, with Spearman's rho as the chosen correlation coefficient. Fig. 4 visualizes the results.

With the exception of lemma-based distance profiles for relatively few words, all correlations are strongly positive, with a rho above 0.9. With larger sample sizes, there is a tendency for the correlations to increase in strength, except when word profiles are scaled to their raw instead of log frequency. This is plausible since the effect of the scaling will increase with a wider range of raw frequencies, which in turn increases as more low-frequency words are considered. However, after an initial decrease, at about N=1,000, the correlation stabilizes to a rho of ~0.95. Without going into any further details, Fig. 4 indicates a surprising robustness of the CUP method against manipulation of individual parameters. The results are encouraging, for instance, in relation to developing CUP analyses on the basis of other data, which may not come in lemmatized and part-of-speech tagged form. They also indicate that consideration of a

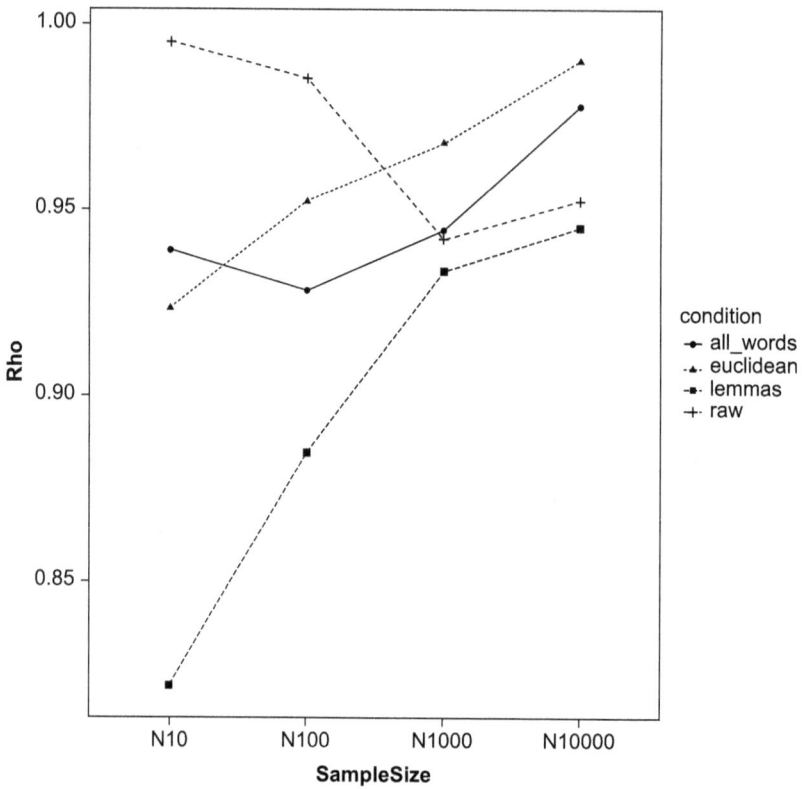

Fig. 4: Spearman's correlations for CUP results with various modifications at different levels of aggregation.

relatively small sample of all words may be enough to reach robust CUP results, thus promising computational efficiency where needed.

6 Discussion

The results presented above are encouraging. Without any information beyond co-occurrences of surface forms, the CUP procedure was able to uncover relationships among varieties, both in regards to individual words and in an aggregate view, in good accordance with theoretical expectations. Against the context of World Englishes research in particular, the results indicate a system of inter-varietal differentiation that is structured along two axes. First, former settlement countries in what is traditionally referred to as the "Inner Circle" (Kachru 1985) behave significantly differently from formerly colonized ones. Secondly, the latter are not so much differentiated by their linguistic emancipation as per Schneider (2007) but rather pattern into areal groups. The role of British and American English as competing spheres of influence – a popular notion at least since Strevens (1980) – was not confirmed in the CUP analysis. Most other varieties are different both from British and American English rather than being more drawn to one or the other.

A key question that remains is how to explain the aggregate dendrograms in Fig. 3. What motivates the relationships between varieties as shown in these diagrams? Does CUP capitalize on cultural discourse patterns, on structural innovations in different countries, on some hidden aspects not considered so far? The fact that word vector models represent usage in a very general sense, comprising various levels of description like semantics, grammar, and style, is a strength in terms of the comprehensive view provided by CUP. When interpreting the results, however, it turns into a double-edged sword. Figures 1 and 2 certainly seem to indicate that both (culturally specific) semantics and grammatical idiosyncrasies are captured by the method, but the extent to which each plays a role deserves further attention.

To that end, it will be necessary to develop methods for post-hoc analyses of a given CUP solution. These should ideally be able to show which groups of words are most relevant for a particular split. For these relevant words, further, more qualitatively informed collocational analyses could then be constructed, thus re-anchoring the method in contextualized corpus data. For instance, comparing the closest neighbours of a given word in each variety's vector space could give insight into what it is that causes cross-varietal differentiations. I am currently in the process of developing principled steps in this direction.

Beyond the specific context of the present study, CUP as a method may be useful for any research interested in contrastive relationships among varieties broadly conceived. These may be defined historically, stylistically, regionally or otherwise. All that CUP presupposes is a sufficiently large collection of electronic text to represent each variety, and that they share large parts of their respective vocabulary. The question of how large a corpus needs to be for CUP to produce meaningful results is not easy to answer with mathematical precision. Future experience and dedicated simulation studies should be able to shed light on the relationship between corpus size and the robustness of CUP results. The smaller sub-corpora considered are 35 million words large, which can be taken as a preliminary conservative estimate of "large enough." Whether smaller corpora, e.g., the International Corpus of English, which contains 1 million words per variety, may also produce robust CUP results requires further empirical confirmation.

7 Conclusion

Above, I have outlined the methodological steps for an innovative perspective on cross-varietal distance, dubbed contrastive usage profiling (CUP). The method draws on algorithms that have been implemented in popular programming languages like Python and are consequently fairly easily available to the research community at large. The added analytical steps can be computationally expensive, but not prohibitively so. The method can still be implemented on a mid-end personal computer with a couple of hours of runtime.

The results of the case study on differences between national varieties of English have revealed an important differentiation between countries in phase five according to Schneider (2007) and formerly colonized countries that are still in the process of postcolonial linguistic emancipation. The latter further cluster into areal groups. This finding emerges from consideration of relatively few surface forms and remains largely consistent as more forms are considered. It is also robust against manipulation of individual parameters such as the choice of part-of-speech tagged lemmas instead of surface forms or the metric used to calculate the distance between two varieties for a given word. At present, CUP is an experimental method awaiting further methodological refinement and empirical validation. Still, the results so far are promising.

References

Baroni, Marco/Dinu, Georgiana/Kruszewski, Germán (2014): "Don't count, predict! A systematic comparison of context-counting vs. context-predicting semantic vectors." In *52nd Annual Meeting of the Association for Computational Linguistics (ACL), Volume 1. Long Papers. Baltimore.* Association for Computational Linguistics, 238–247.

Biber, Douglas (1988): *Variation Across Speech and Writing*. Cambridge: Cambridge University Press.

Bohmann, Axel (2019): *Variation in English Worldwide. Registers and Global Varieties*. Cambridge: Cambridge University Press.

Bohmann, Axel (2021): "Register in World Englishes research." In: Britta Schneider/Theresa Heyd (Eds.): *Bloomsbury World Englishes*. London: Bloomsbury, 80–96.

Davies, Mark/Fuchs, Robert (2015): "Expanding horizons in the study of World Englishes with the 1.9-billion-word Global Web-based English Corpus (GloWbE)." In: *English World-Wide* 36, 1–28.

Erk, Katrin (2012): "Vector space models of word meaning and phrase meaning: A survey." In: *Language and Linguistics Compass* 6, 635–653.

Goebl, Hans (2006): "Recent advances in Salzburg dialectometry." In: *Literary and Linguistic Computing* 21, 411–435.

Gonçalves, Bruno/Loureiro-Porto, Lucía/Ramasco, José J./Sánchez, David (2018): "Mapping the Americanization of English in space and time." *PLoS ONE* 13(5): e0197741.

Greenbaum, Sidney/Nelson, Gerard (1996): "The International Corpus of English (ICE) project." In: *World Englishes* 15, 3–15.

Grieve, Jack (2016): *Regional Variation in Written American English*. Cambridge: Cambridge University Press.

Heeringa, Wilbert/Nerbonne, John (2013): "Dialectometry." In: Frans Hinskens/Johan Taeldeman (Eds.). *Language and Space. An International Handbook of Linguistic Variation (Handbooks of Linguistics and Communication Science)*. Vol. 3. Berlin: Mouton de Gruyter, 624–645.

Heuven, Walter J. B. van/Mandera, Pawel/Keuleers, Emmanuel/Brysbaert, Marc (2014): "SUBTLEX-UK: A new and improved word frequency database for British English." In: *Quarterly Journal of Experimental Psychology* 67, 1176–1190.

Hoenigswald, Henry M. (1960): *Language Change and Linguistic Reconstruction*. Chicago: The University of Chicago Press.

Hovy, Dirk/Purschke, Christoph (2018): "Capturing regional variation with distributed place representations and geographic retrofitting." In: *Proceedings of the 2018 Conference on Empirical Methods in Natural Language Processing*. Brussels, Belgium: Association for Computational Linguistics, 4383–4394.

Hundt, Marianne (2009): "Colonial lag, colonial innovation, or simply language change?" In: Günter Rohdenburg/Julia Schlüter (Eds): *One Language, Two Grammars? Morphosyntactic Differences Between British and American English (Studies in English Language)*. Cambridge: Cambridge University Press, 13–37.

Ireland (1945): *Bunreacht na hÉireann = Constitution of Ireland*. Dublin.

Kachru, Braj (1985): "Standards, codification and sociolinguistic realism: The English language in the Outer Circle." In: Randolph Quirk/H. G. Widdowson (Eds.): *English in the World. Teaching and Learning the Language and Literatures*. Cambridge: Cambridge University Press, 11–30.

Langfelder, Peter/Zhang, Bin/Horvath, Steve (2016): *DynamicTreeCut: Methods for detection of clusters in hierarchical clustering dendrograms*. Online at: https://CRAN.R-project.org/package=dynamicTreeCut <03.11.2021.>

Langfelder, Peter/Zhang, Bin/Horvath, Steve (2009): *Dynamic Tree Cut: In-depth description, tests and applications*. Online at: https://horvath.genetics.ucla.edu/html/Coexpression Network/BranchCutting/Supplement.pdf <03.11.2021.>

Le, Quoc V/Mikolov, Tomas (2014): "Distributed representations of sentences and documents." arXiv:1405.4053 [cs], 1–9.

Loureiro-Porto, Lucía (2017): "ICE vs GloWbE: Big data and corpus compilation." In: *World Englishes* 36, 448–470.

Mair, Christian (2013): "The world system of Englishes: Accounting for the transnational importance of mobile and mediated vernaculars." In: *English World-Wide* 34, 253–278.

Mikolov, Tomas/Chen, Kai/Corrado, Greg/Dean, Jeffrey (2013): "Efficient estimation of word representations in vector space." *ICLR Workshop*. arXiv:1301.3781 [cs.CL], 1–12.

Mukherjee, Joybrato/Bernaisch, Tobias (2015): "Cultural keywords in context: A pilot study of linguistic acculturation in South Asian Englishes." In: Peter Collins (Ed.): *Grammatical Change in English World-Wide*. Amsterdam: John Benjamins, 411–436.

Nerbonne, John (2006): "Identifying linguistic structure in aggregate comparison." In: *Literary and Linguistic Computing* 21, 463–475.

Poplack, Shana/Tagliamonte, Sali A. (2001): *African American English in the Diaspora.* Malden: Blackwell.

R Core Team (2020): R: A language and environment for statistical computing. Vienna, Austria: R Foundation for Statistical Computing. Online at: https://www.R-project-org/ <03.11.2021>.

Řehůřek, Radim/Sojka, Petr (2010): "Software framework for topic modelling with large corpora." In: *LREC 2010 Workshop on New Challenges for NLP.* 46–50.

Rocci, Andrea/Monteiro, Márcio Wariss (2009): "Cultural keywords in arguments: The case for interactivity." In: *Cogency* 1, 65–100.

Rosenfeld, Alex B. (2019): *Computational models of changes in language use.* Austin, TX: The University of Texas at Austin dissertation.

Schneider, Edgar W. (2003): "The dynamics of New Englishes: From identity construction to dialect birth." In: *Language* 79, 233–281.

Schneider, Edgar W. (2007): *Postcolonial English. Varieties Around the World.* Cambridge: Cambridge University Press.

Strevens, Peter (1980): *Teaching English as an International Language.* Oxford: Pergamon Press.

Szmrecsanyi, Benedikt (2013): *Grammatical Variation in British English Dialects. A Study in Corpus-Based Dialectometry.* Cambridge: Cambridge University Press.

Szmrecsanyi, Benedikt/Grafmiller, Jason/Rosseel, Laura (2019): "Variation-based distance and similarity modeling: A case study in World Englishes." In: *Frontiers in Artificial Intelligence* 2, 1–14.

Ward, Joe H. (1963): "Hierarchical grouping to optimize an objective function." In: *Journal of the American Statistical Association* 58, 236–244.

Axel Bohmann, Julia Müller, Mirka Honkanen,
Miriam Neuhausen

A Large-scale Diachronic Analysis of the English Passive Alternation

Abstract: We present the first large-scale, multivariate study analysing the development of the passive alternation in 19th- and 20th-century American English. Based on 2,318,251 tokens of the BE- and the GET-passive, extracted from the Corpus of Historical American English, we explore the strength and stability of several reported constraints on the GET-passive, such as informality, subject responsibility, adversativity, and non-neutrality. Additionally, our analysis includes a range of syntactic predictors. The results indicate a persistent association of the GET-passive with informal contexts, but weakening of most other constraints. A particularly strong effect size is observed for the semantic group of the passivized verb, developed by clustering over a word-vector representation of all verbs. This finding indicates strong lexical-semantic conditioning of the passive alternation. We discuss several challenges in the big-data approach we use and develop a sketch of future research in this direction.

1 Introduction

The past two centuries have seen an increase in the use of GET to form passive sentences in the English language, especially in American English (Hundt 2001), and an even more dramatic drop in the frequency of the traditional BE-passive (Mair/Leech 2006). This development has been referred to as "one of the most active grammatical changes taking place in English" (Weiner/Labov 1983: 43), but its precise motivations are still not fully understood. Mair/Leech (2006: 332) explain the increase in GET at the expense of BE as part of the wider trend of "colloquialization", whereby writing adopts features of spoken language.

The two passive variants BE and GET are not always interchangeable (Xiao/McEnery/Qian 2006). In the rich previous literature, scholars have suggested differences in the semantics of the two passives, such as implications of adversativity (Chappell 1980), informality (Biber/Conrad/Leech 2003: 112), and agentivity (Toyota 2008: 157) for the GET-construction, as well as lexically conditioned preferences (Rühlemann 2007). Schwarz (2015; 2017) speculates that the restrictions on the GET-passive might be weakening over time, as part of its increasing "grammaticalization" (Hundt 2001; Hopper/Traugott 2003). Schwarz does not, however, find evidence of this, nor does she, in fact, detect clear semantic differences between the two passives; subsequently, she encourages research to "focus on finding the factors that encourage the choice of GET" (2015: 166).

Due to the relative infrequency of passivizing GET and the difficulty of distinguishing it from other formally similar constructions, most previous research on the passive alternation has relied on close readings of constructed examples (e.g., Hatcher 1949; Chappell 1980) or considered bivariate distributional patterns in various digitized corpora (e.g., Collins 1996; Xiao/McEnery/Qian 2006; Coto Villalibre 2015). However, only few studies on the passive have adopted a multivariate statistical analysis, which is able to isolate and quantitatively compare the influence of competing factors. Given the semantic and stylistic nuances of the alternation, such a study on a large scale is needed to tease apart the various constraints on the choice of passive auxiliary.

In this paper, we track changes in passive auxiliary choice in a large corpus of written American English over nearly two centuries, investigating the influence of various semantic, textual, and syntactic factors on this variable. We employ automated sentiment analysis, distributional semantics, and a mixed-effects regression model to provide the first preliminary answers to our research questions:

1. How has the use of the BE- and GET-passive constructions with different lexical verbs changed between 1830–2009?
2. Are the alleged connotations of the GET-passive (informality, subject responsibility, adversativity/non-neutrality) empirically verifiable and historically stable?

2 The English Passive Alternation

The English language has two competing passive constructions. The canonical BE + past participle (hereafter, "the BE-passive"; (1)) varies with the newer variant with GET as the auxiliary verb ("the GET-passive"; (2)). In both cases, the affected patient acts as the syntactic subject, while the agent may be included in a *by*-prepositional phrase (PP) or omitted altogether.

(1)   The burglar was arrested (by the police).

(2)   The burglar got arrested (by the police).

The two constructions are, however, not always interchangeable, and a number of distinct syntactic, semantic, and pragmatic constraints have been suggested for each. The BE-passive has been found to be much more frequent, to be favoured particularly in written genres, and more likely to occur with an overt agent in the form of a *by*-phrase (Xiao/McEnery/Qian 2006).

The GET-passive tends to emerge in informal contexts "with meanings connected with speaker attitude, judgment, and affective posture" (Carter/McCarthy 1999: 51). This is a frequently supposed semantic-pragmatic characteristic of the GET-passive (Biber/Conrad/Leech 2003; Xiao/McEnery/Qian 2006). The construction is further associated with subject responsibility, which refers to the idea that the passive subject is somehow responsible for the situation being brought about on themselves (Chappell 1980; Coto Villalibre 2015; Toyota 2008). Furthermore, it is often claimed that the situations the GET-passive encodes tend to have either adversative (Rühlemann 2007; Chappell 1980; Carter/McCarthy 1999; Toyota 2008) or more generally non-neutral (fortunate or unfortunate) consequences for the subject (e.g., Hatcher 1949; Fleisher 2006). By contrast, Coto Villalibre's (2015) findings indicate that the majority of GET-passives are semantically neutral. Consequently, he suggests that GET-passives are either now converging with the neutral BE-passive or adversativity was solely a "contextual feature" in the first place and not a defining property of the construction itself (Coto Villalibre 2015: 24). Furthermore, the GET-passive encodes only dynamic situations as opposed to the BE-passive (e.g., Xiao/McEnery/Qian 2006), which can be either dynamic or stative (Toyota 2008: 149). The semantic difference between the stative and dynamic variants can serve to avoid potential misinterpretations. The semantic ambiguity of (3), for example, is absent in the GET-variant (4) (Quirk et al. 1985: 162).

(3)   The chair was broken.

(4)   The chair got broken.

Notably, not all instances of BE/GET + past participle carry a true passive meaning. There are formally similar structures where the participle "has both adjectival and verbal properties" (5), or is fully stative and adjectival (6) (Quirk et al. 1985: 169–170). Moreover, GET + past participle may also represent the "middle voice", where the subject is "both the controller of the action and affected by it" (7) (Hundt 2001: 51; Croft 1991: 248).

(5)   Wordsworth said he got so maddened by the sight of it that he threw up the job. (COHA fiction 1970).

(6)   The board can get very excited about building, and there's a lot of energy around it. (COHA news 2007).

(7)   The right has also had trouble getting organized for next spring's presi-
      dential elections. (COHA fiction 1917).

The distinction between central passives as in (1) and (2) and such more periph-
eral cases as in (5)–(7) has led scholars to postulate a "passive gradient" (Quirk
et al. 1985: 167).

Given the fine-grained semantic-stylistic differences between the GET- and
the BE-passive as well as the fact that they co-exist with formally identical non-
passive constructions, circumscribing the variable context for this alternation is
no easy task. Trying to ensure the referential equivalence of any attested form
with its competing variant, most empirical studies to date have qualitatively examined individual instances (e.g., Collins 1996; Xiao/McEnery/Qian 2006; Rühlemann 2007; Coto Villalibre 2015; Schwarz 2015; 2017). Even though this practice
may be effective in guaranteeing accountability, it entails two major problems.

Firstly, formal tests for passive centrality often rely on the (in)acceptability
of constructed modifications to an attested candidate sentence. These include,
for example, whether the auxiliary could be replaced by its competitor, or
whether a corresponding active sentence can be formed. Yet, acceptability
judgments in relation to the GET-passive have been subject to debate and
change over even the past four decades. For example, Banks (1996: 127) claims
utterance (8) to be "of doubtful acceptability", but a search in COHA yields
1,352[1] hits for the underlying structure GET + participle + *by*. For a diachronic
study in particular, this means that a stable point of reference for such judgments is difficult to establish.

(8)   Mary got shot by John.

Secondly, in more practical terms, qualitative analysis of all tokens is costly
and has therefore often been restricted to hundreds or thousands of cases. All the
same, the passive alternation shows a number of characteristics that call for a
larger quantitative approach. For instance, the distribution of the two variants is
heavily imbalanced, with the BE-passive outnumbering the GET-passive by ratios
between 10:1 (Xiao/McEnery/Qian 2006) and 100:1 (this study). This means that,
for several thousand tokens considered, the analysis may only be able to provide
insight into a handful of GET-passive cases. Such a limitation is unfortunate,

---

1 This is the figure the COHA online interface gave us at the time of writing the article. However, it does not seem to be stable either across time or the different search options of COHA.
Search on 3 Nov 2022 yields 941 hits for the same query ("GET _v?n by") in the list display and
1,757 in the chart display.

particularly in this case, where numerous constraints at various levels (semantic-pragmatic, stylistic, syntactic) have been put forward. In order to effectively consider their relative importance, a multivariate analysis on a large scale is required. Below, we detail the methodological steps and initial findings of such a study.

3 Data and Methods

3.1 Data Collection

Our investigation relies on a large diachronic corpus, the Corpus of Historical American English (COHA; Davies 2010), which contains ca. 400 million words from U.S. newspapers and magazines as well as fiction and non-fiction books from the 19th and 20th centuries. For the time period from 1830 to 2009, we investigated 398.1 million lemmatized and part-of-speech-tagged tokens. We downloaded the data and wrote a Python (Python Software Foundation 2019) script to automatically extract all instances of lemma BE/GET + past participle, as tagged in COHA. We also included intervening adverbs and negators.

An accountable study of any alternation requires careful definition of the variable context (Poplack/Tagliamonte 1989). Ideally, only cases where both variants can be used interchangeably should be considered, and those that permit only one of the variants under discussion should be excluded. Similarly, all extracted forms should be genuine instances of the variable under investigation. The nature of the passive alternation as well as the number of observations in our study impose several difficulties in this regard. As there is no direct annotation for passive voice constructions in COHA, the automated search has to rely on the lemma/part-of-speech tagging in the corpus. In addition to tagging errors, constructions on the "passive gradient" (Quirk et al. 1985: 167; Collins 1996) exist where both GET and BE may be used, but where the choice between the two entails a semantic difference, as that between (9) and (10).

(9) Jerry was excited now. (COHA fiction 2017)

(10) Poor old Judge Richmond got excited and had another stroke. (COHA fiction 1921)

Both examples express a similar state of affairs – a person in the role of grammatical subject being in a state of excitement – but are differentiated by a greater focus on the state in (9) and on the change of state in (10). These examples demonstrate that the definition of the variable context is not just a problem of automation, but of linguistic interpretation. Arguments could be found both to include or to exclude cases like this from an analysis of the passive alternation. Moreover, as mentioned above, the semantics of both constructions are not completely stable in diachrony. COHA contains many tokens of the BE-passive with clearly dynamic readings, especially from the 19th century. The tendency towards functional association of BE with stative and GET with dynamic situations develops only gradually over the course of the period covered by our data and is far from categorical even in the late 20th century. As such, it does not provide a categorical distinction that can be taken as underlying the analysis of all our tokens.

We recognize these problems as ongoing challenges for our project. We are in the process of addressing them through a combination of manual coding and writing a supervised classifier to separate true cases of variation from those that entail a semantic difference. For the present analysis, we rely on a fuzzy definition of the variable context and only exclude a handful of participle types that categorically do not participate in the alternation or are erroneously tagged: *married, engaged, betrothed, rid, wet, medicaid, (over)tired, (un)dressed,* and *clothed.* Further, we only retain participles that occur at least once with each auxiliary and at least ten times in total. After these exclusions, we are left with 2,318,251 observations to model, 2,292,328 of which occur with BE and 25,923 with GET.

3.2 Mixed-effects Logistic Regression

We run a mixed-effects logistic regression model, which quantifies the influence of various predictor variables on the likelihood of GET. Our model considers a number of hypotheses suggested in the extant literature. In addition to established predictors, we add two new variables – verb sentiment score and verb semantic group – to better operationalize previous claims in an empirical framework. The following predictors are included, ordered by the hypothesized constraints they operationalize:

Diachronic Change
– **Year** (continuous): For each observation, we include the year in which it is attested. Given the well-documented increase of the GET-passive and decline of the BE-passive, we expect this predictor to correlate positively with the likelihood of the former being selected. Since linguistic changes are

often accompanied by a levelling of constraints, we also consider an interaction term between year and each of the other predictors.

(In)formality

- **Genre** (fiction, magazines, newspapers, non-fiction books): This information is extracted as part of the COHA file meta-data. We hypothesize that fiction writing as the least formal genre is the most favourable towards GET-passives, while we expect the opposite for non-fiction books.
- **F-measure** (continuous): This predictor is based on the proportions of words from different word-classes, on the assumption that more formal texts contain more nouns, adjectives, prepositions, and articles, whereas more "contextual" texts feature more pronouns, verbs, adverbs, and interjections (Heylighen/Dewaele 2002: 8). A higher F-value indicates increased formality and is consequently expected to favour BE-passives.

Subject Responsibility

- **Subject animacy** (inanimate, animate, body part, unknown): Givón/Yang (1994: 120) suggest that the GET-passive disfavours inanimate referents if "the vestment of purpose, control and responsibility in the surface subject are necessary ingredients of the GET-passive". To test this, we classify the nearest noun or pronoun to the left of the passive (supposedly usually the clause subject) as inanimate (11), animate (12), or body part (13), assuming that the latter may meronymically signify animate entities. The "unknown" category comprises polysemous and mis-tagged items, collective nouns, place names, cases where the preceding NP could not be retrieved automatically as well as items that were not coded due to their low frequency. We hand-coded the most common 28,610 NP types, thus covering 1,803,838 instances or 77.81% of all subject tokens in the data. We checked the accuracy of our coding on a sample of 600 items; extrapolating the results to the hand-coded part of the whole data set gives an estimated accuracy of 87% for the animacy coding when the unknown cases are excluded.

(11)   A green salad ($3.73) of beautiful baby mixed greens gets coated in a tart, fruity, unbalanced dressing that suggested sour pineapple juice. (COHA news 1992)

(12)   A bad man gets found out sooner or later. (COHA fiction 1914)

(13)   Throats got cleared and feet were shifted. (COHA fiction 1979)

- **Agent PP with *by*** (present, absent): If an instance of *by* is found to the immediate right of the participle, this is coded as an agent PP. The presence of an additional constituent encoding the agent of the situation is assumed to at least partially mitigate subject responsibility and thus expected to favour BE. According to Xiao/McEnery/Qian (2006), GET-passives occur even less frequently than BE-passives with an overtly expressed agent. We spot-checked a random sample of 200 instances with *by* and found 96.5% to be genuine agent PPs.

Adversativity/Non-neutrality
- **Main verb negative emotion** (continuous): For each verb participle in our data, we extract its sentiment value from SentiWordNet (Baccianella/Esuli/Sebastiani 2010), a sentiment dictionary containing a positivity (14), a negativity (15), and an objectivity score (16) for over 100,000 words. The main verb negative emotion value is simply the negativity score as found in SentiWordNet. If the sentence is negated, the same score is used with its sign reversed. According to both the adversativity and the more general non-neutrality hypothesis, higher scores for this predictor are expected to favour GET.

(14) To-day my eyes will be <u>gladdened</u> by the consummation of my great achievement. (COHA fiction 1859, positivity score: 0.875)

(15) Fred has a horror of being <u>henpecked</u>. (COHA non-fiction 1953, negativity score: 1)

(16) Continue past the bronze statue of the angel to the paved road that is <u>flanked</u> by the fourteen stations of the cross. (COHA fiction 2002, objectivity score: 1)

- **Main verb positive emotion** (continuous): The calculation of the score is analogous to the above. Whereas the adversativity hypothesis expects no effect of positive emotion scores, or potentially one disfavouring GET, the non-neutrality hypothesis suggests that higher scores for this predictor correlate positively with the likelihood of selecting GET. Positive and negative emotion scores are not, as one might expect, highly correlated (κ = 1.98) and can therefore be used as predictors in one model.
- **Main verb semantic group** (21 levels): Beyond emotion scores on a simple linear continuum, we test whether different verb groups show distinct selectional preferences in relation to BE and GET. Rühlemann (2007: 122) demonstrates this for individual verbs, arguing that "grammar and lexis can be

shown to a large extent to merge into one another". Here, we attempt to find systematicity beyond isolated items by clustering the 1,800 main verb participle types in our data into natural groups. This is done on the basis of a distributional semantic model for the entire corpus and a subsequent cluster analysis of the relevant participles. For the distributional semantic model, we rely on the word2vec algorithm (Mikolov et al. 2013) as implemented in Python's Gensim module (Řehůřek/Sojka 2010). The output is a representation of each participle in a 100-dimensional vector space based on its co-occurrence with other words in the corpus. A model-based cluster analysis with Gaussian mixture models (Fraley/Raftery/Scrucca 2019) is performed to find the appropriate number of clusters and establish each participle's cluster membership.

Space does not permit us to introduce each verb group here; please consider the appendix for suggested labels and the ten verbs most strongly associated with each cluster. In general, the clusters are characterized by a high degree of semantic coherence, but overall frequency plays a role as well, such that there are several clusters whose main feature is that their members occur only a handful of times in the entire corpus.

Since Gensim's word vector representation is based on single words, we could not treat different phrasal and prepositional, as well as polysemous, verbs separately.

Finally, we code each observation for a number of morpho-syntactic features. Some of these have been remarked on in the literature but are not immediately connected to any of the hypotheses above. Others are included for more exploratory reasons and based on the general assumption that any element making the construction more complex (such as a negator or intervening adverb) tends to disfavour GET.

Morpho-syntactic Constraints

- **Negator** (presence, absence)
- **Form of auxiliary verb** (present (16), preterite (13), perfect (17), infinitive (18), *-ing* (19))
- **Intervening adverb** (presence, absence): Carter/McCarthy (1999: 53) find that "no adverbials occur in medial position between *get* and the main verb past participle".
- **Complementation with a *to*-infinitive** (presence, absence): Xiao/McEnery/ Qian (2006: 112) claim that only the BE-passive allows for an infinitival complement. We automatically code for each observation whether the verb is immediately followed by *to* and an infinitival verb.

(17) Donnie was the one who <u>had gotten nicked</u> by a stray bullet in Donkey Creek, earned himself bragging rights if nothing else. (COHA fiction 2005)

(18) And as it is worth fighting for, the insurance companies here will do all they can to <u>get compensated</u> for their losses. (COHA magazine 1883)

(19) At any rate, those things <u>are getting said</u> nowadays; he'll have to hear them sooner or later. (COHA fiction 1889)

Continuous variables are standardized, i.e., their z-scores are used to allow for better comparisons of predictors on different scales. All correlations between numeric predictors are $r < 0.12$. Therefore, they can all be entered into the model. Generalized variance inflation factors are < 10 for year and *to*-complementation, and < 5 for all other predictors.

Categorical variables are treatment-coded, with the following baseline levels: the largest semantic verb cluster 13, no following *by*-PP, no *to*-complementation, unknown animacy (i.e., infrequent nouns), no negation, no adverb, and infinitive for the form of the auxiliary.

A logistic mixed-effects model with verb lemma as a random effect and random slopes for year was fitted in Julia (Bezanson et al. 2017). A random-effects Principal Component Analysis, as advocated by Bates et al. (2018), indicates that the model is not overparameterized and both the random intercept and slope are justified by the data.

4 Results

We present the results of our model with effects plots created using the *ggeffects* package (Lüdecke 2018) in R (RStudio Team 2020). These plots visualize predictions for main effects and significant interactions with their respective confidence intervals. Please refer to the appendix for the full set of model coefficients.

One of the strongest predictors in our model is, as expected, the publication year of the text. Fig. 1 shows how the likelihood of the GET-passive has increased over the past 200 years.

Many of the other predictors show statistically significant interaction with year; these will be discussed below along with other main effects that do not participate in significant interactions. The results are grouped around the relevant hypotheses.

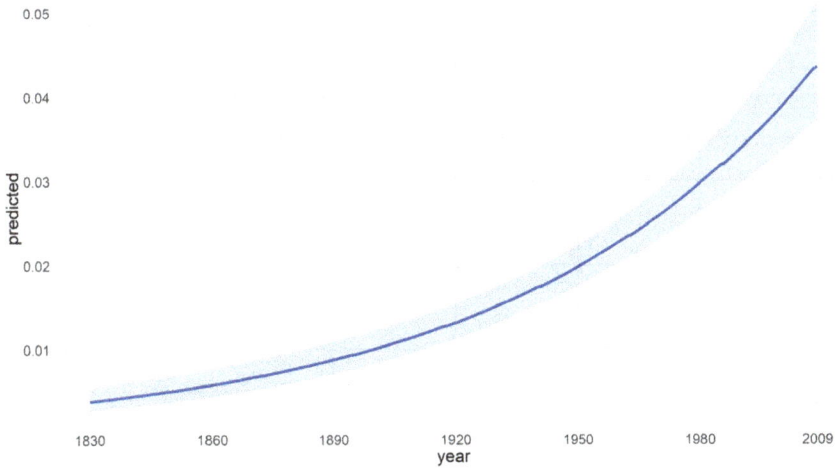

Fig. 1: Predicted likelihood of GET for year as a main effect.

4.1 (In)formality

The GET-passive has become more likely in each of the four genres over time. Notably, this factor interacts with year (Fig. 2) so that the relative increase is greater in magazines and particularly in newspaper writing, which was the genre in which the GET-passive was the least likely in the early 19th century. The likelihood of GET remains the lowest in the most formal genre, non-fiction books, which supports the hypothesis about the informal nature of the GET-passive. Hundt/Mair (1999: 236) suggest that genres differ with regard to "openness to innovation" and "to external socio-cultural influences", finding journalistic writing more "agile" and academic writing more "uptight" and "prone to retain conservative forms". This might explain why the most noticeable increase in the GET-passive is found in newspapers and magazines.

We expected a higher F-value, indicative of formality, to increase the likelihood of BE being selected as the passive auxiliary. Our data confirm this. Furthermore, the likelihood of selecting GET increases most steeply over time for less formal texts with a lower F-value.

4.2 Subject Responsibility

As can be seen in Fig. 3, the significance of *by*-PP as a predictor has decreased over time so that in the early 19th century, its presence disfavours GET even

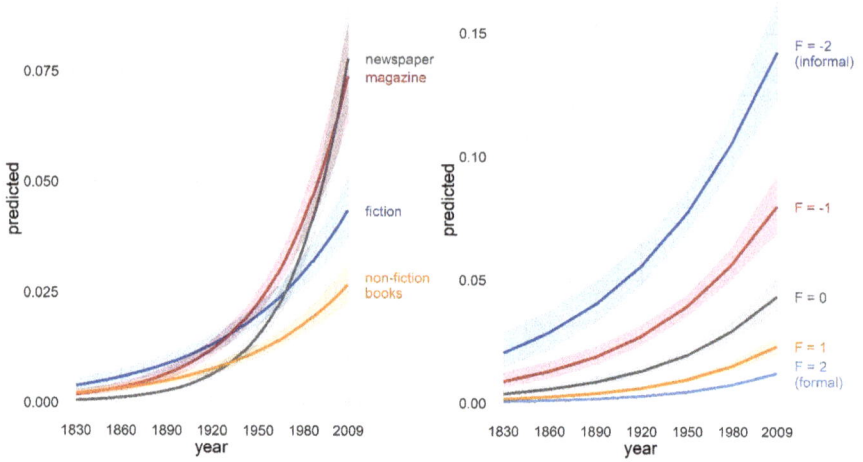

Fig. 2: Predicted likelihood of GET for the interactions between year and genre (left) and z-scored F-measure (right). Higher F-measures indicate higher levels of formality.

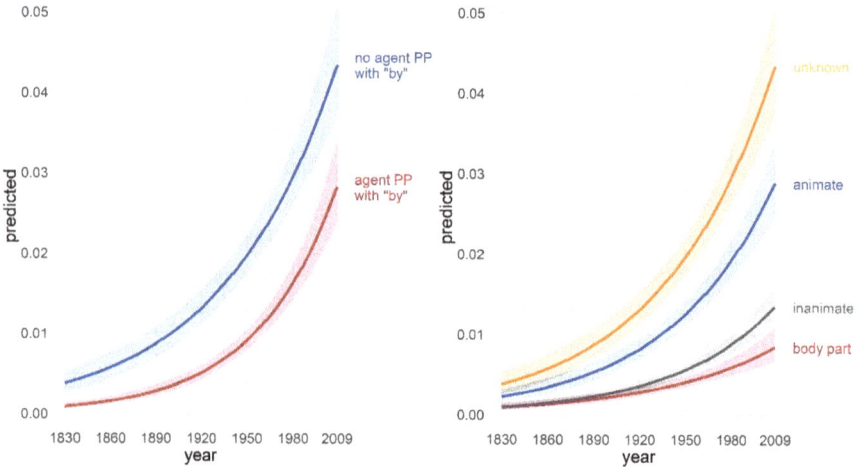

Fig. 3: Predicted likelihood of GET for the interactions between year and *by*-PP (left) and animacy (right).

more strongly than it does by the end of the 20th century. This finding can be related to an overt agent being less compatible with the concept of subject responsibility, lending some support to the hypothesis that the GET-passive may be used to encode situations where the grammatical subject has some agency over the situation. However, the GET-passive appears to be losing this semantic nuance gradually and to be developing in the direction of a more general passive form.

Going in line with this, our model suggests animate subjects to rather co-occur with GET and inanimate subjects with BE. Unexpectedly, body-part subjects show a strong association with the BE-passive; this category, however, covers only 2.7% of the data. The only significant interaction is between inanimate subjects and year; GET becomes relatively more likely to occur with inanimate subjects over time. The significance of subject responsibility seems to be lessening.

4.3 Adversativity/Non-neutrality

A higher sentiment score in either direction – positive or negative – makes the occurrence of GET as the passive auxiliary slightly more likely (Fig. 4). While statistically significant, however, the effect size is quite negligible. Considering the large size of the corpus, the very small coefficients (–0.016 for a negative score; –0.023 for a positive one), and the rather large confidence intervals, we do not think the data offer genuine support to the adversativity or non-neutrality hypotheses.

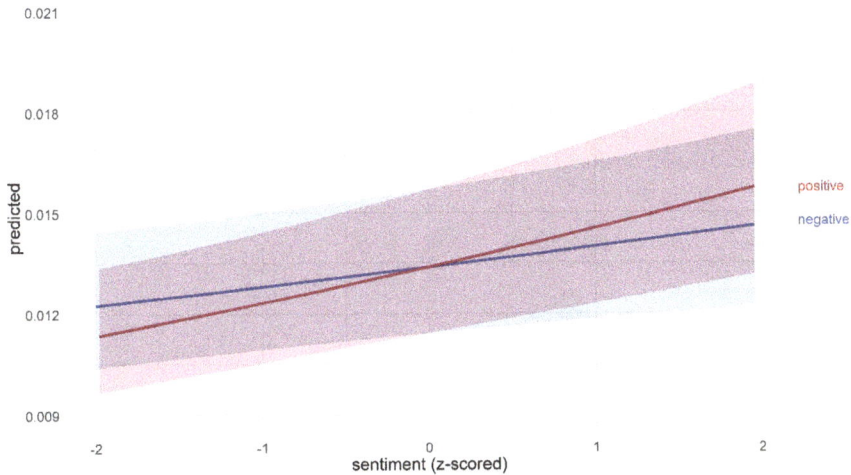

Fig. 4: Predicted likelihood of GET for positive and negative sentiment as a main effect.

Verb semantics, however, does seem to play a role in the choice of the passive auxiliary. Semantic clustering sheds more detailed light on this. The dot-and-whiskers plot in Fig. 5 visualizes the coefficients and their confidence intervals for those 17 clusters that show no significant interaction with year. The groups that differ significantly from the largest, baseline cluster 13 are marked with asterisks.

The clusters that strongly and steadily predict BE contain more formal verbs encoding deontic (*obliged, allowed*) and mental actions (*defined, considered*), and changes in quality/quantity (*increased, postponed*). Clusters showing steady relative preference for GET encode physical motion (*stomped, whacked*), and concrete actions, for instance, in the culinary context (*salted, baked*). Additionally, most of the low-frequency verb clusters are located towards the GET-end of the spectrum. Some of them contain primarily negative verbs – for example *short-changed*, *gypped*, and *guillotined* in cluster 17 – which could be seen as tentative support to the adversativity hypothesis. However, we are inclined to think that the main defining feature of these clusters is the low frequency of their members. The relatively higher likelihood of attesting GET with infrequent verbs shows that the construction is by no means restricted to entrenched combinations like "got killed".

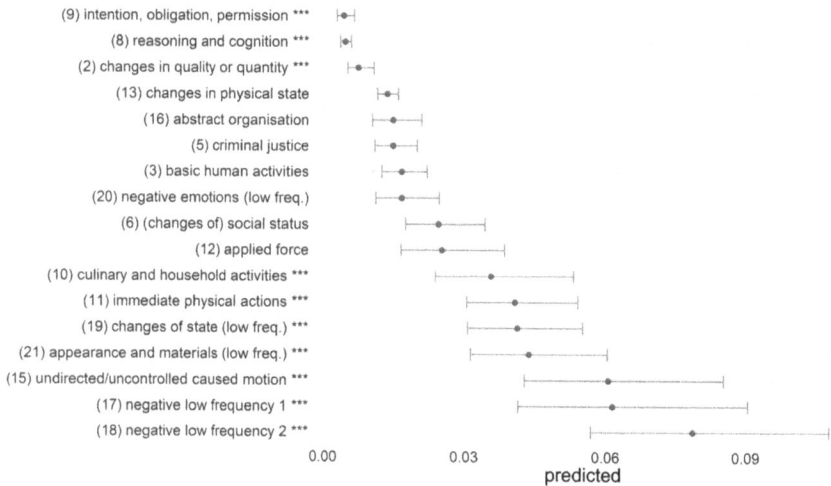

Fig. 5: Predicted likelihood of GET for cluster assignment as a main effect.

Fig. 6 shows the remaining four clusters that display diachronic developments different from the general trend. We see the cluster containing verbs of goal-directed/controlled motion (*thrown, carried*) becoming drastically more likely to combine with GET, and verbs of public communication (*printed, published*) rising relatively more steeply as well, while the likelihood of GET has not increased much with time for verbs that can be expected to be often used statively: clusters

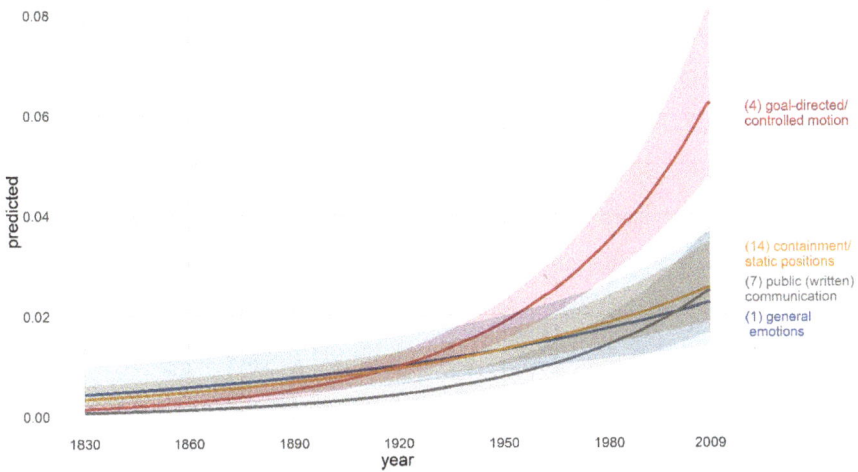

Fig. 6: Predicted likelihood of GET for the interaction between year and cluster assignment.

containing socially accepted emotions (*annoyed*, *excited*) and containment/static positions (*covered*, *stacked*).

4.4 Morpho-syntactic Constraints

The morpho-syntactic predictors are included primarily to explore the supposition that as the GET-passive grammaticalizes (Hopper/Traugott 2003), it becomes increasingly available for different and more complex sentence structures as well. We do see a trend in this direction regarding the presence of a *by*-PP, a negator, and/or a *to*-complement (Fig. 7), each of which disfavours GET significantly more strongly in the early 19th century than in the late 20th and early 21st century; in the newest data, in fact, the model predicts a slightly higher likelihood for GET in negated sentences. The presence of an intervening adverb, however, now lowers the likelihood of GET even more than before.

The form of the auxiliary was included as a variable rather for exploratory reasons with no specific hypothesis attached to it. The results, while statistically significant, are not easy to interpret or explain (Fig. 7). Perfect forms lag clearly behind in the general trend towards more use of GET over time, and while one still finds the highest likelihood of GET with -*ing*-forms, this preference has become less strong over time. The avoidance of GET with perfect and preterite may have to do with a need to differentiate the GET-passive from possessive (HAVE) *got*.

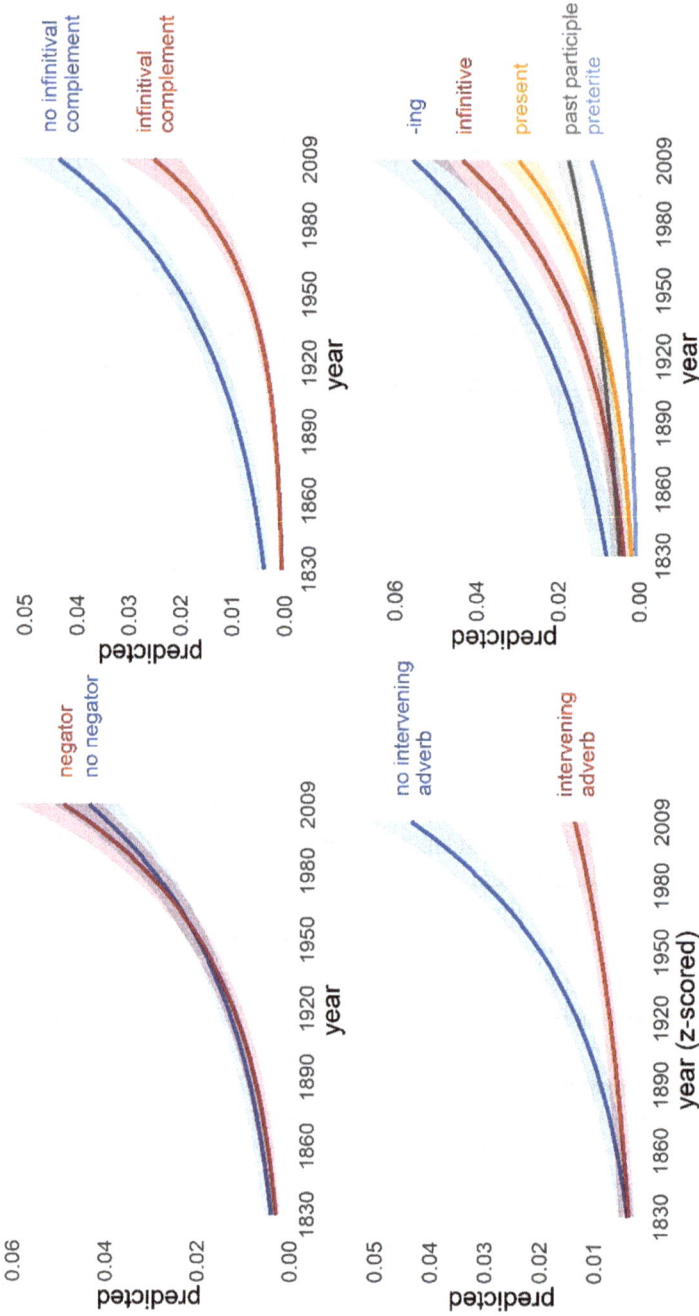

Fig. 7: Predicted likelihood of GET for the interactions between year and negator (top left), infinitival complement (top right), intervening adverb (bottom left), and tense of auxiliary verb (bottom right).

5 Discussion

The first thing to note is the number of main effects and interactions that emerge as significant. Before interpreting any of these in detail, the results of the statistical analysis speak to the complexity of linguistic conditioning in the case of the passive alternation. Investigations of isolated predictors based on raw frequency counts or individual bivariate tests are not ideally suited to do justice to this level of complexity. Our study is the first to our knowledge that grounds its analysis of the English passive alternation in a fully accountable multivariate design, which we maintain is necessary to disentangle the influence of competing conditioning factors.

As regards the specific hypotheses about such conditioning, our results offer partial confirmation for many of these but also suggest a need for further qualification. Unsurprisingly, our data corroborate the general rise of the GET-passive, a process that picks up speed in the latter half of the period covered by our data, i.e., during the 20th century. This change is accompanied by an encroachment of GET into initially disfavouring contexts, as seen in the weakening of morpho-syntactic constraints. The fact that the presence of an intervening adverb shows an effect in a different direction, emerging as a constraint only as time progresses, is an interesting reversal of this general trend in need of further analysis in the future. One explanation might be that many of these sentences are not true passives at all, but that the adverb pre-modifies an adjectival usage of the participle, as for example in (20). However, initial qualitative analysis of a subset of the data does not offer conclusive confirmation of this hypothesis; see for example (21).

(20) If insurance companies cannot go directly to the client where such recourse is morally justified, they will simply step up their rates. (COHA news 1928)

(21) The silence of midnight was almost constantly interrupted by the howling of wild beasts. (COHA magazine 1835)

The innovative GET-variant maintains its informal stylistic profile throughout the time period covered in this study, as seen in the effects plots for both genre and F-measure. The divergent paths of different genres over time speak to general developments in the register ecology of written English (Hundt/Mair 1999) rather than calling the informality hypothesis into question in general. We do not see a weakening of the formality constraint; on the contrary, lower F-measure values (indicating less formality) become more strongly associated with GET over time.

The results are less conclusive concerning the related hypotheses of subject responsibility and adversativity/non-neutrality. The former constraint is found to operate in our data, but to be weakening over time, as seen in the interactions of year with both *by*-PPs and inanimate subjects. This trend is indicative of an expansion of the GET-passive into more general passive contexts. Currently, our operationalization of subject animacy achieves accuracy in about two-thirds of all cases. With sufficient data, such a level of precision is able to offer meaningful results, but nonetheless, more work needs to be dedicated to improving classification accuracy for subject animacy.

While the effects of verb sentiment scores reach statistical significance, their magnitudes are among the smallest in our model. This might either weaken the non-neutrality hypothesis, or be due to the operationalization of sentiment. Specifically, we simply derived verb sentiment scores from an available sentiment lexicon. Missing entries for many lemmas in our data, in addition to insensitivity to the wider sentential context, render the sentiment scores somewhat suspect, and may partially explain their very small effect sizes. We already consider the presence of a negator, thus improving the accuracy of the sentiment scores, but we are convinced that the more appropriate level of sentiment analysis is the entire sentence embedding the given passive instance. Yet, in small-scale comparisons of manually and automatically scored sentiments we observed that automated sentiment scores on the sentence-level suffer from accuracy issues. The older data in particular present challenges to scoring algorithms, most of which have been trained on contemporary language. All in all, compared to other conditioning effects, we see little reason to attach strong meaning to adversativity or non-neutrality as an explanatory variable.

Perhaps our most important finding is the importance of verb semantic cluster. This predictor's effect size outshines that of all others, lending strong support to Rühlemann's (2007) account of the GET-passive as largely lexically conditioned. However, the fact that cluster membership holds such explanatory power, even after accounting for individual verb lemmas with random intercepts, indicates that the behaviour of isolated lexemes is not the appropriate level of generalization. Instead, groups of related verbs that can be identified through corpus-based, quantitative methods show similar passivation profiles. We see our key contribution in sharpening the focus on the relevance of this constraint and in outlining a principled method for operationalizing it quantitatively by means of a distributional word vector model.

Given that our key finding concerns the influence of verb cluster membership, critical attention to this variable is particularly warranted. As with any clustering solution, it is difficult to justify our choice in absolute terms. In order to maximize accountability, we opted for model-based clustering, which has the advantage of identifying the optimal number of clusters in a mathematically principled way. However, a hierarchical, density-based, or any other cluster solution could also have been chosen, yielding potentially different results. We do not see a choice of method immune to criticism. However, in experimenting with various techniques and parameter settings, we noted largely convergent patterns in how individual verbs are grouped together. The difference, then, is more one of detail than of substance. Should different clustering solutions produce highly divergent results, this should be taken as evidence that the underlying vector representation of the words is not reliable, a problem we do not face in this analysis.

The behaviour of the various morpho-syntactic predictors indicates the expansion of GET to more general contexts. *By*-PPs, negators, and *to*-complements used to disfavour GET more strongly in the older data than now. The usage of different tense and aspectual forms does not paint a clear picture, other than the perfect and the preterite being the least GET-friendly forms. This behaviour may be explained by a need to differentiate the GET-passive from possessive (HAVE) *got*. Furthermore, the presence of adverbial premodification strongly mediates the diachronic rise of GET, such that the increase is much more pronounced in bare cases without an intervening adverb. Our tentative working hypothesis is that the presence of an adverb strongly correlates with adjectival uses of the past participle, i.e., marginal instances on the passive gradient. It is possible that these do not constitute valid variable contexts, an issue that will be addressed in future work.

To boil the discussion down to its essence, our large-scale quantitative approach marks a radical divergence from previous research on the GET-passive. Both the potential insights and the problems entailed by this approach are considerable. It is our position that the former more than justify the general choice of method and the latter can, and will, be addressed more comprehensively in future research.

6 Outlook

The present paper contains preliminary findings from our investigation into the factors influencing the passive alternation in American English. More precisely, we investigate change in the choice between BE and GET as the passive auxiliary over the past two centuries, drawing on data provided by COHA. To our knowledge, this big data approach is the first study embedding a large range of variables into a multivariate framework and is therefore able to account for the multitude of predictors and their interactions. Our method allows for an in-depth analysis of the passive construction and offers potential for similar studies of other syntactic and semantic phenomena, such as changes in the use of the progressive.

To summarize the results, we observed a general rise of GET both in absolute numbers and as a competitor to BE throughout the observed time period (1830–2009). Our informality hypothesis was confirmed: GET is more likely in less formal texts, and this tendency has actually strengthened over time. We have further shown that, unlike previously assumed, the constraint of subject responsibility has weakened over time and GET has expanded its reach to more general passive contexts. This is suggested by the decline of the inhibiting effect of both *by*-PPs and inanimate subjects over time. The behaviour of the morpho-syntactic constraints also lends support to this interpretation. In terms of adversativity/non-neutrality, our findings were less conclusive, but in general, we did not find strong support for the significance of these suggested semantic characteristics of the GET-passive. Furthermore, our results corroborate our supposition that the grouping of verbs into semantic clusters is more revealing than an analysis based on isolated lexemes, such as verb sentiment. The highly effective and methodologically innovative process of semantic clustering supports the notion of lexical conditioning of the GET-passive, fitting with current usage-based approaches that see grammar and meaning as tightly integrated.

Several challenges remain to be addressed. Most importantly, we have adopted a very general notion of the variable context, focusing on all cases of BE/GET + past participle, as tagged in COHA, with only very few exclusions. This fuzzy context comprises individual forms that cannot be counted as 'true passives' and lack full referential equivalence to a competing variant. Whether it makes sense to treat, for example, GET *excited* and BE *excited* as directly competing variants is questionable. We therefore recognize that further pruning of the data is desirable in order to keep the analysis more accountable. Currently, we are working on semi-automated as well as fully qualitatively guided ways of narrowing down the variable context to central passives, excluding adjectival uses. The semi-automated measures will include, among others, how often an assumed participle is used with a copula, adjectives, or *very* and other degree elements in COHA, as well as whether it allows *un*-prefixation. The extent to which the results reported here are corroborated by these analyses will be an important touchstone for our method.

Beyond the factors discussed in this paper, we are planning on extending the investigation to other sources of variation in the passive. One such factor potentially contributing to variation is dynamicity, which would be highly interesting to consider, but difficult to operationalize and extract automatically. We have only begun to scratch the surface of the potential offered by the big data approach considering a wide range of variables. The results so far are encouraging and call for further investigations, such as comparing the two constructions across varieties of English.

7 Appendix

Tab. 1: Top ten verbs per cluster.

	Cluster	Verbs
1	general emotions	*annoyed, excited, embarrassed, puzzled, confused, alarmed, shocked, irritated, perplexed, frightened*
2	changes in quality or quantity	*increased, reduced, postponed, delayed, diminished, improved, accelerated, removed, eliminated, changed*
3	basic human activities	*lived, sat, stood, talked, spent, waited, told, said, loved, listened*
4	goal-directed/controlled motion	*thrown, carried, swept, driven, flung, brought, poured, hurled, dragged, put*
5	criminal justice	*murdered, hanged, convicted, slain, jailed, accused, sentenced, imprisoned, raped, fined*
6	(changes of) social status	*excommunicated, naturalized, proscribed, flogged, impeached, beheaded, reprimanded, reunited, martyred, paroled*
7	public (written) communication	*printed, published, issued, written, signed, circulated, mailed, quoted, delivered, copied*
8	reasoning and cognition	*defined, considered, exercised, imposed, characterized, represented, criticized, known, dealt, deemed*
9	intention, obligation, permission	*obliged, allowed, forced, prepared, let, tempted, needed, accustomed, invited, refused*
10	culinary and household activities	*fried, salted, stewed, broiled, baked, boiled, buttered, pickled, roasted, canned*
11	immediate physical actions	*bumped, tripped, bounced, beat, hammered, scrambled, hopped, spun, pounded, rattled*
12	applied force	*cocked, clutched, tugged, tightened, braced, bent, stroked, straightened, tilted, rubbed*
13	changes in physical state	*withered, distorted, bruised, starved, purified, shed, smothered, chilled, spoiled, shattered*
14	containment/static positions	*lined, covered, stacked, littered, packed, loaded, crowded, surrounded, crammed, filled*
15	undirected/uncontrolled caused motion	*throwed, whacked, plopped, bailed, blowed, bowled, chucked, stomped, shooed, gobbled*
16	abstract organisation	*targeted, coordinated, subsidized, monitored, programmed, evaluated, publicized, oriented, mapped, channeled*

Tab. 1 (continued)

Cluster	Verbs
17 negative low frequency 1	*bushwhacked, zonked, jobbed, short-changed, gypped, guillotined, propositioned, jugged, articled, resupplied*
18 negative low frequency 2	*bulldozed, bluffed, cloned, sensitized, sidelined, circumcised, electrocuted, trashed, shacked, bedeviled*
19 changes of state (low freq.)	*overheated, winded, overdone, readjusted, freshened, unhooked, flurried, dehydrated, primed, unmade*
20 negative emotions (low freq.)	*incensed, infuriated, humiliated, embittered, thwarted, enraged, angered, intimidated, harassed, cowed*
21 appearance and materials (low freq.)	*rumpled, matted, creased, freckled, discolored, patched, knitted, glazed, laced, rusted*

Tab. 2: Model coefficient estimates.

term	estimate	standard error	z-value	p-value
(Intercept)	−6.29927	0.0825846	−76.28	<1e-99
year_z	1.00038	0.06697	14.94	<1e-49
genre: mag	−0.0770036	0.0338057	−2.28	0.0227
genre: news	−0.70799	0.0714953	−9.90	<1e-22
genre: nf	−0.554269	0.0423025	−13.10	<1e-38
fMeasure_z	−0.744673	0.0161895	−46.00	<1e-99
animacy_cat: animate	0.352907	0.0234325	15.06	<1e-50
animacy_cat: body part	−0.711412	0.0566091	−12.57	<1e-35
animacy_cat: inanimate	−0.466123	0.0267487	−17.43	<1e-67
by: by	−0.471775	0.0280702	−16.81	<1e-62
participleNegative_z	0.0450047	0.016817	2.68	0.0074
participlePositive_z	0.0840761	0.0165777	5.07	<1e-6
ClusterAssignment: 1	−0.5899	0.220049	−2.68	0.0073
ClusterAssignment: 2	−0.916412	0.171836	−5.33	<1e-7
ClusterAssignment: 3	−0.0941738	0.125678	−0.75	0.4537
ClusterAssignment: 4	−0.585104	0.104404	−5.60	<1e-7
ClusterAssignment: 5	−0.212574	0.131247	−1.62	0.1053
ClusterAssignment: 6	0.305356	0.15939	1.92	0.0554
ClusterAssignment: 7	−1.43674	0.195456	−7.35	<1e-12
ClusterAssignment: 8	−1.4051	0.1066	−13.18	<1e-38
ClusterAssignment: 9	−1.47553	0.201912	−7.31	<1e-12
ClusterAssignment: 10	0.695088	0.193572	3.59	0.0003
ClusterAssignment: 11	0.833613	0.129664	6.43	<1e-9
ClusterAssignment: 12	0.335724	0.203223	1.65	0.0985
ClusterAssignment: 14	−0.646327	0.132854	−4.86	<1e-5
ClusterAssignment: 15	1.25195	0.165797	7.55	<1e-13

Tab. 2 (continued)

term	estimate	standard error	z-value	p-value
ClusterAssignment: 16	−0.213618	0.162823	−1.31	0.1895
ClusterAssignment: 17	1.26807	0.192014	6.60	<1e-10
ClusterAssignment: 18	1.53212	0.157929	9.70	<1e-21
ClusterAssignment: 19	0.846663	0.135071	6.27	<1e-9
ClusterAssignment: 20	−0.0925117	0.188688	−0.49	0.6239
ClusterAssignment: 21	0.906087	0.155566	5.82	<1e-8
aux_tense: ing	0.503215	0.0343079	14.67	<1e-47
aux_tense: perf	−0.364226	0.0270991	−13.44	<1e-40
aux_tense: pres	−0.522158	0.0257872	−20.25	<1e-90
aux_tense: pret	−1.43234	0.0280256	−51.11	<1e-99
adverb: rr	−0.317307	0.0187147	−16.95	<1e-63
to_compl: toComp	−0.64692	0.053865	−12.01	<1e-32
negator: neg	−0.0451412	0.0269028	−1.68	0.0934
year_z & genre: mag	0.374067	0.0293471	12.75	<1e-36
year_z & genre: news	0.777004	0.0560803	13.86	<1e-42
year_z & genre: nf	0.0285464	0.03764	0.76	0.4482
year_z & fMeasure_z	0.0563708	0.0141633	3.98	<1e-4
year_z & animacy: animate	0.027297	0.0211088	1.29	0.1960
year_z & animacy: body part	−0.0789024	0.0509244	−1.55	0.1213
year_z & animacy: inanimate	0.052503	0.0241587	2.17	0.0298
year_z & by: by	0.145539	0.0239594	6.07	<1e-8
year_z & participleNegative_z	−0.0164403	0.0143878	−1.14	0.2532
year_z & participlePositive_z	−0.0229869	0.0146535	−1.57	0.1167
year_z & ClusterAssignment: 1	−0.2683	0.128219	−2.09	0.0364
year_z & ClusterAssignment: 2	−0.028102	0.107379	−0.26	0.7935
year_z & ClusterAssignment: 3	−0.0540112	0.0819367	−0.66	0.5098
year_z & ClusterAssignment: 4	0.349616	0.0713911	4.90	<1e-6
year_z & ClusterAssignment: 5	0.155091	0.0909364	1.71	0.0881
year_z & ClusterAssignment: 6	0.147213	0.107106	1.37	0.1693
year_z & ClusterAssignment: 7	0.287328	0.125378	2.29	0.0219
year_z & ClusterAssignment: 8	0.101418	0.0662312	1.53	0.1257
year_z & ClusterAssignment: 9	0.121376	0.116831	1.04	0.2988
year_z & ClusterAssignment: 10	−0.119907	0.124978	−0.96	0.3373
year_z & ClusterAssignment: 11	−0.0560703	0.0839791	−0.67	0.5043
year_z & ClusterAssignment: 12	−0.254271	0.13054	−1.95	0.0514
year_z & ClusterAssignment: 14	−0.160681	0.0802212	−2.00	0.0452
year_z & ClusterAssignment: 15	0.00868104	0.128198	0.07	0.9460
year_z & ClusterAssignment: 16	0.00729065	0.110859	0.07	0.9476
year_z & ClusterAssignment: 17	0.261172	0.150832	1.73	0.0834
year_z & ClusterAssignment: 18	−0.0999417	0.112238	−0.89	0.3732
year_z & ClusterAssignment: 19	−0.166637	0.0982637	−1.70	0.0899
year_z & ClusterAssignment: 20	0.00322216	0.1208	0.03	0.9787
year_z & ClusterAssignment: 21	−0.200298	0.10481	−1.91	0.0560

Tab. 2 (continued)

term	estimate	standard error	z-value	p-value
year_z & aux_tense: ing	−0.141531	0.0308343	−4.59	<1e-5
year_z & aux_tense: perf	−0.33251	0.0256249	−12.98	<1e-37
year_z & aux_tense: pres	0.0749081	0.0234108	3.20	0.0014
year_z & aux_tense: pret	0.060927	0.0256607	2.37	0.0176
year_z & adverb: rr	−0.162972	0.0176527	−9.23	<1e-19
year_z & to_compl: toComp	0.213035	0.044595	4.78	<1e-5
year_z & negator: neg	0.0627364	0.0239071	2.62	0.0087

References

Baccianella, Stefano/Esuli, Andrea/Sebastiani, Fabrizio (2010): "SENTIWORDNET 3.0: An enhanced lexical resource for sentiment analysis and opinion mining." In *Proceedings of the International Conference on Language Resources and Evaluation, LREC 2010.* 17–23. May 2010, Valetta. 2200–2204.

Banks, David (1986): "Getting by with Get." In: *La Linguistique* 22, 125–130.

Bates, Douglas/Kliegl, Reinhold/Vasishth, Shravan/Baayen, Harald (2018): "Parsimonious Mixed Models." arXiv:1506.04967 [stat.ME], 1–21.

Bezanson, Jeff/Edelman, Alan/Karpinski, Stefan/Shah, Viral B. (2017): "Julia: A fresh approach to numerical computing." In: *SIAM Review* 59, 65–98.

Biber, Douglas/Conrad, Susan/Leech, Geoffrey (2003): *Student Grammar of Spoken and Written English.* 2nd edn. Harlow: Longman.

Carter, Ronald/McCarthy, Melissa (1999): "The English get-passive in spoken discourse: Description and implications for an interpersonal grammar." In: *English Language and Linguistics* 3, 41–58.

Chappell, Hilary (1980): "Is the get-passive adversative?" In: *Papers in Linguistics* 13, 411–452.

Collins, Peter C. (1996): "Get-passives in English." In: *World Englishes* 15, 43–56.

Coto Villalibre, Eduardo (2015): "Is the get-passive really that adversative?" In: *Miscelánea: A Journal of English and American Studies* 51, 13–30.

Croft, William (1991): *Syntactic Categories and Grammatical Relations. The Cognitive Organization of Information.* Chicago: The University of Chicago Press.

Davies, Mark (2010-): *Corpus of Historical American English (COHA).* Online at: https://www.english-corpora.org/coha/ <03.11.2021>.

Fleisher, Nicholas (2006): "The origin of passive get." In: *English Language and Linguistics* 10, 225–252.

Fraley, Chris/Raftery, Adrian E./Scrucca, Luca (2019): *Mclust: Gaussian mixture modelling for model-based clustering, classification, and density estimation.* Online at: https://cran.r-project.org/web/packages/mclust/index.html <12.05.2022>.

Givón, Thomas/Yang, Phil (1994): "The rise of the English GET-passive." In: Barbara Fox/Paul J. Hopper (Eds.): *Voice. Form and Function.* Amsterdam: John Benjamins, 119–150.

Hatcher, Anna G. (1949): "To get/be invited." In: *Modern Language Notes* 64, 433–446.
Heylighen, Francis/Dewaele, Jean-Marc (2002): "Variation in the contextuality of language: An empirical measure." In: *Foundations of Science* 7, 293–340.
Hopper, Paul J./Traugott, Elizabeth C. (2003): *Grammaticalization.* 2nd edn. Cambridge: Cambridge University Press.
Hundt, Marianne (2001): "What corpora tell us about the grammaticalisation of voice in get-constructions." In: *Studies in Language* 25, 49–88.
Hundt, Marianne/Mair, Christian (1999): "'Agile' and 'uptight' genres: The corpus-based approach to language change in progress." In: *International Journal of Corpus Linguistics* 4, 221–242.
Lüdecke, Daniel (2018): "ggeffects: Tidy data frames of marginal effects from regression models." In: *Journal of Open Source Software* 3, 772.
Mair, Christian/Leech, Geoffrey (2006): "Current changes in English syntax." In: Bas Aarts/April McMahon (Eds.): *The Handbook of English Linguistics.* Malden: Blackwell, 318–342.
Mikolov, Tomas/Chen, Kai/Corrado, Gred/Dean, Jeffrey (2013): "Efficient estimation of word representations in vector space." arXiv:1301.3781 [cs.CL], 1–12.
Poplack, Shana/Tagliamonte, Sali A. (1989): "There's no tense like the present: Verbal -s inflection in early Black English." In: *Language Variation and Change* 1, 47–84.
Python Software Foundation (2019): *Python 2.7.10.*
Quirk, Randolph/Greenbaum, Sydney/Leech, Geoffrey/Svartvik, Jan (1985): *A Comprehensive Grammar of the English Language.* London: Longman.
Řehůřek, Radim/Sojka, Petr (2010): "Software framework for topic modelling with large corpora." In: *Proceedings of Workshop on New Challenges for NLP Frameworks, LREC 2010,* 17–23 May 2010, Valletta, 46–50.
RStudio Team (2020): *RStudio. Integrated Development for R.* Boston.
Rühlemann, Christoph (2007): "Lexical grammar: The GET-passive as a case in point." In: *ICAME Journal* 31, 111–127.
Schwarz, Sarah (2015): "Passive voice in American soap opera dialogue." In: *Studia Neophilologica* 87, 152–170.
Schwarz, Sarah (2017): "'Like getting nibbled to death by a duck': Grammaticalization of the get-passive in the TIME Magazine Corpus." In: *English World-Wide* 38, 305–335.
Toyota, Junichi (2008): *Diachronic Change in the English Passive.* Basingstoke: Palgrave Macmillan.
Weiner, Judith E./Labov, William (1983): "Constraints on the agentless passive." In: *Journal of Linguistics* 19, 29–58.
Xiao, Richard Z./McEnery, Tony/Qian, Yufang (2006): "Passive constructions in English and Chinese: A corpus-based contrastive study." In: *Languages in Contrast* 6, 109–149.

Gavin Brookes

'The Fat Gap': Discourses around *Social Class* in UK Press Coverage of Obesity

Abstract: This study examines how discourses around social class contribute to representations of obesity in the British press. A sample of articles explicitly mentioning social class is subjected to a qualitative, critical approach to discourse analysis and newspapers are compared in terms of both their formats (broadsheets and tabloids) and political orientations (left-leaning and right-leaning). Left-leaning broadsheets present social class as central to the development of obesity, with individuals' life circumstances and lack of means framed as causing it. On the other hand, right-leaning newspapers (including tabloids and broadsheets) mitigate the influence of social class on obesity, for example presenting it as something that affects people at all class levels and foregrounding instead the importance of factors connected to lifestyle 'choices'. It is argued that the right-leaning press's discourses are intended to uphold, and to inflict as little harm as possible upon, the neoliberal agenda that characterises its more general coverage of obesity. This chapter considers the potential for such discourses to contribute to the further stigmatisation of society's already least-fortunate, with class-based discrimination compounded by weight stigma, all of which can lead to internalised shame.

1 Introduction

This chapter examines discourses around social class in British press coverage of obesity. The starting point for this chapter is the view that language and discourse have the power to shape the ways in which health and illness are experienced and understood by societies. As Fox (1993: 6) puts it, "illness cannot be just illness, for the simple reason that human culture is constituted in language [. . .] and that health and illness, being things which fundamentally concern humans, and hence need to be 'explained', enter into language and are constituted in language, regardless of whether or not they have some independent reality in nature" (see also Brookes/Hunt 2021). In this sense, I take a broadly social constructionist view of discourse, following Burr (1995: 48) who defines a discourse as "a set of meanings, metaphors, representations, images, stories,

Acknowledgements: This research was funded by the ESRC grant ES/R008906/1.

statements and so on that in some way together produce a particular version of events" (see also Foucault 1972: 49).

The discursively constituted nature of health and illness is arguably most clearly evident in the case of so-called "contested" illnesses (see Brookes 2018; 2020; Hunt/Brookes 2020), such as obesity, which as we will see is subject to a range of competing explanatory discourses within society. For as Baker et al. (2020: online) contend, "our understanding and experience of contested health issues like obesity are based not just in their so-called biological 'realities' but, crucially, in the language used to talk about them, including in (print) media portrayals". Social class is, as will be seen, one of a number of social factors that are put forward by some as an explanation for differing rates of obesity, while others contest such a notion and instead locate obesity's causes with the individual, as arising due to individuals' genetics or personal lifestyle choices, for example. The aim of this study is to examine how discourses around social class contribute to press representations of obesity, taking a corpus-based approach to critical discourse analysis (introduced later).

This chapter is divided into five sections. Following this brief introduction, the next section introduces the central concepts of obesity and social class in more depth, and considers the role of the media in generating and circulating discourses around these. Section 3 introduces the corpus data assembled for this study and the corpus-based approach to critical discourse analysis that is taken to studying it. The analysis of social class discourses is then reported in Section 4 and discussed in the concluding Section 5.

2 Obesity, the British Press and Social Class

Obesity is a diagnostic label that is applied to people who are severely overweight and have a Body Mass Index (BMI) score of 30 or above. Almost two-thirds of adults in the UK have either overweight or obesity, with prevalence being higher amongst people aged 55–74, in some Black, Asian and Minority Ethnic (BAME) groups and, of most relevance to the present study, people who live in more deprived parts of the country (Public Health England 2020). Although the conceptual and diagnostic practices surrounding obesity are, as noted, fiercely contested (see Lupton 2018) for a discussion), many public health authorities around the world (including in the UK) regard obesity as a disease of 'crisis' or 'epidemic' proportions (Boero 2007). This is because, in addition to its high global prevalence, particularly in so-called 'developed countries', obesity has been attributed to heightened risk of diseases like diabetes and some types of cancer, as well as reduced life expectancy overall (Public Health England 2020).

Media representations of health and illness topics have been found to have the potential to alter audiences' health-related attitudes and behaviours, as well as influencing and garnering support for Government policies in this area (Atanasova/Koteyko 2017). This is because, when creating news, journalists and editors make motivated choices respecting their use of language and discourse, with such choices often serving to prioritise certain perspectives on a given issue over others (Richardson 2007). Indeed, experimental evidence indicates that different media discourses around obesity can lead to different ways of assigning responsibility for it, including creating support for particular policies (Liu et al. 2019).

Any exploration of the societal discourses surrounding a health issue like obesity can therefore benefit immensely from taking into account the discourses that characterise (print) media coverage of that issue. Indeed, media representations of obesity have been examined from a wide range of disciplinary and methodological perspectives (see Atanasova/Kuteyko/Gunter 2012 for a review).

The present chapter is part of a wider, ongoing programme of research which explores UK media representations of obesity based on an (approx.) 36-million-word corpus of obesity-related newspaper articles published between 2008 and 2017 (Brookes/Baker 2021). This research has found that press representations of obesity largely rely on discourses of personal responsibility. Such discourses constitute a neoliberal tactic, underpinned by the key notion of individualization, whereby health issues such as obesity are framed as a moral failing by individuals to take 'responsibility' for themselves and their families by preventing and/or eradicating their risk of developing obesity through their lifestyle choices (in this case, relating to diet and exercise). This discourse was found to be particularly prominent in the tabloids (especially the right-leaning ones), which were also likely to stigmatise and shame people with obesity through, for example, euphemistic and humorous language. The broadsheet newspapers, or 'quality' press, meanwhile, were more likely to frame obesity as being caused by wider socio-political factors, with more responsibility being placed with powerful institutions like the Government, food marketers and manufacturers, and supermarkets (For more on the distinction between broadsheet and tabloid newspapers in the UK, see Baker/Gabrielatos/McEnery 2013: 7–8).

This chapter contributes to this ongoing research by analysing discourses around social class in this corpus of UK press articles about obesity. Social class is a complex phenomenon which has its intellectual basis in social and political economic theories advanced by figures such as Karl Marx and Max Weber during the nineteenth century (see Savage 2000 for a discussion). For this chapter,

I adopt the definition of social class put forward by Meyerhoff, who describes it as "a measure of status which is often based on occupation, income and wealth, but also can be measured in terms of aspirations and mobility" (2006: 295). Since social class can be considered a "function of the intersection of a whole lot of different social (and sometimes even personal) attributes" (ibid.), it can be measured in numerous ways. Thus, while traces of Marx's and Weber's influence are evident in contemporary treatments of social class, such treatments also take a broader perspective (Block 2013). Bourdieu (1984: 102), for example, who is influenced by both Marx and Weber, argued that

> class or class fraction is defined not only by its position in the relations of production, as identified through indices such as occupation, income, or even educational level, but also by a certain sex-ratio, a certain distribution in geographical space (which is never socially neutral) and by a whole set of subsidiary characteristics which may function, in the form of tacit requirements, as real principles of selection or exclusion without ever being formally stated (this is the case with ethnic origin and sex).

Relative to other aspects of identity, such as gender, ethnicity and sexuality, social class has received less interest from discourse analysts. As Rampton (2010: 1) points out, "there is a great deal of contemporary work on discourse, culture, power and social inequality, but this generally focuses on gender, ethnicity and generation much more than class". Savage (2000) contends that an initial focus on social class has been usurped by increased interest in other social variables, such as race/ethnicity, gender, and sexuality, while Mills (2017) suggests that the decreased focus on social class may be a consequence of the difficulties associated with categorising individuals into particular class groups, as well as the problems that arise from discussing class differences in terms of deficit.

Another factor that is likely to be relevant is the sense in which social class is no longer as relevant to societies, including British society, as it once was. Indeed, as Charteris-Black/Seale (2010: 23) point out, "[c]lass is often, in the popular imagination, pronounced to be 'dead' and class-based politics rejected". These authors and others attribute this notion, in the UK at least, to the rise of centrist politics and political parties, notably Tony Blair's New Labour and its political legacy evident in recent Governments which have sought to "eliminate class-based discourse through concepts such as 'hard working families'" (ibid.). A consequence of this, Charteris-Black/Seale contend, is that "public and political awareness of the objective importance of social and income inequality has declined" (ibid.). More recently though, Jones (2012: vii) and others have argued that although the true nature and extent of socioeconomic disparities in the UK were previously obscured by the wide availability of cheap credit, the economic crisis of 2008 has since served to "refocus attention on the unjust distribution of wealth and power in society" and that, as a result, class, or at least our aware-ness of and societal discourses around class, are now "back with a vengeance". Likewise, Mills (2017: 81) points out that while some argue that class is no longer relevant to British society, it is also true that society has become more unequal, with lack of employment, precarious zero hours contracts, and reliance on food banks, now all norms for certain sections of society. Mills (2017: 81) describes so-cial class and inequality as "inextricably linked", while Guy (2011: 159–160) ar-gues that [c]lass divisions are essentially based on status and power in a society', where '[s]tatus refers to whether people are respected and deferred to by others in their society (or, conversely, looked down on or ignored), and power refers to the social and material resources a person can command, and the ability (and social right) to make decisions and influence events.

The underlying motivation for this analysis, then, is the view that unequal class relations may contribute to obesity incidence and wider health inequalities in the UK. As Bissell et al. (2016: 14) put it, "obesity shows a well-established so-cial gradient in its prevalence, with the most socio-economically disadvantaged having the highest rates" (see also: Ulijaszek 2014). Bissell et al. also note how evidence increasingly points to "material lack and precarity which are increas-ingly features of daily life across many countries", with "rising levels of material and financial hardship [. . .] clearly impact[ing] the food decisions of many" (ibid.). It is with this in mind that Marsh (2004: online) argues obesity to be a "symptom of social impoverishment".

The study reported in this chapter answers the call, from the likes of Ramp-ton (2010: 1), for research to "resuscitate" the issue of social class in linguistics. It does so by examining how discourses around social class contribute to press representations of obesity. In doing so, the present study will contribute to a re-cent revival in the interest in social class from discourse analysis (see e.g., the studies by Bennett 2013; Baker/McEnery 2015; Toolan 2018; Paterson/Gregory 2019; as well as the collection of corpus-assisted discourse studies of economic inequality representation assembled by Gomez-Jimenez/Toolan 2020). Rampton (2006: 222–223) avers that class can be studied in terms of "primary realities" (i.e., accounting for individuals' material conditions and everyday experiences, activities, practices and discourses) and/or in terms of secondary or "meta-level" representations (including the various ideologies and discourses that surround social class and social class groups). The present study clearly orients to the lat-ter level identified by Rampton. Nevertheless, such "meta-level" representations can have ramifications for the "primary realities" of people belonging to these different groups – a point which will be revisited at the end of the chapter.

3 Data and Analytical Approach

The data examined in this chapter is a sample of articles about obesity taken from a large corpus representing general British press coverage of obesity (described in Brookes/Baker 2021). This corpus comprises all articles, from all UK national newspapers, mentioning either *obesity* or *obese* published between 1st January 2008 and 31st December 2017. For the purpose of the study reported in this chapter, I used the corpus analysis tool, *CQPweb* (Hardie 2012), to extract a sub-sample of all articles in this corpus mentioning the phrase social class* (where the asterisk acts as a wildcard to include cases like social classes). This retrieved two terms: social class (n= 101) and its less frequent plural variant, social classes (n= 37). Articles in which social class is referenced explicitly represent a very small subsample relative to the size of the corpus overall (112 articles; 0.26 per cent). I considered broadening the search by removing the term 'social' from the query, leaving just 'class*'. However, while this search term gave considerably more results (3,646 total occurrences), the vast majority (98 per cent) were false positives, for example referring to school and fitness classes, so weren't relevant for my purposes. For this reason, I proceeded with the more restrictive search-term (social class*), with the comparatively lower frequency at least able to facilitate a qualitative, more granular critical discourse analysis of the social class discourses in the corpus. Tab. 1 gives a breakdown of mentions of social class* across the newspapers, also expressed as normalised frequencies, along with their distributions across texts.

Tab. 1: Mentions of social class* by newspaper, ranked by relative frequency.

Newspaper	Frequency	Frequency per million words	In texts
Times	25	6.52	21
Express	16	4.90	12
Independent	12	4.47	10
Guardian	22	4.20	19
Telegraph	20	4.16	17
Mail	37	3.11	28
Star	1	2.70	1
Mirror	4	1.82	3
Sun	1	0.92	1

As this table indicates, in terms of relative frequency the *Times* mentions social class* more than any other newspaper. In terms of raw frequency, the *Mail* actually mentions *social class** more than any other newspaper. However, because this newspaper contributes so many more words than any other, the relative frequency of this search-term is not as high as it is for the *Times* but also for the *Express, Independent, Guardian* and *Telegraph*. Notably, the bottom half of this table, which represents the newspapers that tend to talk about social class the least, is occupied by tabloids, with the bottom three newspapers – the *Star, Mirror* and, *Sun* – all being so-called 'popular' newspapers. This is consistent with the more general observation that tabloids tend to engage in less political commentary than the broadsheets (see Baker/Gabrielatos/McEnery 2013), so this trend is perhaps to be expected. However, given that social class is an inherently political issue, it is important to consider press discourses of social class not just in relation to newspaper format but also political leaning. If we group the newspapers according to political leanings as well as format (i.e., Broadsheet-Left, Broadsheet-Right, Tabloid-Left, and Tabloid-Right), we see the distinction between (relative) frequencies in the tabloids and broadsheets more clearly.

Tab. 2: Breakdown of frequency of *social class** by corpus section, ranked by relative frequency.

Section	Frequency	Frequency per million words	In texts
Broadsheet-Right	45	5.21	38
Broadsheet-Left	35	4.10	30
Tabloid-Right	55	3.31	42
Tabloid-Left (the *Mirror*)	4	1.77	3

As well as demonstrating more clearly the tendency for the broadsheets to explicitly address the topic of social class more regularly than the tabloids, the ranking in Tab. 2 also suggests that the right-leaning publications are more likely to discuss social class than those situated on the political left. However, political orientation also appears to be less significant to this trend than publication type, as the left-leaning broadsheets were still more likely to discuss social class than the right-leaning tabloids.

Another way of looking at the newspapers in the corpus which is relevant to the analysis of social class relates to which social class groups tend to make up the newspapers' respective readerships. This is because newspaper articles are written, or 'designed', in ways that their editors think will appeal to the perceived sensibilities and worldviews of their 'imagined' readerships (Bell 1984).

With this in mind, it is likely that articles will be written in ways that are designed to appeal to the social class groups that make up the newspapers' perceived readerships. Tab. 3 gives the daily circulation of the newspapers in the data, divided by social class using the NRS social grades system (a system of demographic classification developed by the UK National Readership survey to classify readers). The column ABC1 represents readers in the categories A (upper middle class; higher managerial, administrative or professional occupation), B (middle class; intermediate managerial, administrative or professional occupation) and C1 (lower middle class; supervisory or clerical and junior managerial, administrative or professional occupation). The column headed C2DE represents readers in the categories C2 (skilled working class; skilled manual workers), D (working class; semi-skilled and unskilled manual workers) and E (non-working; state pensioners, casual and lowest grade workers, unemployed with state benefits only).

Tab. 3: Daily reach of UK national newspapers (2000s) (Pamco) (Statistics reflect circulation through phone, tablet, desktop, and print from July 2018 to June 2019. Figures for Sunday and online editions combined).

Category	Newspaper	ABCI		C2DE	
		N (000)	%	N (000)	%
Broadsheet-Left	*Guardian*	4,140	75.55	1,340	24.45
	Independent	2,035	68.33	943	31.67
Broadsheet-Right	*Telegraph*	3,563	71.81	1,399	28.19
	Times	1,830	81.66	411	18.34
Tabloid-Left	*Mirror*	8,093	54.96	6,631	45.04
Tabloid-Right	*Express*	3,652	58.80	2,561	41.20
	Mail	7,345	63.52	4,219	36.48
	Star	874	45.95	1,028	54.05
	Sun	7,654	52.99	6,789	47.01

It is important to note, from Tab. 3 that all newspapers are read more by the higher social class groups than the lower ones, except for the *Star*, which is read more by people in the lower groups. Proportionally, the gaps are tighter between the tabloids than the broadsheets, which indicates that readers at the lower end of the class spectrum make up a much bigger proportion of the readerships of the tabloids compared to the broadsheets. Specifically, readers in the C2DE categories account for an average of 25.66% of broadsheet readerships but 44.76% of tabloid readerships.

The sample of social class-related articles represented in Tab. 2 was then subjected to a manual, qualitative critical discourse analysis which set out to identify the presence of social class- and obesity-related discourses. According to Mills (1997: 17), the linguistic manifestations of discourses can be identified through the "systematicity of the ideas, opinions, concepts, ways of thinking and behaviours which are formed within a particular context". Thus, this analysis focused on linguistic choices that contributed to recurring ways of thinking about and conceiving of social class and its relationship with obesity in the articles. All 112 texts mentioning 'social class' and/or 'social classes' were analysed. While concordance output for the phrase social class* was used as the analytical entry point, in all cases the examination of discourses went beyond the solitary concordance line to interpret the discourses and the functions these performed within the wider contexts of the entire articles.

The analysis reported in this chapter orients to Fairclough's (2015 [1989]) three-tier approach to critical discourse analysis, which incorporates interpretation of discourse at the levels of: i) text, ii) discursive practice and iii) social practice. At text level, discourses are identified through their linguistic manifestations and interpreted in terms of how they contribute to local (i.e., text-level) representations of social class and obesity. The creation of the news texts is then interpreted as a discursive practice in which particular discourses are drawn upon by the text creators on the basis that such discourses fulfil their ideological motivations and reflect the views of their 'imagined' readers. Finally, as a form of social practice, the discourses identified in the analysis will be interpreted in terms of their possible ramifications for readers and wider societal understandings of obesity, in this case as it relates to social class. The readership statistics presented in Tab. 3 are therefore important to understanding news discourses as forms of discursive and social practice, as the choice of discourses is driven by editors' imagined audiences and will, if reaching these groups, likely have particular ramifications for their understandings of, and attitudes towards, obesity. The analysis is reported in the next section. To facilitate comparison of the different sections of the press, the analysis is structured according to the categories in Tab. 2, beginning with the left-leaning broadsheets.

4 Analysis

4.1 Left-leaning Broadsheets

As a reminder, the left-leaning broadsheets were ranked second in terms of normalised frequency of *social class**. Analysing the uses of this term, I observed an overwhelming tendency, accounting for 27 of the 35 uses, for obesity and poor diet to be framed as consequences of social class, with social inequalities construed as the cause not only of obesity but also of health inequalities more widely. Such representations also paved the way for criticism towards the media for idolising slender bodies, as well as towards public health strategies underpinned by a neoliberal logic for failing to address the fact, as the articles' authors see it, that a person's ability to lose weight and maintain a slender physique are contingent on their ability to afford, for example, nutritious food and a gym membership, as the examples below demonstrate.

(1) Education, income and **social class** all have a bearing on the diseases we get and how long we live, but a study like this can make allowances for all these factors to get a clear and unbiased picture of the effects of particular aspects of one's lifestyle. (*Guardian* 2009)

(2) No public health campaign could begin to compete with the message sent out every day in every way that thin is beautiful, and fat is ugly, undesirable and a sign of moral uselessness. That's not a nudge, it's a daily knock on the head with a cudgel. 'You can't be too rich or too thin,' said Dorothy Parker. What no one says explicitly enough is that fat is a **social class** issue. Most of the seriously obese are poor. This is tiptoed around, but those with a body-mass index in the red zone, those whose children risk swelling up at a young age, in danger of losing limbs and eyesight to diabetes as they grow up, are the poorest. The hyper-rich are called 'fat cats', but privilege is usually thin and sleek, its body well-exercised by gyms and personal trainers on diets of kale and goji berries. (*Guardian* 2016)

In a minority of cases, the newspapers in this category presented a counter argument to this position that social class influences obesity risk, and the association between obesity and the lower classes in particular, by presenting obesity as something that affects people equally, regardless of social class. However, this only appeared in 4 of the mentions of *social class** in this section of the data and, overall, the left-leaning broadsheets were much more likely to construct social class as something that has profound influence on obesity incidence.

4.2 Right-leaning Broadsheets

Moving on now to the right-leaning broadsheets, which exhibited the highest relative frequency of *social class**, and the representation here was less decisive, with no clear overall pattern. Here, the relationship between social class and obesity appears to be conceived in a way that is less straightforward and more variable. For example, where articles which constructed obesity as something that affects people regardless of social class were in the minority in the left-leaning broadsheets, such stories account for a larger proportion of the right-leaning broadsheet sample, found in 10 of the 45 mentions of *social class**. As this and the forthcoming examples will demonstrate, a characteristic of the right-leaning broadsheets' discourses on social class is that they are recontextualised from scientific research articles.

(3)   It's not just poor children who have a poor diet. The findings come from a team of nutritionists who tracked the food intake, from birth to the age of eight, of 4,000 children. They took into account **social class** and access to books and toys, and other brainboosting environmental factors, before concluding that poor diet alone leads to a deficit of five IQ points. (*Telegraph* 2011)

Such studies and their findings are not selected and recontextualised at random but are likely selected for coverage because they have been deemed to be newsworthy and/or because they support an argument or position that the particular newspaper is interested in advancing. In this case, the findings from such studies could be newsworthy because their findings are surprising, assuming that readers would likely associate obesity with those at the poorer end of the social class spectrum. However, it is also in these newspapers' interest to publish such stories, since they confer the authority of expertise to legitimise (van Leeuwen 2008) the potentially contentious notion that all social class groups are affected by obesity. Or more precisely, to legitimise the logical implication that social class is not a decisive factor in the development of obesity.

In a further four articles, obesity was construed not just as something which affects all people regardless of social class but was even framed as something which affected people in the 'middle classes' more than people lower down the socio-economic ladder. For example, this extract from the *Times* reports on a study suggesting that obesity affects middle class girls more than girls from 'poor' or 'very rich' families. Note how, as well as legitimating this position by again invoking the authority of scientific knowledge, the newspaper places particular stock in this finding by describing the study from which it originates as 'more reliable than other studies', perhaps placing it above that majority of other studies which imply a connection between obesity and the lower social classes.

(4)   The findings of the report are published in the International Journal of Obesity and suggest that results drawn from a three-year study of 13,000 11-year-olds in Leeds, using data on the wealth of neighbourhoods to assign **social class** [. . .], may be more reliable than previous studies. Middle-class girls, it found, were fully twice as likely to be fat as those from poor (or very rich) families. (*Times* 2013)

Obesity was also depicted in this section of the press as being contingent on factors other than social class, with factors such as marital conflict, genetics, gender, time of birth, number of siblings, and a child's rate of development all put forward instead. For example, the extract below reports on a study which found that people with obesity had especially low levels of vitamin D.

(5)   The Aberdeen study did indeed find that obese people had lower levels of vitamin D than those of healthy weight, after other controlling for factors such as diet and **social class**. It is also true that sunlight is the primary source of vitamin D (though it is also found in foods such as oily fish and eggs). This association led much of the media to make the jump to a simple headline that absolves obese people from some responsibility for their shape, while indulging our national obsession with the weather. (*Times* 2008)

In addition to mentioning twice that this study controlled for social class (helping to background the effects of this variable), it is also worth noting that the article is critical of other sections of the media for utilising the attested link between obesity and vitamin D to 'absolve obese people from some responsibility for their shape', touching on a theme of responsibility which looms large in this section of the press.

The representation of social class was not straightforward in the right-leaning broadsheets, though, and in 8 of the mentions of *social class** obesity was represented as something that affects people at the bottom of the socio-economic ladder more than those at the top, reflecting the type of discourse that dominates in the left-leaning broadsheets. However, in contrast to their left-leaning counterparts, claims around the lower classes being disproportionately affected by obesity were mitigated in the right-leaning broadsheets, orienting again to other factors such as those which are presented as being more influential above. For example, in the extract below, although fathers' social class is presented as influencing health inequalities, this is reframed through a biomedical perspective and reduced to as a 'hormone profile':

(6) Professor Diana Kuh, of the Medical Research Council's Unit for Lifelong Health and Ageing at UCL said the hormonal differences showed how societal factors literally 'get under the skin' and affect health. 'In the UK, substantial health inequalities exist; those in less socioeconomically advantaged circumstances have worse health,' said Prof Kuh. 'We found that socioeconomic disadvantage across life, based on father's **social class** and on the study member's education, social class and income, was associated with an adverse hormone profile.' (*Telegraph* 2015)

At other points, articles alluding to a link between obesity and low social class did so in the wider context of a neoliberal discourse which responsibilised individuals into managing their obesity risk. For instance, extract (7) below, taken from the *Telegraph*, constructs "poor nutrition" as a "result of poverty" which is "itself closely related to social class". However, rather than take this opportunity to explore and critique the social conditions leading to poverty, the article then develops a decidedly neoliberal flavour, citing doctor Dame Sally Davies to contend that physical unfitness results from "mental unfitness, since the obese refuse to do anything about it", before seemingly advocating a more judgmental approach to public health to address this.

(7) Many 'obesity-related conditions' are caused by limited exercise capacity resulting from pre-existing medical conditions, or from poor nutrition as a result of poverty, itself closely related to **social class**. Dame Sally implies that physical unfitness is caused by mental unfitness, since the obese refuse to do anything about it. In the meantime, the NHS actually promotes promiscuity with its studiously 'nonjudgmental' approach. (*Telegraph* 2014)

Similarly, in this extract from the *Times*, overall health in old age is construed as being contingent on both social class but also "whether you have taken responsibility for your health". Perhaps in an attempt to preclude either age or social class from being used as an excuse for individuals failing to fulfil this neoliberal obligation, the author then describes how they chat with "*older* folks" at their "*council* gym".

(8) A recent report by Help the Aged (now part of Age UK) Future Communities, remarks that the division between the rich and poor will be starker than ever in old age. As the Big Society shrinks the State, the quality of your final decades will be starkly defined by **social class** and whether you have taken responsibility for your health. At my council gym, I often

chat with older folks who were referred by GPs after strokes or heart attacks. (*Times* 2011)

4.3 Right-leaning Tabloids

Staying with the right-leaning newspapers but moving on to the tabloids, the first thing to note about this section of the corpus is that, in raw terms, it contained the most mentions of *social class** (55 across 42 texts). However, this is the largest section of the corpus, and in relative terms this translates to 3.31 mentions per million words, which is less than in both the left- and right-leaning broadsheets. The second thing to note is that the mentions of *social class** in the popular newspapers in this section of the corpus (i.e., the *Star* and *Sun*) were not relevant to the representation of obesity. The analysis here is therefore based on the other two newspapers in this quadrant (i.e., the *Express* and *Mail*), of which 33 of the 53 mentions of *social class** were relevant to the representation of obesity. Here, we can observe a striking similarity between these tabloids and the right-leaning broadsheets, including drawing extensively on scientific studies. Like the right-leaning broadsheets, obesity's relation to social class, and the lower social classes in particular, was frequently obscured or mitigated. For example, in ten cases, obesity was constructed as something that affects not just people from lower down the social class scale (referred to here as 'the ignorant'), but all people regardless of social class:

(9)   It isn't just the ignorant affected by obesity, it goes across all **social classes**. (*Mail* 2009)

Like the right-leaning broadsheets, in eleven cases the tabloids also framed other factors as being more relevant to the development of obesity, such as diet, gender, mothers' age, the low price of alcohol, hormones, season of birth, and mental health. This also presented an opportunity for social class to be backgrounded in favour of more individualising, personal responsibility factors, specifically physical activity and, as in extract (10), diet.

(10)   OF COURSE, comparisons like this don't factor in **social class**, or whether you eat chocolate or take a run after work, but that's the whole point – compared with factors like what we snack on, hard manual labour just doesn't make as much of a difference. Even if your day is spent shovelling

gravel, you're still going to develop a pot belly if you lunch on pizza and fizzy drinks every day. (*Mail* 2009)

Again, in parallel with their broadsheet counterparts, of the sixteen cases when the right-leaning tabloids *did* present a link between social class and obesity, half were infused with a neoliberal discourse which once more framed individual responsibility as being more influential than social class. For example, although this excerpt from the *Mail* acknowledges the presence of an 'increasing social class divide in health', lexical choices respecting the representation of members of the lower social classes help to convey a sense in which they are actively "choosing" to lead unhealthy lifestyles; decisions which are framed as having implications not only for their health but also for the health service.

(11)   Meanwhile an influential health think tank has said NHS efforts to tackle the obesity epidemic are failing to impact on less well-off Britons – creating an increasing **social class** divide in health that will put 'unavoidable pressure' on the service. The King's Fund report said that while the middle-classes are getting healthier by giving up bad habits, many poorer people are still choosing to smoke, eat junk food, and live a largely sedentary lifestyle. (*Mail* 2012)

Likewise, extract (12) from the *Express* positioned people from the lower social classes as being most affected by rising obesity rates, before alluding to causes such as a lack of material means to afford healthy food but also the "resistan[ce]", as the article put it, of people from this group towards health advice – a lexical choice which constructs them as actively disregarding and thus failing the obligations on them to maintain a healthy weight.

(12)   Epidemiologist Dr Emmanuel Stamatakis, of University College London, said: 'If trends continue as they have been between 1995 and 2007, in 2015 the number and prevalence of obese young people is projected to increase dramatically – and these increases will affect lower **social classes** to a larger extent. [. . .] The 'fat gap' between rich and poor is the result of food poverty – a term used to explain why those on low incomes often can not provide a healthy diet for their children. Poorer families are also sometimes resistant to health messages aimed at changing their lifestyle.' (*Express* 2009)

Another way in which this neoliberal, responsibilising discourse manifested in the right-leaning tabloids' treatment of social class, but which could not be

seen in the broadsheets, was the provision of health advice to readers as a resolution to class-related differences in obesity prevalence.

(13) The family appears blessed with good genes and their love of horse riding
      and other outdoor pursuits provides a health boost but Office for National
      Statistics Figures show that **social class** counts for a lot when it comes to
      health. Their neighbours in upmarket Kensington and Chelsea enjoy the
      highest life expectancy in the UK. Residents can expect to live to 86.7
      years, 10 years more than those living in Manchester, where the Royle
      family holds court in front of the telly. Predominantly working-class Glas-
      gow has the lowest life expectancy in the UK, with an average of just 74.3
      years. Here we look at some of the ways **social class** affects our health
      and what we can do in order to swing the odds in our favour. (*Express*
      2011)

This extract is taken from an article about the British royal family. It begins
with a description of the good health of the royal family, which is initially attributed to their genetics and enjoyment of outdoor pursuits. The article then
segues into a discussion of the disparities in life expectancy across different social class groups, pointing out that people in Kensington can expect to live ten
years longer than people in Manchester and even longer than people in Glas-
gow. However, this passage (extract (13)) is interwoven with hints at a responsibilising, blaming discourse, with reference the Royle family (a British sitcom
based on the lives of a working class family) "hold[ing] court in front of the
telly" arguably indexing a sedentary lifestyle that contrasts with the actual roy-
als' "love of horse riding and other outdoor pursuits". This subtle nod is then
followed up with an invitation to readers to take responsibility for their health
by considering what they can do in order to "swing the odds in [their] favour".
The gambling metaphor invoked here serves moreover, to obscure the unequal
social systems that lead to these health disparities, presenting life expectancy
instead as a game or sport, individuals' success at which depends on their ability and willingness to exercise and diet. One explanation for why we see this
kind of explicit, reader-directed health advice in articles concerned with social
class in the tabloids and not the broadsheets is perhaps that the former is
aware of and thus targeting more consciously its largely lower social class readership, who in such cases are at more acute risk of developing obesity.

4.4 Left-leaning Tabloids (the *Mirror*)

There is only one left-leaning UK tabloid that mentions *social class** (the *Mirror*). Of these, only one mention has direct relevance to the representation of obesity: an article discussing the impact that having an allotment and gardening can have in terms of addressing obesity at all levels of class.

(14) This week a study has found that just 30 minutes a week working on an allotment can improve mood and self-esteem as well as physical fitness. Researchers from the Universities of Westminster and Essex said the positive impact was found across all **social classes** and suggested that allotments could help cut back growing NHS costs caused by lack of exercise and obesity. (*Mirror* 2015)

This extract could be interpreted as echoing some of the themes identified across different sections of the press, including the employment of a neoliberal, responsibilising logic to overcome obesity (i.e., by being physically active through gardening), and also points out that the benefits of this can be felt by people across all social class groups, thereby potentially flattening out class differences on this issue. However, this is just one article and what is perhaps more telling here is the general absence of explicit discussion of social class, as it relates to obesity at least, in the 'popular' press.

5 Discussion and Concluding Remarks

The study reported in this chapter has examined the role of discourses around a complex social phenomenon, social class, in British press representations of obesity. Comparing newspapers along the lines of both their publication formats and political leanings, the analysis has identified a range of discourses which position obesity in relation to social class in various ways. The decision to compare the newspapers at these two levels of variation was beneficial in terms of better capturing the complexity of newspaper registers (and subregisters) and the discourses that characterise their varying representations of two particular, equally complex, social issues.

This perspective was productive for the analysis, as the social class discourses identified varied according not only to their formats but also their political leanings. The left-leaning broadsheets presented social class as central to the development of obesity, as individuals' life circumstances and lack of means were framed as causing obesity. On the other hand, the right-leaning newspapers, including both tabloids and broadsheets, offered discourses that mitigated the influence of social class on obesity. For example, both of these sections of the press presented obesity as something that affects people at all class levels (in some cases even affecting middle- and upper-classes more), and foregrounded other factors, most frequently those connected to lifestyle 'choices', as being more influential in the development of obesity. This was the case even when the articles acknowledged heightened rates of obesity prevalence among people from lower down the social class ladder, with these groups accordingly depicted as making poor decisions respecting diet and exercise and even as 'resisting' health advice. The only left-leaning tabloid that discussed social class with respect to obesity, the *Mirror*, did so in just a single article across ten years, and that article echoed some of the discourses associated with other tabloids.

Overall, then, the left-leaning press can be contrasted with those on the political right in terms of the relationship that is (or is not) constructed between obesity and social class. For the left-leaning newspapers, obesity tends to be framed as a social justice issue that is linked to, and indeed driven by, other forms of social and health inequality. On the other hand, for right-leaning publications obesity is not determined by social class but is first and foremost a failing of individual responsibility (and tenets of neoliberal political agendas) and, if people lower down the socio-economic ladder *are* affected disproportionately by obesity, it is only because they make poorer life choices and do not eat as well as, or exercise as much as, those belonging to higher social class groups. These distinctions largely reflect the differing ways in which obesity is reported on across these sections of the press (Brookes/Baker 2021).

I would argue that, in the case of the right-leaning press, the discourses identified in this chapter are intended to uphold, and inflict as little harm as possible upon, the neoliberal agenda that characterises its general coverage of obesity. To attribute obesity to social class, as the left-leaning press does, arguably has the potential to illuminate to readers the particular social and political systems (and powerful institutions) which, knowingly or otherwise, create and maintain health inequalities through the unequal distribution of resources within society. Instead, in this coverage focus is placed on individuals and their life choices, with "good" or "bad" choices framed as the cause of not just obesity but other forms of social inequality, too. Characteristic, though it is, of general coverage of obesity in the right-leaning press, the centrality of neoliberal ideologies to articles published by this section of the press can nevertheless be viewed as problematic when we consider, as we have seen, that these newspapers (and the tabloids in particular) are read mostly by people lower down the socio-economic ladder, who are also more likely to be affected by obesity. This is because the neoliberal, individualising discourses – and the related suppression or discrediting of social class-related explanations of obesity – is likely to lead to individuals with obesity being blamed for having obesity and their other health challenges, which may be perceived by others as 'just reward' for making poor life choices and even actively resisting health advice. Such discourses could therefore contribute to the further stigmatisation of society's already least-fortunate, with class-based discrimination only compounded by weight stigma, all of which can lead to internalised shame (Obesity UK 2020).

A possible counterargument, and one in favour of the neoliberal discourses that characterise much press coverage of obesity and which underpin depictions of social class in the right-leaning press, is that such representations may motivate their audiences into changing their lifestyles and even advise them on how to go about it. However, such an argument can itself be swiftly countered. Not only are shaming strategies unlikely to instigate positive health change (see Brookes/Harvey 2015 for a discussion), but health policies predicated on personal behaviour and responsibility usually have limited success with people from poorer socio-economic backgrounds, mostly because they fail to grasp that

> when individuals behave in ways that may be damaging to their health, this may not necessarily be due to their lack of awareness about adverse health effects; rather the constraints of their life experiences and environments may mean that they are simply unable to change their behaviours (Atanasova/Koteyko 2017: 652)

In other words, lifestyle change is only really possible for those who possess the resources to do it. To conclude this study on a methodological note, it is important to acknowledge that the approach employed in this study will not have captured all instances where social class is indexed in press coverage of obesity, particularly as the search-term used focussed on explicit, rather than implicit, linguistic 'occasionings' of social class in the data. For complex social issues, like social class, any comprehensive investigation will require a more nuanced approach, and ideally one that is better able to account for cases where social class is indexed implicitly. This notwithstanding, the approach adopted in this chapter has afforded new insights into the ways in which discourses around obesity and social class intersect in the press.

References

Atanasova, Dimitrinka/Koteyko, Nelya/Gunter, Barrie (2012): "Obesity in the news: Directions for future research." In: *Obesity Reviews* 13, 554–559.
Atanasova, Dimitrinka/Koteyko, Nelya (2017): "Obesity frames and counter–frames in British and German online newspapers." In: *Health* 21, 650–669.

Baker, Paul/Brookes, Gavin/Atanasova, Dimitrinka/Flint, Stuart (2020): "Changing frames of obesity in the UK press 2008–2017." In: *Social Science & Medicine* 264, 113403.

Baker, Paul/Gabrielatos, Costas/McEnery, Tony (2013): *Discourse Analysis and Media Attitudes. The Representation of Islam in the British Press.* Cambridge: Cambridge University Press.

Baker, Paul/McEnery, Tony (2015): "Who benefits when discourse gets democratised? Analysing a Twitter corpus around the British Benefits Street debate." In: Paul Baker/ Tony McEnery (Eds.): *Corpora and Discourse Studies. Integrating Discourse and Corpora.* Basingstoke: Palgrave Macmillan, 244–265.

Bell, Allan (1984): "Language style as audience design." In: Nikolas Coupland/Adam Jaworski (Eds.): *Sociolinguistics. A Reader and Coursebook.* New York: St Mattin's Press, 240–250.

Bennett, Joe (2013): "Moralising class: A discourse analysis of the mainstream political response to occupy and the August 2011 British riots." In: *Discourse & Society* 24, 27–45.

Bissell, Paul/Peacock, Marian/Blackburn, Joanna/Smith, Christine (2016): "The discordant pleasures of # everyday eating: Reflections on the social gradient in obesity under neo-liberalism." In: *Social Science & Medicine* 159, 14–21.

Block, David (2013): *Social Class in Applied Linguistics.* London: Routledge.

Boero, Natalie (2007): "All the news that's fat to print: The American 'obesity epidemic' and the media." In: *Qualitative Sociology* 30, 41–60.

Bourdieu, Pierre (1984): *Distinction. A Social Critique of the Judgement of Taste.* Cambridge: Harvard University Press.

Brookes, Gavin (2018): "Insulin restriction, medicalisation and the Internet: A corpus–assisted study of diabulimia discourse in online support groups." In: *Communication & Medicine* 15, 14–27.

Brookes, Gavin (2020): "Corpus linguistics in illness and healthcare contexts: A case study of diabulimia support groups." In: Zofia Demjén (Ed.): *Applying Linguistics in Illness and Healthcare Contexts.* London: Bloomsbury, 44–72.

Brookes, Gavin/Baker, Paul (2021): *Obesity in the News. Language and Representation in the Press.* Cambridge: Cambridge University Press.

Brookes, Gavin/Harvey, Kevin (2015): "Peddling a semiotics of fear: A critical examination of scare tactics and commercial strategies in public health promotion." In: *Social Semiotics* 25, 57–80.

Brookes, Gavin/Hunt, Daniel (2021): "Discourse and health communication." In: Gavin Brookes/Daniel Hunt (Eds.): *Analysing Health Communication: Discourse Approaches.* Basingstoke: Palgrave Macmillan, 1–17.

Burr, Vivien (1995): *An Introduction to Social Constructionism.* London: Routledge.

Charteris–Black, Jonathan/Seale, Clive (2010): *Gender and the Language of Illness.* Basingstoke: Palgrave Macmillan.

Fairclough, Norman (2015[1989]): *Language and Power.* 3rd edn. London: Routledge.

Foucault, Michel (1972): *The Archaeology of Knowledge.* New York: Pantheon.

Fox, Nick (1993): *Postmodernism, Sociology and Health.* Maidenhead: Open University Press.

Gomez–Jimenez, Eva M./Toolan, Michael (Eds.) (2020): *The Discursive Construction of Economic Inequality. CADS Approaches to the British Media.* London: Bloomsbury.

Guy, Gregory R. (2011): "Language, social class, and status". In: Rajend Mesthrie (Ed.): *The Cambridge Handbook of Sociolinguistics.* Cambridge: Cambridge University Press, 159–185.

Hardie, Andrew (2012): "CQPweb: Combining power, flexibility and usability in a corpus analysis tool." In: *International Journal of Corpus Linguistics* 17, 380–409.

Hunt, Daniel/Brookes, Gavin (2020): *Corpus, Discourse and Mental Health*. London: Bloomsbury.

Jones, Owen (2012): *Chavs. The Demonization of the Working Class*. London: Verso.

Leeuwen, Theo van (2008): *Discourse and Practice. New Tools for Critical Discourse Analysis*. Oxford: Oxford University Press.

Liu, Jiawei/Lee, ByungGu/McLeod, Douglas M./Choung, Hyesun (2019): "Framing obesity: Effects of obesity labelling and prevalence statistics on public perceptions." In: *Health Education & Behavior* 46, 322–328.

Lupton, Deborah (2018): *Fat*. 2nd edn. London: Routledge.

Marsh, Peter (2004): *Poverty and obesity: Social issues research centre*. Online at: http://www.sirc.org/articles/poverty_and_obesity.shtml <03.11.2021>.

Meyerhoff, Miriam (2006): *Introducing Sociolinguistics*. London: Routledge.

Mills, Sara (1997): *Discourse*. London: Routledge.

Mills, Sara (2017): *English Politeness and Social Class*. Cambridge: Cambridge University Press.

Public Health England (2020): *Excess weight and COVID–19: Insights from new evidence. Online report*. Online at: https://assets.publishing.service.gov.uk/government/uploads/system/uploads/attachmnt_data/file/903770/PHE_insight_Excess_weight_and_COVID–19.pdf <03.11.2021>.

Paterson, Laura L./Gregory, Ian N. (2019): *Representations of Poverty and Place. Using Geographical Text Analysis to Understand Discourse*. Basingstoke: Palgrave Macmillan.

Rampton, Ben (2006): *Language in Late Modernity. Interaction in an Urban School*. Cambridge: Cambridge University Press.

Rampton, Ben (2010): "Social class and sociolinguistics." In: *Applied Linguistics Review* 1, 1–21.

Richardson, John E. (2007): *Analysing Newspapers. An Approach from Critical Discourse Analysis*. Basingstoke: Palgrave Macmillan.

Savage, Michael (2000): *Class Analysis and Social Transformation*. Oxford: Oxford University Press.

Toolan, Michael (2018): *The Language of Inequality in the News*. Cambridge: Cambridge University Press.

Ulijaszek, Stanley J. (2014): "Do adult obesity rates in England vary by insecurity as well as by inequality? An ecological cross–sectional study." In: *BMJ Open* 4, e004430.

Steven Coats

Dialect Corpora from YouTube

Abstract: This paper introduces two new large corpora comprised of YouTube Automatic Speech Recognition (ASR) transcripts of the speech of videos from geographically localized channels in the United States, Canada, and the British Isles, a promising resource for more in-depth study of regional language variation in spoken English. The procedure used to create the corpora bypasses the web API for YouTube, instead relying on web scraping and open-source scripts or software for the automatic identification and downloading of suitable channel content as well as dealing with the rate-limiting issues that arise thereby. In order to assess the accuracy of downloaded transcripts, word frequency statistics are compared for ASR and manual transcripts of city council meetings of Philadelphia, Pennsylvania, USA, and a transcript classification task is undertaken using vector-based distributed representations of transcript content. Despite errors, corpora of ASR transcripts may prove useful for the characterization and study of regional language variation, particularly when analytical techniques are employed that are relatively robust to low-frequency phenomena.

1 Introduction

Large corpora of geographically localized speech transcripts are an important resource for the analysis of regional variation in English (Szmrecsanyi 2011), but despite the appearance of new corpora in recent years and the proliferation of corpus-based methods for linguistic analysis, particularly in the UK (Busse 2018), relatively few corpora of regionally-located speech exist for North America or the British Isles. Considering the time and resources required for manual transcription of audio and video data, advances in Automatic Speech Recognition (ASR) present opportunities for the creation of corpora of orthographic transcripts that may be useful for corpus linguistic-based research into variation in spoken language. Corpus creation from ASR transcripts, however, raises new methodological issues pertaining to data access and to transcript accuracy. Obtaining ASR transcripts, for example from YouTube, in volumes sufficient for the creation of a

Acknowledgements: Thanks to two anonymous reviewers for suggestions to a draft version of the manuscript and to Finland's Centre for Scientific Computing for access to computing resources.

geographically representative corpus may present difficulties: Access to data via YouTube's web API (Application Programming Interface) is by default limited, and web scraping can result in IP blocking, limiting the researcher's ability to access data.

Although ASR algorithms can achieve accuracy levels comparable to those of human transcribers for recordings with high acoustic fidelity or for specific transcription tasks (Chiu et al. 2018; Xiong et al. 2017), and ASR transcripts may be accurate enough for certain types of transcript-based analysis (Ziman et al. 2018), the accuracy of ASR transcripts of naturalistic speech is typically lower, and has been judged to be insufficient for some corpus creation projects. McEnery, for example, discussing the methods used for the creation of the spoken portion of the BNC2014 corpus, found ASR to be "not at all helpful" (2018: 11); the project instead utilized a team to manually transcribe audio data recorded on mobile telephones.

Nevertheless, not all research projects will have the time and resources necessary for large-scale manual transcription. While a corpus of ASR transcripts, which typically contain a certain amount of "noise" (i.e., textual errors), may be unsuitable for analyses of (for example) rare lexical items, it may, given sufficient size, still be useful for a range of linguistic analyses, including a broad range of language processing tasks that can support such analyses, for example topic modelling, content summarization, or word-vector-based approaches. The usefulness of noisy transcripts for such tasks is a result of the law of large numbers: For a given feature, if a sufficient proportion of transcriptions are accurate, the resulting signal in a corpus will be strong enough to make reliable predictions, despite the existence of inaccurate transcriptions of that feature.

Starting from the premise that ASR transcripts will indeed be useful for a variety of analyses of regional English in North America and the British Isles, despite inaccuracies, this paper is organized as follows: First, an overview of some previous work on ASR transcripts is provided. Then, the procedure used for the creation of corpora of geographically localized ASR transcripts from YouTube is presented; two corpora (one for the United States and Canada and one for the United Kingdom and Ireland) are described. In Section 4, two preliminary analyses are conducted: ASR transcripts for a subset of the material (40 transcripts totalling ~500,000 words) are compared to manual transcripts of the same videos in terms of word error rate (WER). Then, word embeddings are used to create a language model from a subset of the North American corpus; word vectors are used to predict the regional provenance of unknown speech transcripts from California or New York and to visualize state-level similarity in lexis. The results are discussed and possible directions for future work are presented in the final sections.

2 Previous Research

The accuracy of ASR transcripts has increased in recent years due to the use of sophisticated machine learning models and large amounts of training data (Chiu et al. 2018; Halpern et al. 2016; Liao/McDermott/Senior 2013; Sainath et al. 2015; Xiong et al. 2017). Ziman et al. (2018) found that Google's speech-to-text service offers high accuracy in terms of word identification and timing. An ASR-based system used to create transcripts of sessions of the Japanese parliament is reported to have accuracy of up to 95% (Kawahara 2012). Ranchal et al. (2013) analysed the use of automatic captioning with IBM's ViaScribe and Hosted Transcription Service for 19 hours of university lectures, finding that error rates ranged from 45%, for spontaneous real-time transcription of speech using an untrained model, to 9.1%, when input parameters of the acoustic signal were carefully prepared and the speech model trained in advance with acoustic data from a specific lecturer. Tatman (2017) found YouTube English ASR captions to be generally accurate, but that accuracy can also depend on speaker gender and dialect.

Bokhove/Downey (2018) discussed the advantages of using ASR transcripts in research requiring speech transcripts in terms of time and expenditure, compared to manual transcriptions. They analysed the automatic transcripts created by YouTube for three videos: a one-to-one interview of a lecturer at an English university with high audio fidelity, a video of a mathematics lesson for 8th-graders at an American school, and a video of a UK parliamentary inquiry interview with a British Army officer. They found textual similarity rates between 64% and 92% for the YouTube ASR transcripts and manual transcripts.[1] Këpuska/Bohouta (2017) found that Google Cloud's speech-to-text system outperformed Microsoft's ASR service and a system created at Carnegie-Mellon University in terms of WER. Kim et al. (2019) evaluated the performance of several ASR transcription services by calculating WERs for transcripts of medical conversations with Australian medical school students. They found WERs between 0.28 and 0.55, with YouTube showing the lowest rates.

In natural language processing, 'noisy' text has been shown to be useful for a number of analytical tasks. Agarwal et al. (2007) conducted an experiment in which machine learning was used to automatically classify collections of texts using the "bag of words" approach (i.e., on the basis of word frequencies,

---

1 The method used to measure accuracy was unorthodox: ASR and manual transcripts were compared using the similarity score of the commercial plagiarism detection software *Turnitin*, rather than standard measures such as WER.

but not considering word order). Tests were undertaken in classifier performance after increasing levels of random noise (i.e., spelling errors) had been introduced into the text data. The authors found that the performance of naïve Bayes and Support Vector Machine classifiers remained relatively stable even when noisy data, with errors in 40% of the words, was utilized. Similarly, Eder working with texts in English, German, Polish, Latin and Ancient Greek, found that textual error rates of up to 20% do not significantly affect the results of an authorship attribution task.

Franzini et al. (2018), applying authorship attribution to a corpus of correspondence between Jacob and Wilhelm Grimm, found that error-containing OCR (optical character recognition)-generated texts can serve as a reliable proxy for more accurate manually-keyboarded texts. Pentland et al. (2019) reported on a project that investigates the relationship between ASR transcript accuracy and text classification model performance using transcripts of company earnings call audio files and ASR transcripts of the audio. They reported a relatively high WER of 34% for the ASR transcripts. In follow-up work, they found that when used to train a machine-learning model, manual transcripts and ASR transcripts do not differ substantially in model performance, even for ASR transcripts with relatively high WER values (S. Pentland, pers. comm. of paper under review, 17 November 2020).

Coats (2019) described a method for the creation of corpora from ASR transcripts of local government and community organization channels by using a script to send multiple search terms to YouTube's API, then downloading channel content using open-source tools. Word timings from this data were used to investigate regional variation in speech articulation rate in spoken American English in Coats (2020).

3 YouTube, Data, Channel Identification, and Data Collection

YouTube transcripts are available for download through the site's API or through URLs that are generated automatically when a user accesses a video on the platform's website. The API is a convenient means of accessing transcript (and other) data, but may not be suitable for the creation of larger corpora due to access and rate limitations. Accessing transcripts through a URL and downloading them with the open-source YouTube-DL software (Yen/Remite/Sergey 2020) is an alternative.

3.1 YouTube ASR Transcripts and API

YouTube makes video content and metadata, including speech-to-text captions, available for download through an API (Google Developers 2021). Access to API content is limited by a system that assigns a "quota cost" to each HTTP request sent to YouTube's servers: For example, listing the various types of metadata associated with a specific video or channel has a quota cost of 3, conducting a search of all YouTube content a cost of 100, and downloading a specific transcript a cost of 200 quota points. In the spring of 2019, YouTube reduced the daily default quota for API access to 10,000 quota units (1% of the volume previously available), making the collection of a large number of transcripts via the API less feasible (cf. Coats 2019). Because YouTube content, including transcripts, are stored at publicly available URLs, however, they can be scraped directly from web pages, rather than collected via the API. A web-scraping method, utilizing Python scripts and libraries, was used to collect transcript data in order to create the corpora described below.

3.2 Channel Identification and Data Collection

Two scaping-based approaches were adopted for data collection by using pre-existing lists of websites. In the first approach, a large list of local government entities from the U.S. Census Bureau was scraped for websites; these websites were then scraped for links to YouTube channels. In a second approach, an automated browser script sent lists of search terms to YouTube's public web interface (rather than the API). Both of these methods made use of the browser automation tool *Selenium* in Python (Muthukadan 2018).

3.2.1 United States

For the United States, a list of 35,924 websites was extracted from a comprehensive listing of 91,386 local government entities provided by the U.S. Census Bureau (2017). These websites, mostly homepages of cities, towns, school boards, public utility districts, or other administrative entities, were then scraped for links to You-Tube channels, resulting in 2,534 channels. After removal of false positives,[2] all

---

2 Some local government websites are built from templates which include icons that can link to social media such as Facebook, Twitter, and YouTube. If the default templates are not

available English-language ASR transcripts were downloaded from 2,376 channels using YouTube-DL (Yen/Remite/Sergey 2020) routed through the Tor network (see below; Loesing/Murdoch/Dingledine 2010). Exact locations for channels were assigned using a geocoder by passing a string consisting of the Census Bureau entity name, the YouTube channel name, and the city and state location to a geocoder (Esmukov et al. 2018). Channels with the same location (for example, city government and city school district channels resolved to the same street address) were then merged. Tokenization of the 322,677 individual transcript files was undertaken with Spacy (Honnibal 2019). Transcripts with fewer than 100 words, as well as transcripts with textual features indicating they were not generated by the YouTube ASR algorithm and transcript files without individual word timings were removed,[3] resulting in a corpus of 270,931 transcripts from 2,189 channel locations, comprising 1,149,031,002 words and corresponding to over 141,455 hours of video from locations in all 50 U.S. states and the District of Columbia (Tab. 1).

3.2.2 Canada

For Canada, a list of Canadian municipalities or other local administrative entities and their official or semi-official government websites was created by scraping public web resources such as web pages, PDF files, and databases of the 13 Canadian provincial and territorial governments, as well as Wikipedia lists of municipalities.[4] In total, the list comprised 3,401 localities or local government agencies (mostly cities, counties, towns, villages, rural municipalities,

---

altered, the link may direct to the social media presence of the service provider that created the template, rather than the account of the local government entity.

3 If only manually-uploaded transcripts are available for a YouTube video, YouTube-DL will download these transcripts, even if scripts are configured to download only automatic subtitles. Some of these manually-uploaded transcripts are identifiable on the basis of their textual features, such as all-capital-letter orthography.

4 Alberta: http://municipalaffairs.gov.ab.ca/cfml/officials/Official.xls; British Columbia: https://www.ubcm.ca/EN/main/about/ubcm-members/municipalities.html; Manitoba: https://www.gov.mb.ca/mr/contactus/pubs/mod.pdf; New Brunswick: https://www2.gnb.ca/content/gnb/en/de partments/elg/local_government/content/community_profiles.html, Newfoundland and Labrador: https://en.wikipedia.org/wiki/List_of_municipalities_in_Newfoundland_and_Labrador; Northwest Territories: https://www.maca.gov.nt.ca/en/community-contact-listing; Nova Scotia: https://beta.novascotia.ca/sites/default/files/documents/1-1759/municipal-statistics-annual-report-2018-en.pdf; Nunavut: https://en.wikipedia.org/wiki/List_of_municipalities_in_Nunavut; Ontario: https://www.amo.on.ca/AMO-Content/Municipal-101/Ontario-Municipalities.aspx; Prince Edward Island: https://www.princeedwardisland.ca/sites/default/files/publications/municipal_directory.pdf; Quebec: https://www.donneesquebec.ca/recherche/fr/dataset/repertoire-des-municipalites-du-

districts, or settlements, but also other entities) with websites in all 13 Canadian territories or provinces, representing 65% of census subdivisions of the 2011 Canadian Census (Statistics Canada lists 5,253 census subdivisions for the 2011 Canada Census (Statistics Canada 2011).

Two approaches were used to find YouTube channels associated with the Canadian administrative bodies aggregated in this list. First, each website was scraped directly for links to YouTube channels present on the homepage, in the same manner as employed for the US Census list. For Canada, 205 of the homepages had links to YouTube channels, of which 112 were unique.[5] In a second approach, a script iteratively sent the name of each of the 3,401 locations and its province/territory name (e.g., "City of Calgary, Alberta") to YouTube's web search interface and the first two channel results were harvested. This method resulted in 679 channels, some of which were the YouTube channels of commercial entities or channels with no connection to a Canadian place.[6]

After manual filtering to remove commercial channels, non-Canadian channels, channels automatically generated by YouTube algorithms,[7] channels with no obvious locality, and channels for which transcripts were automatic translations of French videos,[8] the lists of YouTube channels identified using the two methods were merged. All available automatic speech-to-text transcripts were downloaded from the 407 channels identified in this manner, resulting in a corpus of 30,916 video transcripts and 103,035,369 words, corresponding to over 12,586 hours of video, from all 13 of Canada's provinces and territories. Summary statistics are presented in Tab. 2.

---

quebec/resource/19385b4e-5503-4330-9e59-f998f5918363; Saskatchewan: http://www.mds.gov.sk.ca; Yukon: http://www.gov.yk.ca/aboutyukon/communities.html.

5 Many municipal websites link to the same YouTube channel: For example, most of the homepages for Nunavut municipalities link to the YouTube channel of the Government of Nunavut.

6 YouTube's search function for channels returns hits if any video in a channel contains the search term in its title or the description on the "About" page.

7 Channels with the string "- Topic" in the title are automatically generated by YouTube; they contain videos that have been aggregated based on individual video metadata. In many cases "Topic" channels will contain content about a particular place, but as such content is not necessarily representative of speech in that place (for example, in the case of tourism videos profiling a particular location), they were removed from the download list.

8 This is the result of an issue with the YouTube-DL code: https://github.com/ytdl-org/youtube-dl/issues/13646.

Tab. 1: US Subcorpus Summary Statistics.

State	Channels	Videos	Words	Length (h)	State	Channels	Videos	Words	Length (h)
Alabama	27	2827	10,581,345	1,315.67	Montana	3	145	926,229	143.20
Alaska	6	451	1,854,654	248.37	Nebraska	16	677	2,487,171	312.51
Arizona	35	6356	26,393,272	3,063.73	Nevada	5	2,759	6,110,915	638.06
Arkansas	14	986	6,748,658	882.77	N.H.	11	1,305	10,913,552	1,469.04
California	211	18278	83,915,246	10,146.57	New Jersey	88	6,982	29,523,334	3,977.57
Colorado	56	8802	36,551,218	4,299.68	New Mexico	14	1,895	6,750,477	883.10
Connecticut	25	3731	24,549,746	3,010.04	New York	97	8,037	37,560,959	4,856.87
Delaware	3	148	242,073	25.45	N. Carolina	97	11,357	46,231,979	5781.40
District of Columbia	3	242	261,209	32.90	N. Dakota	10	768	3,616,363	442.05
Florida	89	17625	64,647,923	7,468.48	Ohio	97	7,647	33,695,476	4,268.46
Georgia	49	5487	18,565,796	2,421.53	Oklahoma	19	1,977	5,271,339	643.35
Hawaii	1	152	123,617	15.42	Oregon	38	2,769	15,675,898	1,992.84
Idaho	11	1547	8,747,885	1,012.14	Pennsylvania	74	6,984	32,571,217	3,970.32
Illinois	151	14243	54,613,612	6,725.31	Rhode Island	7	822	3,195,777	530.94
Indiana	46	4017	12,958,084	1,643.88	S. Carolina	24	3,894	8,716,589	1115.20
Iowa	43	7516	24,286,940	3,072.57	S. Dakota	12	1,819	18,619,258	2,172.97
Kansas	35	4444	19,862,293	2,504.08	Tennessee	33	7,194	43,286,858	5,127.52
Kentucky	26	4965	17,834,978	2,092.75	Texas	155	21,330	44,736,009	5,789.44
Louisiana	16	2018	10,500,407	1,221.96	Utah	21	2,561	7,766,782	940.21
Maine	12	819	5,879,165	797.01	Vermont	3	94	131,558	16.62
Maryland	32	7373	34,009,832	4,100.84	Virginia	42	9,209	34,806,149	4,059.67
Massachusetts	44	17596	11,517,230	14,682.19	Washington	51	6,178	28,949,403	3,387.77
Michigan	90	9832	51,293,982	6,079.47	W. Virginia	6	101	196,479	25.86
Minnesota	80	8666	31,366,468	3,661.89	Wisconsin	83	9,514	45,983,568	5,744.59
Mississippi	18	1448	2,613,901	346.07	Wyoming	7	251	2,638,963	348.39
Missouri	53	5093	15,094,086	1,946.43					

Tab. 2: Canada Subcorpus Summary Statistics.

Province/territory	Channels	Videos	Words	length (h)
Alberta	95	6,623	21,239,251	2,497.45
British Columbia	102	10,002	26,853,481	3,246.83
Manitoba	20	3,286	2,771,200	318.21
New Brunswick	8	382	2,347,141	278.05
Newfoundland and Labrador	2	108	186,070	29.99
Northwest Territories	3	32	21,404	3.27
Nova Scotia	11	332	1,229,149	148.38
Nunavut	1	6	1,230	0.23
Ontario	112	8,404	45,970,092	5,774.59
Prince Edward Island	6	753	777,772	95.87
Quebec	6	166	486,265	60.29
Saskatchewan	10	663	895,143	103.12
Yukon	7	159	257,171	30.48

3.2.3 CoNASE

The U.S. and Canadian resources were combined with the corpus described in Coats (2019) to create the Corpus of North American Spoken English (CoNASE) of more than 1.25 billion words (CoNASE; Coats 2021). Fig. 1 shows the locations of the channels from which transcripts were downloaded in this combined corpus. Circle sizes are proportional to the number of videos sampled from the channel(s) at that location.

3.2.4 British Isles

For the British Isles, a method similar to that employed for North America was employed: A list of the names of local government authorities in England, Scotland, Wales, Northern Ireland, and the Republic of Ireland was created in November 2019 from information available on Wikipedia,[9] then searches for the name of the

---

9 https://en.wikipedia.org/wiki/List_of_county_councils_in_England, https://en.wikipedia. org/wiki/Unitary_authorities_of_England, https://en.wikipedia.org/wiki/Metropolitan_bor ough, https://en.wikipedia.org/wiki/London_boroughs, https://en.wikipedia.org/wiki/Non-metropolitan_district, https://en.wikipedia.org/wiki/Subdivisions_of_Scotland, https://en.wi kipedia.org/wiki/List_of_Welsh_principal_areas_by_area, https://en.wikipedia.org/wiki/ Local_government_in_Northern_Ireland, and https://en.wikipedia.org/wiki/Local_govern ment_in_the_Republic_of_Ireland. The council for the Isles of Scilly was added manually.

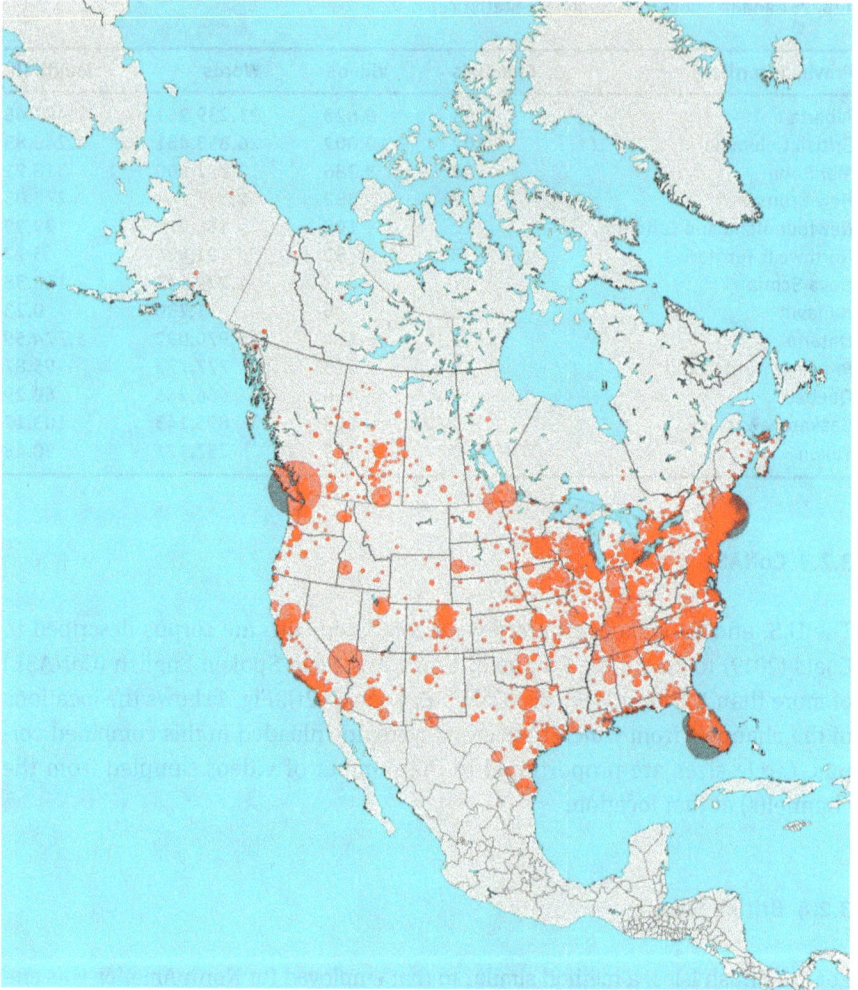

Fig. 1: Locations and sizes of sampled channels in CoNASE.

authority plus the string "Council" were sent to the search function on YouTube's web page for each of the 413 local government entities (e.g., "Dorset Council", "East Ayrshire Council", "Mayo County Council", etc.). The first three "channel" results ranked in order of relevance were retrieved. Results were then filtered to retain channels that included the strings "council" or "cc" in the channel name. Almost all of these were the official YouTube channels of the regional authorities targeted by the search procedure, although in a few cases, both an official and an unofficial channel existed for a given local authority with the same name or very similar names.[10] In addition to these 'unofficial' channels, likely created automatically by scripts, channel duplicates, channels automatically generated by YouTube, and channel false positives (e.g., the channel "Boston City Council" from the United States, rather than Lincolnshire, or "Ipswich City Council TV" from New South Wales, Australia) were removed after a content check.

In 2021, websites of local governments in England, Scotland, and the Republic of Ireland were scraped to retrieve several additional channels.[11] In total, the British Isles corpus contains transcripts from 453 geolocated channels, comprising 38,680 transcript files and 111,563,614 tokens, and corresponding to more than 12,801 hours of video. A summary of the results by country is presented in Tab. 3.

Tab. 3: UK and Ireland Corpus Summary Statistics.

Country	Channels	Videos	Words	Length (h)
England	324	23,657	72,879,173	8,521.71
Northern Ireland	10	1,898	6,508,505	770.84
Republic of Ireland	26	2,525	6,264,276	680.81
Scotland	75	8,135	17,111,396	1,845.35
Wales	18	2,465	8,800,264	982.66

The map in Fig. 2 depicts the locations assigned to the channels by the geocoding procedure with circle sizes proportionate to the number of videos in each location. As can be seen, channel density is high in relatively densely-populated parts of the British Isles such as London, the Midlands, and the 'Central Belt' of Scotland, but lower in the North of England, Wales, most of Scotland, and Ireland.

---

10 For example, the channel "Stoke-on-Trent City Council" (https://www.youtube.com/chan nel/UCTrvOc-4pd_ME-RyuN5ZBMQ) contains a large number of videos and is the official channel of the authority. "Stoke City Council" (https://www.youtube.com/channel/UCngBVsm9 z3OAR3j7vV2AF8Q) contains only four videos.

11 The channels listed at https://www.local.gov.uk/our-support/guidance-and-resources/ communications-support/digital-councils/social-media/go-further/a-z-councils-online plus channels scraped from sites listed at https://www.mygov.scot/organisations#scottish-local-au thority and https://www.gov.ie/en/organisation-information/fd139-local-government-coun cils-and-councillors.

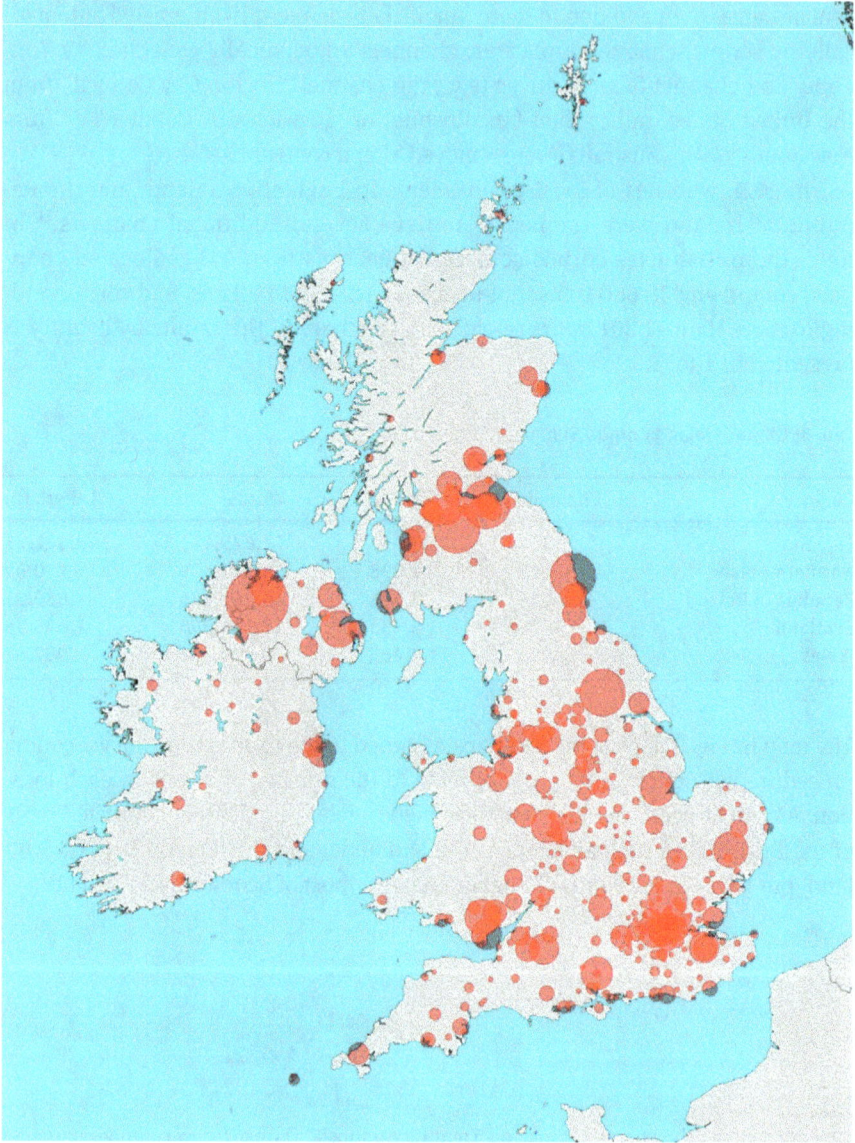

Fig. 2: Locations and sizes of sampled channels in the United Kingdom and Ireland.

3.3 Use of the Tor Network

The procedures described above require large numbers of requests to be sent iteratively by scripts to YouTube servers, which can result in the sender's IP address being blocked for 24 hours, 48 hours, or longer. To surmount this problem, scripts can be designed to send requests from multiple IP addresses, automatically switching addresses after a certain number of requests. Most researches do not have access to multiple IP addresses, and the cost of acquiring multiple IPs via a virtual private network may be prohibitive. For this reason, the Tor network was used to send requests to YouTube servers. Tor, an open-source software protocol for anonymous internet use, sends encrypted HTTP requests to a target via a randomized network of node servers (Loesing/Murdoch/Dingeldine 2010). Periodically generating a new Tor connection changes the Tor 'exit node' and thus the IP address of the server from which the request is passed YouTube. For the collection of transcripts described in this paper, the Tor exit node was changed every 1,000 calls to YouTube made by the YouTube-DL library. While using Tor can circumvent IP blocking, it reduces the download speed of the script pipeline. To generate the corpora described in this paper, it was necessary to run the download scripts for several weeks.

Although the methods described above focus on the creation of corpora of ASR transcripts from specific locations, they could also be used for the creation of other types of specialized corpora, for example pertaining to specified content, communicative situations, or speaker demographic attributes. In addition, because the functionality of YouTube-DL allows users to download the original video file as well as captions or other metadata, the basic procedure described above can be employed for the creation of specialized corpora of video or audio files from YouTube or other websites; these could then be subjected to acoustic or audio-visual analysis.

4 Test Cases

YouTube ASR transcripts can be considered a type of 'noisy' data: they contain errors, which can be due to low acoustic fidelity in the audio source, inaccurate identification of the language being spoken by the ASR algorithm, overlapping speech, music in the background, or other causes. In the following two subsections, the accuracy of the ASR transcripts is measured and an example of transcript classification using noisy corpus data is described.

4.1 WER of ASR Transcripts

The WER of ASR transcripts was calculated by comparing them with publicly-available manual transcripts of council sessions of the American city of Philadelphia, Pennsylvania. The city of Philadelphia, like many larger American cities, hires stenographers to produce official transcripts of meetings of local government bodies. In Philadelphia, the service is provided by a stenography firm that specializes in the transcription of courtroom proceedings (which for most types of trials are required by law to be transcribed).

In order to retrieve the official transcripts of the 40 Philadelphia City Council meetings whose ASR transcripts were present in the North American corpus described above, a script was written to scrape the website of the city of Philadelphia for links to the corresponding transcript files, which were then downloaded.

```
                          Stated Meeting
                        September 28, 2017

                                                              Page 22
    1           9/28/17 - STATED - COMMUNICATIONS

    2                  (Applause.)

    3              MS.      :  And then, finally,

    4       I'd like to ask all of our partners with

    5       MED Week to stand up as well.

    6                  (Applause.)

    7              MS.      :  And I want to say

    8       that these are the individuals that are

    9       out here every single day fighting,

   10       advocating, supporting, and making sure
```

Fig. 3: Excerpt of official transcript of the Philadelphia City Council meeting of 28 September of 2017.

The files, in PDF format (an example excerpt is provided in Fig. 3), were converted to text using Apache Tika (2021), then processed to remove all text that did not correspond to speech, such as the title of the transcript, the time and location of the transcribed meeting, the list of participants, page headers and page numbers, the name and telephone number of the company that prepared the transcript, the certification of the stenographer that the transcript is accurate, the index at the end of the transcript, and all indications of speaker diarization (names of speakers followed by colons).[12] Parenthetical annotations that did not correspond to speech were also removed, such as "(Councilmember and guests approached podium.)", "(No response.)", "(Applause.)", or "(The council is at ease.)". After the cleaned texts were stripped of remaining punctuation and excess whitespace and converted to lower case, they were used to calculate the WERs of the corresponding ASR transcripts.

Word error rate is calculated with

$$WER = \frac{S+D+I}{N}$$

where S is the number of substitutions, D the number of deletions, and I the number of insertions necessary to transform the 'hypothesis' text (i.e., the text whose accuracy is to be tested, in this case the ASR transcript) to the 'ground truth' text (i.e., the manual transcript); N is the number of words in the 'ground truth' text. WER ranges from 0 (texts are identical) to 1 (texts have zero overlap). For example, the WER of the strings "welcome to our council meeting" and "welcome to the city council meeting", where the first string is the hypothesis and the second string the ground truth, would be 2/6 or 0.333. Word error rate (WER) was calculated using the *jiwer* library in Python (Vaessen 2020). For the 40 transcript pairs, the mean WER was 0.22, with a standard deviation of 0.03 and a range from 0.15 to 0.29.

This WER is comparable to some values reported in the literature, but does not give a good indication of how useful the ASR transcripts may be for linguistic analysis. In order to gauge the comparability of the ASR and manual transcripts, word frequencies in aggregated transcripts were compared. ASR transcripts were aggregated into one text, and manual transcripts into another. The relative frequencies of all word types were then calculated in both aggregated texts. The log-likelihood score (Dunning 1993; Rayson/Garside 2000) and corresponding p-value were used to compare the frequencies of the 14,433 word types with at least one occurrence in each of the aggregated texts. For 13,929 types (96.5% of the shared word types), no significant difference in usage was found at an alpha level of $p = 0.05$. For 504 word types (3.5% of the shared word types), a significant difference in frequency was found at $p = 0.05$. The types that exhibit significant differences in use between the manual and automatic transcripts are various: Many are personal names ("Clarke", "Belen", "Bill") or other proper nouns such as place names ("Roxborough", a suburb of Philadelphia, "Leverington", a street name). Legal terminology ("writ", "mandamus") and words common in the

---

12 YouTube ASR transcripts do not contain diarization metadata as of 2021.

specific context of a council meeting but otherwise relatively rare in spoken language ("rezoning", "councilperson") show significant frequency differences, as do some digits and numerals ("12", "706"), possibly in part due to the various ways in which numbers can be phonetically realized in spoken English.[13] In addition, some words that are homonyms show significant frequency differences between the ASR and manual transcripts, such as "gym" ("Jim") and "I" ("aye"). Among the types that show significant differences in frequency but are otherwise relatively common English words are "teen", "emotion", and "meaning", among others. Further investigation is necessary to determine why such types may inaccurately transcribed in this data.

In Fig. 4, the logarithm of the frequency for each of the 14,433 word types is plotted in the ASR transcripts (x-axis) and the manual transcripts (y-axis). If the two aggregate transcripts were exactly equivalent, all words would have the same frequency in both texts and scatterplot points would fall on a straight line. As can be seen, for low-frequency items there is considerable variation in word frequencies (i.e., many errors), but more frequent words tend to show comparable frequencies.

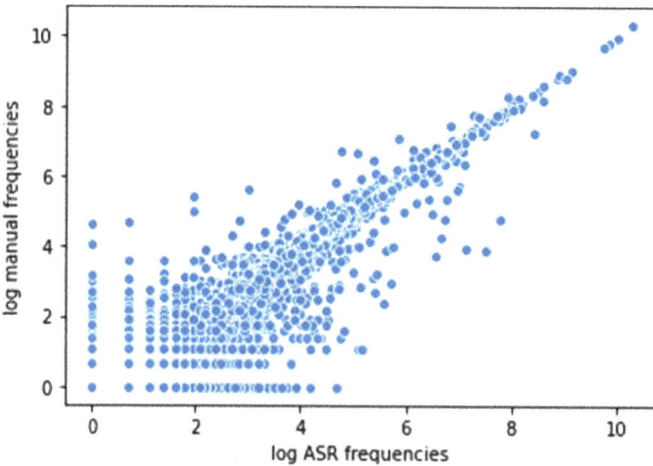

Fig. 4: Log-log plot of frequencies of shared types.

---

13 For example, 344 can be "three hundred and forty four", "three forty four", or "three four four", depending on if it is spoken as part of a residential address, a telephone number, or some other numerical quantity.

Vector representations of documents (individual video transcripts) and vocabulary items were created from a subset of the US corpus comprising 78,238 transcripts whose video titles included the words "council", "session", or "meeting", totalling 691,442,599 words. SpaCy (Honnibal 2019) was used for tokenization, part-of-speech tagging, removal of named entities such as organizations and place names, and restriction of the vocabulary to nouns, verbs, adjectives, and interjections. Doc2Vec (Le/Mikolov 2014), a variant of the popular Word2Vec neural network model (Mikolov/Yih/Zweig 2013) which also allows tagged documents (in this case, individual transcripts) to be embedded in the same multidimensional space as individual words, was employed to generate a model in which each of the 78,238 transcripts was tagged with one of 51 labels (for the 50 US states and the District of Columbia). The Gensim implementation of Doc2Vec was used, with distributed bag-of-words training, a window size of 15 words, 300-dimensional vectors, a minimum frequency of 50 occurrences per word type, and 20 training epochs (Rehurek/Sojka 2011).

This model, which embeds vectors for individual words and vectors for document tags (state names) in the same multidimensional space, makes it possible to see which words are closest to each state. In addition to words denoting activities, geographical features or crops important in some states (for example, the closest words for Alaska included "fisheries" and "harbor", while the closest words for some Midwestern states included "corn" and "vetch"), the model managed to capture some features of American lexis that may be regionally distributed: For example, the vocabulary items "folks", "alrighty", and "sir" were found to be among the vectors nearest to the Southern states of North Carolina, South Carolina, and Georgia.

To test the ability of the model to accurately predict the provenance of regional language, a simple logistic regression classifier was trained for the transcripts from California and New York, using 90% of the transcripts from those two state locations as training material and 10% as test material. Classifier accuracy was 96.7% for the test transcripts: Of the 634 test transcripts from California, 618 were accurately classified; of the 251 New York test transcripts, 238 were accurately classified.

Next, t-SNE (van der Maaten/Hinton 2008) was used to project the 300-dimensional vectors into 2-dimensional space. Fig. 5. visualizes vector similarity for the state-level labels based on the aggregate documents and vocabulary from that state. As can be seen, vector representations derived from ASR transcripts recapitulate to some extent geographical proximity: A Southern cluster, comprising Tennessee, Florida, Louisiana, North Carolina, Virginia, South Carolina, Alabama, Mississippi, and Georgia is evident at the top of the figure. A New England cluster of Maine, Massachusetts, New Hampshire, Rhode Island, and Connecticut is apparent to the left, and the Midwestern states of Illinois, Wisconsin and Minnesota form a cluster to the right of Fig. 5 in close proximity to the neighbouring states of North and South Dakota, Montana, Iowa, and Nebraska. At the bottom of the figure the Western states of Utah, Wyoming, Washington, Oregon, Colorado, and Idaho are clustered together.

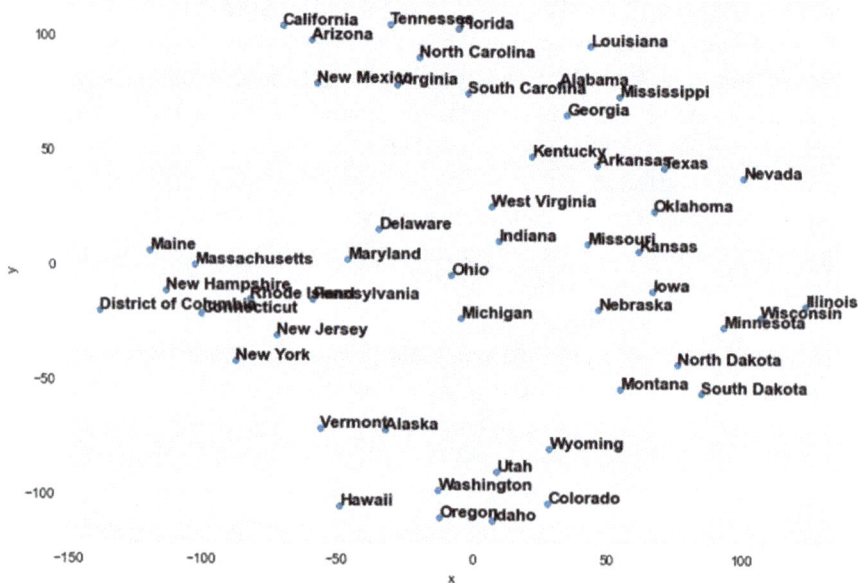

Fig. 5: t-SNE map of vector similarity for US states and Washington, DC.

Document classification or the calculation of cosine similarity for vector representations may not be tasks that directly correspond to analysis of linguistic variation in terms of lexis or morpho-syntax, but they are ultimately also based on frequency information. The high level of accuracy achieved by the classification task and the geographical patterns of similarity generated from vectors suggest that relative frequencies in a constrained vocabulary model can be used to identify basic patterns of regional variation in spoken American English. More sophisticated feature representations, for example in which morpho-syntactic variability is identified using regular expressions, may further increase the accuracy of NLP tasks, as well as provide more direct insight into linguistic variation.

5 Discussion

5.1 Methodological Caveats

Inherent features of YouTube ASR transcripts as well as methodological procedures pertaining to sampling and filtering techniques and the assignment of transcripts to geographical locations need to be kept in mind when considering the types of analysis that can be undertaken using these and similar corpora.

ASR transcripts contain errors, and rare lexical items are often incorrectly transcribed. In addition, some potential phonological or morpho-syntactic linguistic features are subject to normalization by the ASR algorithm and therefore may be inaccurately recorded in the transcripts. These include non-standard stem vowels in past tense forms of strong verbs ("I sot" for *to sit*) or non-standard weak past tense forms for verbs that are typically conjugated according to the strong paradigm (e.g., *blowed, dealed, drinked*), which are attested as features in some varieties of English dialectal speech, but are have not been found in the ASR transcripts, likely due to the ASR model having been trained mainly on transcripts of standard speech. Similarly, non-standard verbal agreement (e.g., "I likes", "they was") in speech may be rendered according to the standard paradigm in ASR transcripts due to the preponderance of standard forms in the training data for YouTube's ASR algorithms.

The transcripts used for the creation of these corpora do not contain speaker metadata or any indication of speaker diarization. However, the structure of the corpora facilitates manual annotation of this and other metadata: Because the word tokens in the corpora contain timing information, the corresponding videos can be checked at the time of utterance for a given phenomenon of interest, and relevant metadata recorded.

The WER analysis presented in Section 4 shows that ASR and manual transcripts are not equivalent, but the manual transcripts from Philadelphia may also be inaccurate: Taylor et al. (2019) tested a sample of Philadelphia courtroom stenographers and found that their transcripts of recordings of speech of African-Americans who had a history in the criminal justice system did not necessarily correspond to the researchers' own transcripts, either for verbatim transcripts or for a "paraphrase task" in which the speech was translated into Standard American English, particularly for the representation of aspectual properties of the verbal phrase.[14] The assessment of transcript accuracy in Section 4, however, is

---

14 The authors found that the accuracy of transcripts prepared by experienced court stenographers varied from 8.8% to 41.6%, with black court reporters showing higher WERs.

based on language delivered in the relatively formal situational context of a city council meeting and hence more likely to correspond to the norms of standard American English than to African-American Vernacular English.

5.2 Potential Features for Analysis

Due to the normalization of the ASR transcripts, variation that occurs within the constraints of standard orthographical forms is better suited for the exploration of regional variation in the YouTube corpora. A large number of potential morphological and syntactic features have been identified in previous studies, including lexical and word order variation features that could be examined in orthographic transcripts. In a study of patterns of negation in spoken British English, Anderwald (2002) made use of orthographic transcripts from the BNC as well as smaller corpora. Kortmann/Szmrecsanyi (2004) summarized morphosyntactic variation in global English varieties on the basis of 76 grammatical features grouped into 11 categories. Szmrecsanyi (2011), in a discussion of the outlook for corpus-based dialectological studies, used the frequencies of 57 morphosyntactic features in the *Freiburg Corpus of English Dialects* (Szmrecsanyi/Hernández 2007) to explore patterns of regional variation in spoken British English. Grieve (2016) showed that lexical and morpho-syntax features in written American letters to the editor of newspapers exhibit regional variation.

Additional features that could be examined in this framework include, for example, politeness words (Culpepper/Gillings 2018), intensifiers (Aijmer 2018), variation manifest in multi-word sequences such as dative alternation (Jenset/McGillivray/Rundell 2018) or non-standard reflexive pronoun deixis (Paterson 2018). The corpora may also be suitable for studies of conversational phenomena such as word repetition or repair sequences.

6 Summary and Future Outlook

Automated methods were used to create large corpora of ASR speech transcripts from YouTube channels of geographically localized local government entities in the United States, Canada, and the British Isles. Web-scraping scripts, the Tor network, and the open-source YouTube-DL library, when used in concert, allow the researcher to create large corpora of ASR transcripts that may be suitable for linguistic analysis of regional variation in English. In addition, with minor script modifications, such a corpus-creation pipeline allows the collection of transcript material according to pre-defined register, genre, or other parameters, as well as the download of video and audio data for acoustic analysis.

Word error rates for a subset of the ASR transcripts in the US corpus were found to be approximately 22%, making some types of analysis less feasible. However, in aggregate, only 3.5% of the word types attested in both ASR and manual transcripts showed a significant difference in frequency, according to a log-likelihood test.

The findings of Agarwal et al. (2007), Eder (2013), Franzini et al. (2018) and Pentland et al. (2019), as well as the simple classification presented in this study, suggest that some tasks may be relatively robust to high error rates in transcripts, presumably due to the fact that the even in transcripts with many errors, with sufficient sample sizes, distinct patterns emerge in the relative frequencies of accurately transcribed features (i.e., words). Vector representations of corpus vocabulary and corpus transcripts can be used to investigate patterns of geographical variability – a simple embeddings model using a restricted vocabulary was found to recapitulate some state-level geographical clusters, and some lexical items associated with particular regions in the US were found to be among the items closest to state labels.

Future work could be organized along the following lines: First, similar corpora are planned for other countries in which local government business is conducted in English, such as Australia, New Zealand, and South Africa. Continual refinements to YouTube's language models should allow ASR corpora in other languages to be compiled, as well. Second, the investigation of variation in spoken English in North America and the British Isles can proceed, for example, by using regular expressions to capture morpho-syntactic variants rendered in standard orthography or by using word-vector based methods (Hovy/Purschke 2018). Large corpora of geo-located speech obtained from ASR transcripts will open up new possibilities to explore the diversity and development of spoken English in terms of its geographical variability.

References

Agarwal, Sumeet/Godbole, Shantanu/Punjani, Diwakar/Roy, Shourya (2007): "How much noise is too much: A study in automatic text classification." In: Geetha Jagannathan/ Rebecca N. Wright (Eds.): *Proceedings of the Seventh IEEE international Conference on Data Mining (IDCM 2007), Omaha, NE, 2007*. 3–12.
Aijmer, Karin (2018): "'That's well bad': Some new intensifiers in spoken British English." In Vaclav Brezina/Robbie Love/Karin Aijmer (Eds.): *Corpus Approaches to Contemporary*

British Speech. Sociolinguistic Studies of the Spoken BNC2014. New York: Routledge, 60–95.

Anderwald, Liselotte (2002): *Negation in Non–Standard British English. Gaps, Regularizations and Asymmetries.* London: Routledge.

Tika.apache.org. (2021): *Apache Tika – Apache Tika.* Online at: https://tika.apache.org <05.11.2021>.

Bokhove, Christian/Downey, Christopher (2018): "Automated generation of 'good enough' transcripts as a first step to transcription of audio–recorded data." In: *Methodologican Innovations* 11, 1–14.

Busse, Beatrix (2018): "Current British English: The sociolinguistic perspective." In: Vaclav Brezina/Robbie Love/Karin Aijmer (Eds.): *Corpus Approaches to Contemporary British Speech. Sociolinguistic Studies of the Spoken BNC2014.* New York: Routledge, 16–26.

Chiu, Chung–Cheng/Sainath, Tara/Wu, Yonghui/Prabhavalkar, Rohit/Nguyen, Patrick/Chen, Zhifeng/Kannan, Anjuli/Weiss, Ron J./Rao, Kanishka/Gonina, Ekaterina/Jaitly, Navdeep/ Li, Bo/Chorowski, Jan/Bacchiani, Michiel (2018): "State–of–the–art speech recognition with sequence–to–sequence models." arXiv:1712.01769v6 [cs.CL], 1–5.

Coats, Steven (2019): "A corpus of regional American language from YouTube." In: Constanza Navarretta/Manex Agirrezabal/Bente Maegaard (Eds.): *Proceedings of the 4th Digital Humanities in the Nordic Countries Conference (DHN 2019).* CEUR, 79–91.

Coats, Steven (2020): "Articulation rate in American English in a corpus of YouTube videos." In: *Language and Speech* 63, 799–831.

Coats, Steven (2021): *Corpus of North American Spoken English* (CoNASE). Online at: http://cc.oulu.fi/~scoats/CoNASE.html <12.05.2022>.

Culpeper, Jonathan/Gillings, Matthew (2018): "Politeness variation in England: A North–South divide?" In: Vaclav Brezina/Robbie Love/Karin Aijmer (Eds.): *Corpus Approaches to Contemporary British Speech. Sociolinguistic Studies of the Spoken BNC2014.* New York: Routledge, 33–59.

Dunning, Ted (1993): "Accurate methods for the statistics of surprise and coincidence." In: *Computational Linguistics* 19, 61–74.

Eder, Macei (2013): "Mind your corpus: Systematic errors in authorship attribution." In: *Literary and Linguistics* 28, 603–614.

Esmukov, Kostya (2018): *Geophy* [Python module]. Online at: https://github.com/geopy/ geopy <14.04.2022>.

Franzini, Greta/Kestemont, Mike/Rotari, Gabriela/Jander, Melina/Ochab, Jeremi K./Franzini, Emily/Byszuk, Joanna/Rybicki, Jan (2018): "Attributing authorship in the noisy digitized correspondence of Jacob and Wilhelm Grimm." *Frontiers in Digital Humanities* 5, 1–15.

Google Developers (2021): *API Reference.* Online at: https://developers.google.com/youtube/ v3/docs <14.04.2021>.

Grieve, Jack (2016): *Regional Variation in Written English.* Cambridge: Cambridge University Press.

Halpern, Yoni/Hall, Keith/Schogol, Vlad/Riley, Michael/Roark, Brian/Skobeltsyn, Gleb/Bäuml, Martin (2016): "Contextualizing prediction models for speech recognition." In: *Proceedings of Interspeech 2016,* 2338–2342.

Honnibal, Matthew (2019): *SpaCy* [Python Module]. Online at: https://github.com/explosion/ spaCy <14.04.2022>.

Hovy, Dirk/Purshke, Christoph (2018): Captioning regional variation with distributed place representations and geographic retrofitting. In *Proceedings of the 2018 Conference on Empirical Methods in Natural Language Processing*, 4383–4394.

Jenset, Gard B./McGillivray, Barbara/Rundell, Michael (2018): "The dative alternation revisited: Fresh insights from contemporary British spoken data." In: Vaclav Brezina/ Robbie Love/Karin Aijmer (Eds.): *Corpus Approaches to Contemporary British Speech. Sociolinguistic Studies of the Spoken BNC2014*. New York: Routledge, 185–208.

Kawahara, Tatsuya (2012): "Transcription system using automatic speech recognition for the Japanese parliament (Diet)." In: *Proceedings for the Twenty–Fourth Innovative Applications of Artificial Intelligence Conference*, 2224–2228.

Këpuska, Veton/Bohouta, Gamal (2017): "Comparing speech recognition systems." In: *International Journal of Engineering Research and Applications 7*, 20–24.

Kim, Joshua Y./Liu, Chunfeng/Calvo, Rafael A./McCabe, Kathryn/Taylor, Silas C. R./Schuller, Björn W./Wu, Kaihang (2019): "A comparison of online automatic speech recognition systems and the nonverbal responses to unintelligible speech." arXiv:1904.12403, 1–13.

Kortmann, Bernd/Szmrecsanyi, Benedikt (2004): "Global synopsis: Morphological and syntactic variation in English." In: Bernd Kortmann/Edgar W. Schneider/Kate Burridge/ Rajend Mesthrie/Clive Upton (Eds.): *A Handbook of Varieties of English, Vol. 2. Morphology and Syntax*. Berlin/New York: Mouton de Gruyter, 1142–1202.

Le, Quoc V./Mikolov, Tomas (2014): "Distributed representations of sentences and documents." In: *Proceedings of the 31st International Conference on Machine Learning (ICML–14)*, 1188–1196.

Liao, Hank/McDermott, Erik/Senior, Andrew (2013): "Large scale deep neural network acoustic modelling with semi–supervised training data for YouTube video transcription." In: *Proceedings of the 2013 IEEE Workshop on Automatic Speech Recognition and Understanding (ASRU)*. New York: IEEE, 368–373.

Loesing, Karsten/Murdoch, Steven J./Dingledine, Roger (2010): "A case study on measuring statistical data in the Tor anonymity network." In: Radu Sion/Reaz Curtmola/Sven Dietrich/Aggelos Kiayias/Josep M. Miret/Kazue Sako/Francesc Sebé (Eds.): *Financial Cryptography and Data Security. FC 2010 Workshops, RLCPS, WECSR, and WLC 2010 Tenerife, Canary Islands, Spain, January 2010, Revised Selected Papers*. Springer, 203–215.

Maaten, Laurens van der/Hinton, Geoffrey E. (2008): "Visualizing high–dimensional data sing t–SNE." In: *Journal of Machine Learning Research 9*, 2579–2605.

McEnery, Tony (2018): "The spoken BNC2014: The corpus linguistic perspective." In: Vaclav Brezina/Robbie Love/Karin Aijmer (Eds.): *Corpus Approaches to Contemporary British Speech. Sociolinguistic Studies of the Spoken BNC2014*. New York: Routledge, 10–15.

Mikolov, Tomas/Yih, Wen–Tau/Zweig, Geoffrey (2013): "Linguistic regularities in continuous space word representations." In: *Proceedings of HTL–NAACL 13*, 746–751.

Muthukadan, Baiju (2018): *Selenium with Python*. Online at: https://selenium–python.readthe docs.io/ <14.04.2022>.

Peterson, Laura L. (2018): "'You can just give those documents to myself': Untriggered reflexive pronouns in 21st century spoken British English." In: Vaclav Brezina/Robbie Love/Karin Aijmer (Eds.): *Corpus Approaches to Contemporary British Speech. Sociolinguistic Studies of the Spoken BNC2014*. New York: Routledge, 235–255.

Pentland, Steven/Spitzley, Lee/Fuller, Christie/Twitchell, Doug (2019): "Data quality relevance in linguistic analysis: The impact of transcription errors on multiple methods of linguistic analysis." In: *AMCIS 2019: Proceedings of the 25th Americas Conference on Information Systems*. Online at: https://aisel.aisnet.org/amcis2019/human_computer_interact/human_computer_interact/12 <05.09.2022>.

Ranchal, Rohit/Taber–Doughty, Teresa/Guo, Yiren/Bain, Keith/Martin, Heather/Robinson, J. Paul/Duerstock, Bradley S. (2013): "Using speech recognition for real–time captioning and lecture transcription in the classroom." In: *IEEE Transactions on Learning Technologies* 6, 299–311.

Rayson, Paul/Garside, Roger (2000): "Comparing corpora using frequency profiling." In: *WCC '00 Proceedings of the Workshop on Comparing Corpora*, 1–6. ACM: New York.

Rehurek, Radim/Sojka, Petr (2011): "Gensim–python framework for vector space modelling." In: *NLP Centre, Faculty of Informatics* 3. Masaryk University: Brno, Czech Republic.

Sainath, Tara N./Vinyals, Oriol/Senior, Andrew/Sak, Hasim (2015): "Convolutional, long short–term memory, fully connected deep neural networks." In: *Proceedings of the 2015 IEEE International Conference on Acoustics, Speech and Signal Processing*. New York: IEEE, 4580–4584.

Statistics Canada (2011). Tab. 5 Census subdivision types by province and territory, 2011 Census.

Szmrecsanyi, Benedikt (2011): "Corpus based dialectometry: A methodological sketch." In: *Corpora* 6, 45–76.

Szmrecsanyi, Benedikt/Hernández, Nuria (2007): *Manual of Information to Accompany the Freiburg Corpus of English Dialects Sampler ("FRED–S")*. Freiburg: University of Freiburg. Online at: http://www.freidok.unifreiburg.de/volltexte/2859/ <14.04.2022>.

Tatman, Rachael (2017): "Gender and dialect bias in YouTube's automatic captions." In: *Proceedings of the First Workshop on Ethics in Natural Language Processing, April 4th, 2017, Valencia, Spain*. Stroudsburg, PA: Association for Computational Linguistics, 53–59.

U.S. Census Bureau (2017): *Public Use Files*. Online at: https://www.census.gov/data/data sets/2017/econ/gus/public–use–files.html <14.04.2022>.

Vaessen, Nik (2020): *JiWER: Similarity measures for automatic speech recognition evaluation* (version 2.1.0). Online at: https://pypi.org/project/jiwer <14.04.2022>.

Xiong, Wayne/Droppo, Jasha/Huang, Xuedong/Seide, Frank/Seltzer, Michael/Stolcke, Andreas/Yu, Dong/Zweig, Geoffrey (2017): "Toward human parity in conversational speech recognition." In: *IEEE/ACM Transactions on Audion, Speech and Language Proceedings* 25, 2410–2423.

Yen, C. H./Remite, A/Sergey, M. (2020): *YouTube–dl* [Software]. Online at: https://github.com/rg3/youtube–dl/blob/master/README.md <14.04.2022>.

Ziman, Kirsten/Heusser, Andrew/Fitzpatrick, Paxton/Field, Campbell/Manning, Jeremy (2018): "Is automatic speech–to–text transcription ready for use in psychological experiments?" In: *Behavior Research Methods* 50, 2597–2605.

María Isabel González-Cruz

A Pragmatic Approach to a Corpus of Anglicisms Used in Canarian-Spanish Digital Headlines

Abstract: This paper examines a corpus of 1710 headlines with at least one Anglicism taken from the Spanish digital newspaper *Canarias 7*, published in the Canary Islands. The headlines, which were collected between March 1st 2019 and June 30th 2020, illustrate the use of a total of 677 different Anglicisms. The study follows the relatively recent shift from formal towards pragmatic aspects in the analysis of linguistic borrowings, underlining their stylistic motivations or pragmatic functions and confirming the high impact English is currently having on the Spanish language, more specifically in the Canary Islands. The work focuses on the analysis of the pragmatic functions and the effects that the Anglicisms collected seem to produce in digital journalese. The results prove the pragmatic nature of many of the phenomena the headings illustrate, such as the need of contextual background for adequate interpretation, the role of pragmatic marking with Anglicisms used with a primarily referential or expressive function and the use of Anglicisms for brevity and precision or to indicate attitudes, such as humour, word-play, connotations of modernity and/or euphemism. In addition, there are a few cases of headlines with presuppositions and implicatures, as well as headings with pragmatic Anglicisms, i.e., those involving the transfer of "interjections, expletives, discourse markers and focus-marking devices, which are external to propositions but contribute as signals of how an utterance is to be understood in its communicative context" as Andersen (2014: 22) puts it.

1 Introduction

The widespread influence of English and the incorporation of Anglicisms into almost all of the world's languages have been the focus of attention of so many studies that the current literature on these topics is overwhelming. In the case of Spanish this is proved by the bibliographical compilations carried out in recent decades (Rodríguez-Medina 2000; Núñez-Nogueroles 2017). Evidence of the pervasive presence of Anglicisms in today's Spanish is also provided by Rodríguez-González's (2017) latest dictionary with its more than 4,500 entries, confirming the high impact English is currently having on the Spanish language. This is not in the least surprising, given the increasing process of Anglicization throughout the world. Anglicisms have been attested in all European languages (Görlach 2001; Furiassi/Pulcini/Rodríguez-González 2012), as well as in Latin American varieties of Spanish and Portuguese (Delgado Álvarez 2005; Vázquez 2011; Finardi 2016; Sanou et al. 2017). In addition, the growing relevance of the field of World Englishes (Melchers/Shaw/Sundkvist 2019; Nelson/Proshina/Davis 2019) can be explained by the unprecedented sociocultural and sociolinguistic role of English worldwide.

Traditionally, the study of Anglicisms has adopted a language contact approach, mainly "concerned with lexical and terminological aspects of borrowing" (Andersen 2017: 123). Actually, many authors have focused on the building of periodical inventories, as well as on studying "the semantics of individual forms and their degree of morphological and phonological adaptation" (Andersen/Furiassi/Ilic 2017: 71). In the last decades, however, some scholars have shifted from formal towards pragmatic aspects in their analyses of linguistic borrowings, underlining their stylistic motivations or pragmatic functions (e.g., Rodríguez-González 1996; Rosenhouse/Kowner 2008; Núñez-Nogueroles 2019). Thus, they adopt usage-based approaches (Drange 2009; González-Cruz/Rodríguez-Medina 2011; Estornell-Pons 2012; Andersen 2014; 2015; 2017; Fiedler 2017; Peterson 2017), which are more concerned with "the use of context to make inferences about meaning" (Fasold 1990: 119), i.e., relating to Pragmatics.

On the other hand, it is a fact that nowadays Anglicisms pervade every area of our daily life (Luján-García 2012), from information sciences (Pano 2007; Bolaños-Medina/Luján-García 2010), the economy (López-Zurita 2005) and sports (Rodríguez-González 2012), to fashion and beauty (Balteiro 2014), TV-advertising (García-Morales et al. 2016), or even leisure (González-Cruz 2015). These are some of the many fields where Anglicisms abound, thence spreading into more general spheres. Interestingly, all these areas are usually covered by most newspapers in their various sections. In fact, newspapers recognizably reflect current linguistic usages and play a key role in the diffusion of neologisms, especially Anglicisms, in various national settings, particularly in Spain (Morín 2006; González-Cruz 2012; Nuñez-Nogueroles 2018).

Although this chapter deals with a case of remote language contact "due to the effects of English as a global language" (Andersen 2014: 22), it is worth-noticing that Anglicisms have been used in the Canarian press since the nineteenth century. Between 1880 and 1930 there was close English/Spanish sociocultural and linguistic contact in the main capital cities of the Canaries. In those days many British subjects settled there for business (González-Cruz 1995; 2012) and played a crucial role in the islands' economy, mainly in the development of tourism and trade. This explains why the press has been the focus of attention of the many studies on Anglicisms carried out locally over the years (González-Cruz 1995; 2012; Luján-García 1998; Brito-Pérez 2002; González-Cruz/Luján-García 2003). That said, I concur with Andersen (2017: 24) that the validity of using a written corpus such as the press cannot be denied, "since forms which have entered the written medium, and indeed reached the stage where they are used by journalists and published by newspaper editors, can be considered linguistically integrated to such a degree that they are conventional and relatively stable borrowings." Thus, using the press as a suitable source to examine the presence of Anglicisms is very frequent (Erling/Walton 2007; Gani 2007; Rogoyska/Zboch 2016) and justified, even more so with the growing impact of online journalism (cf. Develotte/Rechniewski 2001; Planchon 2014). With the extraordinary development of the Internet, both the digital editions of traditional papers and the many

> online news sites vie for the latest scoop, giving priority to rapidity and being the most up-to-date so as to attract as many readers as possible (Planchon 2014: 43).

Following the relatively recent pragmatic turn in studies of linguistic borrowing, this essay will analyse the corpus of headlines taken from the Spanish regional digital newspaper *Canarias 7,* in order to answer the following research questions:

i)   Do the Anglicisms used in this corpus serve any pragmatic function or play any role of a pragmatic nature, such as pragmatic marking?
ii) If so, what kind of effects do they have on readers?

Having posed my general aims in this piece of research, in the next section I will outline the basics of the framework that shapes my study of the pragmatic functions and effects Anglicisms seem to produce in digital journalese, i.e., the discourse of the online press. Then, I will briefly describe the corpus, the method used and the more specific aims of our study, before offering the main findings and some final remarks.

2 Newspaper Headlines, Anglicisms and Digital Discourse through Pragmatics

The academic study of newspapers is intrinsically interesting and by all means justified because of the significant social role the press plays in our contemporary world. In fact, it is recognized as one of the most influential powers with its reality-pronouncing function. As Ibáñez-Rosales (2019: 61) put it, "society relies on the media as the source of truth in this brave new world," even though their discourse can never be neutral or objective. Actually, many scholars (Fowler 1991; Fairclough/Wodak 1997; Van Dijk 1998) have proved that the news is imbued with ideologies. Likewise, Partington/Taylor (2018: xvii) state that "[t]he power of persuasion of the media is considerable," despite "its inbuilt privileging of drama, crisis and alarmism."

Generally described as brief and specific types of texts in which one or more words announce the content of the article they precede, headlines have also been defined as "textual negotiators" (Dor 2003: 696) as long as they "constitute the first contact between the reader and the news" (Quintero-Ramírez 2019: 142). Regarding their communicative functions, it is true that they tend to work as an initial summary, but Dor[1] notes that some headlines merely promote one or more secondary details of the story, rather than summarize it; while others simply quote or "even contain material which does not appear in the news item itself" (2003: 697). Besides introducing or summarising the news item, another important function[2] of headlines is to attract the readers' attention so that they feel the need to read the article. Dor (2003: 697) also quotes Iarovici/Amel, who describe this double function of headlines in the following terms:

> a *semantic function*, regarding the referential text, and a *pragmatic function*, regarding the reader (the receiver) to whom the text is addressed. The two functions are simultaneous, the semantic function being included in and justified by the pragmatic function [. . .] The main function of the headline [. . .] is to alert the reader (receiver) to the nature or the content of the text. This is the pragmatic function of the headline, and it includes the semantic one. The headline enables the reader to grasp the meaning of the text. The headline functions as a plurality of speech acts (urging, warning, and informing).

In turn, Crystal/Davy (1969: 173) admit that "the function of headlining is complex". This is due to the fact that

> headlines have to contain a clear, succinct and if possible intriguing message, to kindle a spark of interest in the potential reader, who, on average, is a person whose eyes move swiftly down a page and stops when something catches his attention.

---

1 Interestingly, Dor (2003: 698) uses Sperber/Wilson's *Relevance theory* to define headlines functionally as 'relevance optimizers' since "they are designed to optimize the relevance of their stories for their readers". His engaging study reveals the ten features successful headlines tend to possess.
2 Some authors have pointed out one additional function that online headlines perform, namely, the hypertextual function, because the headline is also the hyperlink readers have to "click in order to gain access to the whole article" (Quintero-Ramírez 2019: 142).

On the other hand, Hart (2002) explains that generally

> journalists have used a proven approach called the 'five W's' to answer the questions that the readers of newspaper articles most commonly want writers to answer.

They are *what, where, who, when* and *why*, although some authors include a sixth question word, *how*. In their headlines, writers usually try to reply to some of these W's so that readers will be interested in knowing about the others. For instance, they might omit the doer of an action -as in headlines[3] (1) and (2) below- thus intriguing readers who would need to read the piece of news to find out, or to know more about what exactly is being discussed, as in (3), (4) and (5) below:

(1) Sorprendido con 48 dosis de crack (7/5/2019) [Caught with 48 doses of crack]

(2) Se salta un stop y se da a la fuga (1/3/2019) [Jumps a traffic light and flees]

(3) No caigas en este timo de WhatsApp (12/2/2020) [Don't get fooled by this WhatsApp hoax]

(4) #ChairChallenge, ¿eres capaz de hacerlo? (4/12/2019) [#ChairChallenge, can you do it?]

(5) 148 wasaps y 51 emails al día, ¿es normal? (14/3/2019) [148 WhatsApps and 51 emails a day: is this normal?]

From the arguments given so far, it seems obvious that journalists must possess a variety of skills and linguistic tools which will help them arouse the interest of the audience they have to entertain. This means that headline writers need to resort to communicative tactics, such as selecting words that not only provide information but also carry some emotional weight, in order to create headlines which are "striking and memorable" (Shostack/Gillepie 2014: 277), and which satisfy the constant need and eagerness for innovation and linguistic creativity that is so typical of journalese (Guerrero-Salazar 2007: 12). Thomas states that "certain words are used very often in newspaper headlines because they are short or sound dramatic" (1989: 84). In fact, vocabulary has been widely recognized as one of the

---

3 All these headlines (and the remaining ones throughout the chapter) have been taken from *Canarias 7.*

most significant features in the language of headlines. The words used need to be short since they must fit a limited space, yet they must attract attention and be effective. And it is precisely here that Anglicisms come into play, since, apart from being fashionable, they tend to be concise, usually much shorter than Spanish words. In addition, the fact that much press news is drawn from external news agencies, combined with the necessary rapidity due to the shortage of time, results in poor translations that oftentimes maintain many of the original English words and expressions.

As a concept, the *Oxford English Dictionary* online defines 'Anglicism' as "[a] characteristically English word, phrase, or idiom, especially one introduced into a sentence in another language". In this respect, I agree with Rogoyska/Zboch (2016: 27) that "the notion of an Anglicism is complex, and encompasses a great deal of linguistic units." Nevertheless, for the purposes of this investigation, suffice it to say that, just like them, under the category of 'Anglicism' I will include "all linguistic signs whose form or meaning suggests English origin."

Linguistic borrowing, and particularly Anglicisms, can be described as the complex result of language contact and cultural globalization, a sort of mechanism for transculturation. As Rosenhouse/Kowner explain (2008: 3), the English lexical 'invasion' that most of the world's languages are undergoing can be seen as "a natural and inevitable process, driven by psycholinguistic, sociolinguistic and sociohistorical factors." It also proves that "borrowed loan words constitute part of the normal way languages develop and survive." After all, the main driving force behind lexical borrowing "is apparently the need for efficient and expressive communication" (2008: 3).

In the case of Spanish, the usage of Anglicisms goes beyond the limits of cultural borrowing and affects all linguistic levels[4] (morphology, semantics, syntax, phraseology), due to the tremendous technological, cultural and political influence of the Anglo-American world (Gómez Capuz 2004: 24–25). Undoubtedly, all these factors play a key role but we cannot minimise the impact of technological innovations, which are leaving their imprint on communicative behaviour all over the world, and putting English "at the service of the various digital genres," as Kortmann notes. In his foreword to Taimo's edited volumes on *Discourse Behavior and Digital Communication,* he argues that "digital communication has significantly strengthened the role of English as the global lingua franca" (Kortmann 2010: xxxiii).

---

4 Although a few Spanish authors have noted the use of Anglicisms for humorous, stylistic or euphemistic purposes, as Nuñez-Nogueroles (2019) shows, no specific study overtly addressing their role at the pragmatic level has been carried out, to the best of my knowledge.

Finally, we must underline the fact that Pragmatics provides an ideal background for our analysis of the use of Anglicisms in digital discourse, as long as it focuses on "the study of the factors that govern our choice of language in social interaction and the effects of our choices on others" (Crystal 1987: 120). As Padilla (2013: 1) explains,

> pragmatics assumes that meaning is not an inherent property of lexical items and grammatical structures, but a by-product of the intentions of the users of language

as long as speakers and writers have an informative but also a communicative intention, and they are expected to do their best to enable their interlocutors or readers to recognise it. In Padilla's (2013: 1) words,

> Pragmatics conceives of communication as a [. . .] complex activity: an inferential one wherein speakers [and writers] do not always encode all they intend to communicate, but leave some gaps for hearers [readers] to fill. Hearers [and readers] can fill those gaps thanks to their deductive abilities [. . .] or to the knowledge they store. Understanding utterances is seen as a process of mutual adjustment of both their explicit and implicit content [. . .] In it they carry out a series of tasks: disambiguation, conceptual adjustment, reference assignment, constructions of descriptions of the attitude the speaker [or writer] expresses or of the action they have performed, supplying some premises or relating the content of the utterance [sentence] to contextual information in order to draw some conclusions.

In short, Pragmatics reveals "how language users make and interpret meaning in context through language and accompanying nonverbal signals" (Chapelle 2013: xiii). As stated above, the influence of English at the pragmatic level is a relatively recent research strand that encompasses two specific aspects; on the one hand, it deals with the study of the motivations and effects Anglicisms can have as marked choices versus other local or native alternatives; while, on the other, it covers "the transfer of pragmatic items" (Andersen 2014: 22). For this essay, I have re-examined the corpus of headings with Anglicisms collected through grant CEI2018-32 in the light of this pragmatic perspective. The next section will describe the corpus, the methodology and the more specific aims of the study.

3 Corpus Description, Method and Aims

As stated above, this work is part of a research project funded by the Canary Islands Government (grant CEI2018-32)[5] with the aim of compiling and studying the Anglicisms used in the local media. I was in charge of compiling the *Canarias 7* corpus, which turned out to include a total of 1710 headings with at least one Anglicism in it and amounting to a total of 677 different Anglicisms. They were collected after three phases of daily monitoring between March 1st 2019 and June 30th 2020. The following Tab. 1 summarizes the results of the quantitative analysis of the general types of Anglicisms found.

Tab. 1: Number of different Anglicisms and their general types.

Types of Anglicism	Amount of different Anglicisms
Registered in DLE	123
New (not registered)	130
Proper nouns	424
Total amount of different Anglicisms	**677**

As Tab. 1 shows, three general types of Anglicisms were collected, namely, i) those which have already been registered in the *Diccionario de la Lengua Española (DLE),* the official dictionary published online by the Royal Academy of the Spanish Language; ii) new Anglicisms i.e., those which have not been registered yet, and iii) proper nouns. Interestingly, the latter were classified into ten categories, which were created on the basis of several related thematic areas. They all appear in Tab. 2 below, showing in decreasing order the number of items each of them contained. Notice that all the Anglicisms that were collected for this corpus are listed in the Appendix at the end of the chapter.

Some of the proper nouns used in headings were names of English-speaking celebrities, mainly actors and actresses, but these were not considered for our frequency count. The relevance of all these naming strategies is undeniable, as they

5 This funding is hereby gratefully acknowledged. The research team, based at the University of Las Palmas de Gran Canaria, studied three of the most popular newspaper published locally both in print and online, for analysis and comparison of the inventory and classification of the Anglicisms used in each. This paper uses the corpus I compiled with the headings published online in *Canarias 7*.

Tab. 2: Number and classification of proper nouns by thematic areas.

Thematic areas	Number of different Anglicisms
Titles of films, plays, songs, TV channels, TV programmes and publications	77
Names of shops, ships, hotels, companies and enterprises	65
Names of organizations, institutions, celebrations, campaigns, challenges and prizes	57
Names of sports, sport teams, gyms, events and tournaments	46
Names of social/musical events, fairs and exhibitions	41
Names of characters, singers or musical groups	38
Names of apps, social networks, videogames, platforms, forums, digital items	29
Acronyms	27
Toponyms and leisure places	23
Commercial brands, names of natural species and diseases	17
Names related to politics	4
TOTAL number of different proper nouns	**424**

are "capable of creating associations and extensions" (Khoutyz 2009: 10) which contribute to pragmatic marking.

Following Furiassi/Pulcini/Rodríguez-González's (2012) formal typology, all the Anglicisms collected could be further classified into the following categories, for which a few examples are provided below:

Unadapted:
drag queen, golf, influencer, online, topless, top model

Adapted:
básquet, castin, estrés, fútbol, jáquer, parquin, selfi, tique

Hybrids:
Black Fraude, Jandíabike, Sitycleta, Plastiman

Pseudo-Anglicisms:
balconing, bunkering, Vueling

Regarding methodology, in the first stage of data collection every occurrence of a headline or a subheading with Anglicisms was registered in an Excel file, together with details about their type (according to Furiassi/Pulcini/Rodrí-guez-González's 2012 typology), date and paper section, form, typographical marks, and any other suitable observations. The data was first used in another study in which I analysed all these Anglicisms from a formal perspective, illustrating their different grammatical categories and uses, and discussing briefly the borrowability of the different word classes (González-Cruz 2021). For the present chapter a pragmatic perspective has been adopted. This has required a second manual analysis of the same data, but now focusing on the stylistic, pragmatic effects and motivations for the use of Anglicisms in those digital headings. To the best of my knowledge, no previous study on pragmatic aspects of the use of Anglicisms in digital headings has been carried out so far in the Canaries. Drawing both on my knowledge and experience as a teacher of and a researcher on Pragmatics, I established the specific aims which will be pursued in this new analysis of the data. For this, I tried to identify the kind of pragmatic phenomena I expected to find in the corpus headings with Anglicisms. They are the following:

a) Headings showing the need of contextual background for adequate interpretation
b) Headings with Anglicisms used with a primarily referential function
c) Headings with Anglicisms used with a primarily expressive function
d) Headings with Anglicisms used for brevity and precision
e) Headings with Anglicisms indicating attitudes: humour, word-play, connotations of modernity and/or euphemism
f) Headings with cases of presuppositions and implicatures
g) Headings with pragmatic Anglicisms, i.e., those involving the transfer of "interjections, expletives, discourse markers and focus-marking devices, which are external to propositions but contribute as signals of how an utterance is to be understood in its communicative context," as Andersen (2014: 22) puts it.

All these phenomena, if found in the corpus, would be important indicators of how Anglicisms can be employed for pragmatic marking (Khoutyz 2009) in Canarian Spanish. The following section will describe the results of this study, regarding the communicative functions, connotations and attitudinal meanings that Anglicisms can convey in the Spanish discourse of the headings.

4 Results and Discussion

In addition to the findings, this section will highlight the various observations I made after analysing from a pragmatic perspective the corpus of *Canarias 7* digital headings with Anglicisms. I will focus on each of the pragmatic phenomena listed above in section 3 in order. As stated, they constitute the specific aims of this study.

4.1 The Need of Contextual Background for Adequate Interpretation

One of the many definitions of Pragmatics is Jenny Thomas's, who describes it as the study of "meaning in context" (1995: 1). In this respect, Develotte/ Rechniewski (2001: 2) say that headlines

> depend on the reader recognising instantly the field, allusions, issues, cultural references necessary to identify the content of the articles.

In addition, they "encapsulate not only the content but the orientation, the perspective that the readers should bring to their understanding of the article".

Undoubtedly, many headings in our corpus require some background knowledge in order to be properly interpreted. This means that any reader who is unfamiliar with the local Canarian context – examples (6) through (9) – or with TV cultural news (10) will probably be unable to interpret correctly the following headings and their referents:

(6)   Un bull terrier acebrado enloquece a Rio (1/3/2019) [A zebra-striped bull terrier captivates Rio]

(7)   Alfredo L. Jones se cansa de obras (9/11/2019) [Alfredo L. Jones is tired of the building works]

(8)   El queque perfecto (28/3/2020) [The perfect cake]

(9)   Entre Coca-cola y Pepsi, Clipper (11/11/2019) [Between Coca-cola and Pepsi, it's Clipper]

(10) Hoy llega 'The Witcher' a Netflix (20/12/2019) ['The Witcher' on Netflix today]

If readers manage to see the picture next to heading (6), they will be able to infer that this news item relates to the winner of the local Carnival contest, which in 2019 was devoted to Río de Janeiro. Similarly, outsiders may not know that Alfredo L. Jones is not a person but the name of a street, an inanimate entity which, obviously, cannot get tired of the building works (*se cansa de obras*); only the neighbours living there can. Likewise, the term *queque* is the local Anglicism used to refer to a cake (*bizcocho,* or *pastel* in standard Spanish). In turn, the referents in (9) are tricky as they go beyond the mere names of these three popular drinks, Clipper being a local brand that in this context is actually evoking a local nationalist party. Actually, this heading corresponds to an opinion article, whose author criticises the latest political events and uses the names of those drinks to represent national and local political forces. As Develotte/Rechniewski (2001: 15) explain,

> headlines draw at least part of their power and meaning from the pool of shared cultural, political and general knowledge on which they draw. Not only can they intrigue and awaken interest, they 'reward' the reader through the intellectual satisfaction gained in successfully decoding them.

4.2 Referential Function

As expected, this is the most frequent communicative function performed by the Anglicisms in this corpus of headings. Examples abound, although they often show some overlap with other communicative purposes, such as brevity, concision or connotations of modernity. The Anglicisms in the examples below ('selfies', 'influencers', 'Black Friday', *hackeo* – from 'hacker'- 'apps', 'web', 'online', 'sexting', 'youtuber') refer to new items or phenomena related to technological innovations, except for (16), where the terms 'derby' and 'Playoff' belong to the domain of sports:

(11) ¡Cuidado con los selfies! (11/3/2019) [Beware of selfies!]

(12) Baby boom entre las influencers (4/11/2019) [Baby boom among influencers]

(13) Todos preparados para el Black Friday (10/11/2019) [Everyone ready for Black Friday]

(14) Los Chancletas sufren un hackeo en Facebook (17/12/2019) [The Chancletas get hacked on Facebook]

(15) Cuidado con las apps para ligar (14/1/2020) [Be careful with dating apps]

(16) El derbi, tren con destino al Playoff (24/1/2020) [The Derby match, the run-up to the Playoff]

(17) Triana crea una web para la venta 'online' (21/4/2020) [Triana sets up a website for online sales]

(18) El sexting comienza ya a los 14 años (11/2/2020) [Sexting starts at 14 now]

(19) El responsable de 'Twin Peaks' aprovecha el confinamiento para hacerse youtuber (15/6/2020) [The Director of 'Twin Peaks' uses lockdown to become a Youtuber]

As shown, all these Anglicisms are used without explanation or definition, which means that they are "assumed to be widespread in the society if the headlines are to have meaning" (Develotte/Rechniewski 2001: 5).

4.3 Expressive Function

According to Salaverría (2005), cyberspace has opened new expressive strategies for journalists who can now take advantage of the hypertextual, interactive and multimedia resources that the Internet offers. In fact, it seems that one of the most significant contributions of the worldwide web has been the enhancement of the emotive or expressive function. Authors such as Moreno-Ortiz (2019: 40–41) believe that the Internet has moved from being a resource for sharing referential information to becoming a sort of repository where opinions and emotional states can be easily dumped.

Thus, in (20) and (21) below, the onomatopoeic word *boom* (made all the stronger by the vowel multi-repetition) can only be interpreted through awareness of the islands' socio-political context, as these expressions are mocking a previous controversial statement made on Twitter by the president of a local governmental institution. Finally, the expression *"A tope de power"* (Power to the max) in (23) is a powerful cry that encourages the fight against the adversities of life; it is uttered in homage to a beloved young businessman who died after fighting a brutal disease.

(20) BOOOOOOOOOM! (7/5/2019)

(21) Caso Grúas, "¡Booooom!" (14/5/2019) [The Cranes file, "¡Booooom!"]

(22) Paseo triunfal al grito de 'Welcome Angelina!' (25/10/2019) [Stroll of triumph to the cries of 'Welcome Angelina!']

(23) "A tope de power!", en memoria de Dany González (21/10/2019) ["Power to the max!" in memory of Dany González

4.4 Anglicisms Used for Brevity and Precision

The following headings include Anglicisms whose use is possibly fostered by the media due to their accurateness or precision and for their brevity, especially when contrasted with their Spanish equivalents or alternatives, namely, the more precise 'smartwatch' – in Spanish, *reloj inteligente* – vs. an ordinary watch; 'pin' for *contraseña*; 'top' for *los más usados*; and 'sold out' for *colgar el letrero de entradas agotadas*. Thus, economy of use (and space) prevails, particularly in (28), where the English acronym SOS and the word 'show' nicely simplify and replace what would be a complex sentence in Spanish (*¿hay que socorrerlo o tomarlo como un espectáculo?*). Particularly interesting is the increasing use of the English prefix *e-* which in (29) replaces the adjectives *electrónico, virtual*. Likewise, forms such as *e-commerce, e-sports, e-biblio* or *e-cigarrillos* have become very popular and widely used.

(24) Detenida por hurtar en Triana un smartwatch (8/3/2019) [Arrested for stealing a smartwatch in Triana]

(25) El pin, entre la censura y el derecho (20/1/2020) [PIN numbers, a dilema between censorship and rights]

(26) Lucas y Martina, nombres 'top' de bebés (13/2/2020) [Lucas and Martina, among the top baby names]

(27) El concierto de Eros en la isla, cerca del 'sold out' (13/4/2019) [The Eros concert on the island, nearly sold out]

(28) Ante un quemado a lo bonzo: ¿SOS o show? (27/3/2019) [Seeing a self-immolation: ¿SOS or show?]

(29) Boom en e-biblio, crece un 1200% (30/3/2020) [Boom in e-libraries, up by 1200%]

4.5 Anglicisms Indicating Attitudes: Humour, Word-play, Connotations of Modernity and Euphemism

Many of the Anglicisms employed in this corpus illustrate the journalist's purpose of providing headlines with a touch of humour, which sometimes includes wordplay and/or the structural paraphrasing of popular sayings, as well as transmitting some sense of modernity or even avoiding Spanish words that may sound harsh, politically incorrect or taboo because of their sexual (cf. Crespo-Fernández/Luján-García's 2018) connotations. The following are examples of all those uses.

(30) Paula Echevarría sorprende con su beauty look (4/4/2019) [Paula Echevarría surprises with her beauty look]

(31) Meghan ya no es royal (1/4/2020) [Meghan: no longer royal]

(32) Inglés para kids (21/3/2020) [English for kids]

(33) Historias de Catalina Park (2/2/2020) [Stories from Catalina Park]

(34) Tetir es 'beautiful' (25/5/2020) [Tetir is beautiful]

(35) ¡Bienvenido Mr Yanes! (20/3/2019) [Welcome Mr Yanes!]

(36) Una campaña llena de 'frikis' (15/5/2019) [A campaign full of freaks]

(37) 50 artistas participan en el festival online 'Canari-On' por el Día de Canarias (26/5/2020) [50 artists take part in the online festival 'Canari-On' on Canary Islands Day]

(38) Cuidado con el 'Black Fraude' (18/11/2019) [Beware of 'Black Fraud-day']

(39) La ciencia con Internet entra (6/3/2020) [Learning science using internet works]

(40) La top model curvy se ha convertido en madre de un niño (21/1/2020) [The curvy top model becomes mother to a boy]

(41) Rosalía, abanderada del fenómeno 'curvy' (30/9/2019) [Rosalía, ambassador for the curvy phenomenon]

(42) Más de 300 swingers evacuados de una orgía (7/11/2019) [Over 300 swingers evacuated from an orgy]

(43) La pareja ha protagonizado la noche más hot de *Supervivientes* (29/5/2019) [The couple were the stars of the hottest night of *Survivors*]

None of the Anglicisms in (30) through (36) above are referentially necessary as there are suitable equivalents in Spanish; they simply add connotations of modernity to the headings. Interestingly, in line with Andersen's (2014: 22) observations regarding the use of 'kids' in German, its occurrence in heading (32) also seems to "portray the modern emancipated child". Likewise, headline (35) evokes the title of a popular Spanish film *(Bienvenido Mr Marshall)* shot in the 1950s, criticizing Francoist society via a parody of a visit by the American politician who planned the European Recovery Program after World War II. Although the headline performs the expressive function with its welcoming message, by using the English term of address 'Mr' it becomes humorous. Similarly, the term 'frikis' (from 'freaky') in (36), elicits humour.

Particularly noticeable is the creativity in the expression 'Canari-on' (37), which plays with the local demonym *canarión*, informally used to refer to islanders native to Gran Canaria, with the Spanish augmentative suffix -ón, and the technically charged English form 'on'. Similarly, in (38) the headline writer is warning readers by playing with the phonetic similarity between 'Friday' and the Spanish term *'fraude'* (fraud), thus suggesting that this commercial event (Black Friday) involves cheating people with apparently lower prices.

In turn, the creativity of headline (39) has to do with its drawing a positive parallel with the sadly familiar Spanish saying, *La letra con sangre entra*, which claims that learning in children is better achieved through pain and physical suffering, even with blood-letting after being beaten or physically punished. Finally, the last four headings illustrate cases of euphemisms, by using 'curvy' instead of the Spanish *gorda* (fat) in (40) and (41), 'swingers' (42) to refer to the participants in an orgy, and 'hot' (43) to avoid using Spanish expressions overtly conveying the idea of 'sexual excitement'.

In sum, these headings show how *Canarias 7* journalists resort to Anglicisms to humorous effect, sometimes including word-play and popular sayings, as well as to express modernity. They also use them for the euphemistic roles they can perform. That said, I must concur with Develotte/Rechniewski (2001: 4) that "[t]he recognition by the reader of various types of puns and plays on words also relies on general and cultural knowledge".

4.6 Presuppositions and Implicatures

Recognized as two of the most engaging pragmatic phenomena, presuppositions and implicatures related to the use of Anglicisms are not particularly plentiful in our corpus. Most of the presuppositions found belong to the existential category, as in (44) through (47) below. Thus, in (44) the existence of doping *(dopaje)* among the members of the political party Coalición Canaria (CC) is assumed to be a fact; the same goes for 'bullying' in (45), Laura's fans in (46) and the dangers of 'likes' in (47); whereas (48) illustrates both the factive type (it is a fact that Maspalomas is not participating in the Fitur Gay trade fair) and the usage of a proper name, 'Fitur Gay':

(44) El dopaje de CC (22/5/2019) [Doping in CC]

(45) El triunfo del bullying (21/1/2020) [The triumph of bullying]

(46) Laura Escanes responde a sus fans (16/1/2020) [Laura Escanes replies to her fans]

(47) Correa indaga en los peligros de los 'likes' (23/2/2020) [Correa looks into the dangers of 'likes']

(48) Los empresarios critican que Maspalomas no esté en el Fitur Gay (19/1/2020) [Business owners criticise non-participation of Maspalomas in Fitur Gay]

As for implicatures, they are rather scarce. The following are a few instances:

(49) Matlab para subir a la ULPGC en los 'ranking' (13/3/2019) [Matlab to push ULPGC higher up the university tables]

(50) ATI, fake news y Wikipedia (19/3/2019) [ATI, fake news and Wikipedia]

(51) La investigación canaria en 'stand by' tras la marcha de Darias (22/2/ 2020) [Research in the Canary Islands on 'stand by' after the departure of Darias]

(52) Illa: "La desescalada no es un sprint" (28/5/2020) [Illa: "Easing the lockdown is not a sprint"]

Thus, in (49) the low position of the ULPGC is implied, as it needs Matlab to climb up the university ranking. Notice the lack of grammatical agreement in "los 'ranking'", with the Spanish article taking the plural form *los*, but the singular being kept for 'ranking'. By simply listing three items, headline (50) establishes some connection between them, which makes readers expect an account of the lies this radical political group (ATI) within the local nationalist party may have published (or not) in that popular online encyclopaedia. In (51) Darias's crucial role in Canarian research is also implied, while (52) suggests that the opening up after Corona virus lockdown should be a slow process.

4.7 Pragmatic Anglicisms

Last, but not least, I will deal with the so-called pragmatic Anglicisms. Andersen (2014: 17) explains that the influence of English at the pragmatic level has to do with "a variety of phenomena whose common feature is that they do not contribute to the propositional content of utterances." What they do instead is to "carry signals about speaker attitudes, the speech act performed, discourse structure, information state, politeness, etc.". In his wide interpretation of pragmatic borrowings, Andersen (2014: 23) includes interjections, expletives, discourse markers, greetings/leave-taking formulae, politeness markers, vocatives, tags, response markers, etc. When thinking about this type of Anglicisms, I anticipated that headlines might not be the best context to find them. However, by experience I knew that, in addition to 'OK', whose use is widely extended in both speech and writing, oftentimes, in informal situations, my friends, colleagues, and even I myself tended to use some Anglicisms of a pragmatic nature, such as *bye* or *goodbye, hello, no comment, thank you,* and *sorry.* In fact, I was aware of the local usage of this type of pragmatic Anglicisms because in another study (González-Cruz/Rodríguez Medina 2011) we had chosen that label to refer to a number of English words and expressions such as *please, hello, bye, no comment* and *darling* whose use in Canarian youngsters' speech was quite frequent, according to a survey conducted previously. These expressions are totally unnecessary in Spanish as discourse markers, since we have highly established and ritualized Spanish equivalents that are employed in similar contexts. Therefore, it is obvious that their use only responds to pragmatic purposes of expressiveness, snobbery or humour, mainly in informal situations and with people we are relatively close to. However, then I remembered having participated in a seminar organized by one of the local governmental institutions, the *Cabildo de Gran Canaria,* in May 2014. Interestingly, this seminar, a formal event dealing with the presence and influence of the British colony settled on the island between 1880 and 1930, was called "Hello Gran Canaria." I knew that the seminar had been reported by the local press, so I decided to search for it, and found the following heading:

(53) Cita con 'Hello Gran Canaria' este martes en la Casa de Colón (20/5/2014) [Date with 'Hello Gran Canaria' this Tuesday in Colombus House]

Then, after examining the *Canarias 7* current corpus (covering the headlines published between March 2019 and June 2020), I found two occurrences of items that belong to the categories classified by Andersen as 'pragmatic Anglicisms', namely, 'OK' and 'bye-bye'. Neither worked as such, though. Firstly, the form 'OK', as can be observed in (54), was used as an adjective, rather than a discourse marker or pragmatic expression:

(54) "El abogado nos dijo que había ido a los juzgados y que estaba todo OK" (11/2/20) ["The lawyer told us he'd been to the courts and it was all OK"]

In much the same fashion, the second item, 'bye-bye', as used in (55), functions more as a noun:

(55) Bye-bye de Meghan en verde sereno (10/3/2020) [Meghan's goodbye in serene green]

Out of curiosity and with the aim of finding more evidence of the reality of these extended pragmatic uses in Canarian Spanish, I carried out a further online search in *Canarias 7* records. It resulted in the following headlines with pragmatic Anglicisms, which proves Canarian readers' familiarity with these forms and their pragmatic functions:

(56) LPA Good Bye (27/5/2015)

(57) Bye bye Pelos Apertura (11/1/2010) [Inauguration of Bye bye Pelos Clinic]

(58) La Otra Orilla. Bye Mr Soria (29/5/2007) [The other side of the pond. Bye Mr Soria]

(59) La Otra Orilla. Hello, again, Mr Soria (26/7/2007) [The other side of the pond. Hello, again, Mr Soria]

(60) 'Hello, my name is Roque Mesa' (6/7/2017)

(61) 'Sorry,' de Justin Bieber (3/2/2016) ['Sorry,' by Justin Bieber]

(62) Maika Makovski presenta su último trabajo 'Thank you for the Boots' en un concierto exclusivo en Mojo Club (3/4/2013) [Maika Makovski presents her new song 'Thank you for the Boots' at an exclusive concert in Mojo Club]

(63) 'Thank you for the Rain,' 'La Tortuga roja', 'Basura' y 'Pulse,' ganadoras de Ficmec (5/6/2017) ['Thank you for the Rain,' 'La Tortuga roja', 'Basura' and 'Pulse,' winners of Ficmec]

(64) Rodríguez: "¿Penalti a Viera? No comment" (20/11/2011) [Rodríguez: "¿Penalty against Viera? No comment"]

It is worth noticing, however, that only the Anglicisms in (56), (58) and (59) directly perform pragmatic functions, those of farewell and greeting; whereas (60) and (64) are quotations respectively illustrating pragmatic uses of 'Hello' and 'No comment' but in the mouths of Roque Mesa, a local football player who was transferred to Swansea City Football Club, and the local team coach at the time. The rest are exceptions, since (57) reports the funny name of a new beauty clinic, *Bye bye Pelos* (hair), while in (61), (62) and (63) the expressions 'Sorry' and 'Thank you' are the titles of two songs and a film, respectively. Interestingly, the addressee in (58) and (59), Mr Soria, is a well-known local politician, José Manuel Soria, who became a member of the Spanish national government. Using the English term of address 'Mr' provides an additional touch of humour to the headline.

In contrast, in continental Spain these expressions and pragmatic usages do not seem to be so common. Nuñez-Nogueroles (2019: 169) argues that

> The possible reasons for the absence of English pragmatic items in [peninsular Spanish] are the low level of competence in English that characterise the population of Spain (in contrast to speakers of other languages), the fact that English is not widely used in this country by the man in the street on a daily basis and the common practice of dubbing rather than adding subtitles to films and TV series.

> Nevertheless, in certain groups of young people whose job is related to languages, have spent an academic year abroad with an Erasmus grant and have studied a degree in the area of philology or translation, the use of these pragmatic English items is spreading nowadays.

5 Conclusion

This chapter has explored the use of Anglicisms in the headings of the digital regional paper *Canarias 7* from a pragmatic perspective. The main aims have been to determine whether the Anglicisms employed in the headlines actually performed any pragmatic function or any case of pragmatic marking, as well as to specify their effects on readers. After justifying the relevance of newspaper headlines for the study of linguistic borrowing, I have described the corpus and the methodology employed. By proving the noticeable presence of Anglicisms in the headlines of this newspaper, the study has confirmed Develotte/Rechniewski's (2001: 1) idea that "headlines are particularly revealing of the social and cultural representations circulating in a society at a given time".

This piece of research is a small contribution to the recent pragmatic turn in studies of linguistic borrowing. In reply to our research questions, the data obtained shows how Anglicisms are often used in the headings of *Canarias 7* for pragmatic marking and for serving different pragmatic functions, particularly the referential and the expressive functions. In addition, Anglicisms tend to be used for their brevity and precision, or to indicate certain attitudes, such as giving a humorous touch (through wordplay or by resorting to familiar phrases). Other important roles played by Anglicisms in the headings studied here are those of providing connotations of modernity and performing a euphemistic role. I have also shown the need for contextual and cultural background information so that readers can appropriately interpret certain headings. A few cases of presuppositions and implicatures were commented on briefly, too.

Finally, the concept of pragmatic Anglicisms was examined. Although no real cases were found in the current corpus, evidence was given that this type of

Anglicisms does exist in the records of *Canarias 7* headlines. Besides, a previous study (González-Cruz/Rodríguez-Medina 2011) dealing with Canarian youngsters' speech strategies, had proved that, in contrast to continental Spain, Canarian Spanish speakers are familiar with pragmatic borrowings from English. In fact, besides provoking humour, another significant effect of the use of so many Anglicisms is that *Canarian 7* readers must have noticeably increased their lexical repertoire.

It goes without saying that further research will be necessary to complement the present study, which at its simplest notes "the existence of pragmatically borrowed items, [. . .] providing minimal descriptions of their functions" (Andersen 2014: 31). I agree with Andersen (2014) that future empirical and cross-linguistic studies will be of great interest if they focus on a comparative analysis that may account for the full richness and complexity of pragmatic borrowing.

6 Appendix

The corpus of Anglicisms in *Canarias 7* headlines

a) Anglicisms Registered in DLE (123)

antiestrés; bar; badmington; basket; béisbol; bikini; blog; blues; boom; bridge; bull-terrier; bungalow/bungalós; camp; camping; castin/casting; catamarán; CD; charter; chat; cheque; chequear; chequeo; claxon; click; cócteles; cómic/s; club/es; coach; container; crack; derbi; dopaje; dron/drones; establishment; estand/stand; estrés; estriptis; exprés; fans; ferry; films; friquis; fútbol; futbolísimo; gasoil; gay; gol; golf; góspel; hackeo; hippies; hockey; iceberg; internet; jazz; kayak; kit/s; láser; líder; lidera; lideradas; liderando; liderará; liderato; liderazgo; lideró; look/s; market-ing; memes; miss; míster; mitin; parking/parquin; penalti; performance; picnic; pin; póker; pop; pop-rock; pub; queque; radar; rally; ránking; rap; rapero; récord/s; relax; remake: resort/s; ring; robots; rock; rol/roles; sandwich; selfie/s/selfi; set; sexy; shock; show; soul; spa; sprint; stock; stop; surf; swing; tableta; taxi; tenis; test; tickets; top; tráiler; trap; tuit; tuitero; videoclip; voley; web/s; wifi; windsurf.

b) New Anglicisms (130)

afterwork; animal flow; antibaby; app/s; baby; baby boom; baby shower; big band(s); bikecenter; beautiful; beauty; beauty look; black; bodyboard; boxcycling; booktuber/s; brunch; bulldog; bullying; burger; camp; coach/es; coaching; cool; cover; coworking; crochet; crowdfunding; curvy; dating show; drag; drag queen; dumper; ecommerce; ecoresort; ecuavoley; email/s; fake; fake news; fam trip; fast ferry; feeling; fitboxing; follower/s; foodies; gliders; hashtag; hip hop; hi-tech; hostels; hot; hub; impeachment; indie; influencer/s; instagrammers; kayak; kickboxing; kids; kitesurf; kitesurfista; K-pop; like/s; lookazos; lover boys; low cost; made in; mails; mansplaining; master class; matches; medical science liaison; (mega)yate; millennials; off-road; online; open; phishing; pitbull; plastiman; play-off/playoff; podcast; pole; power; Private Equity; proficiency; protech [sic]; ramsonware; rapea; rent a car; renting; reseteo; running; rhythm & blues; send nudes; sexting; shishas; smartwatch; snacks; snorkel; sold out; spinning; spin-off; squad; stand by; starlight; startup; stickers; streaming; stripper; superrobots; superyates; surf city; surfero; swingers; talent; top; top ten/10; topless; top model; trail; trail running; transfer; trending topic; turf; USB-killer; vision lab; welcome; WhatsApp/wasaps; Youtuber/s.

c) Proper Names (424)

i. Titles of Films, Plays, Songs, TV Programmes and Publications (77)
Bad Boys for Life; Badman; Beyond The Sun; Big Bang Theory; Billie Jean; Black Beach; Bohemian Rapsody; Boing; Capitana Marvel; Cars; Cinderella; Cocodrilo Dundee; Dead Set; Dummy; Embassy; Endgame; First Dates; Friends; Frozen; Glitter; Good morning, midnight; Got Talent; Grasp Network; Grease; Green Book; Halt & Catch Fire; Heimat is a Space in Time; Homecoming; Human Lost; Hustlers; I will survive; Joker; Killing Eve; Lady Off; La Voz Kids; Love Life; Love me not; Made in Gran Canaria; Masterchef; Monopoly; Onward; Perfect; Personal Assistant; Playground of the Rich; Real Mom; Red Network; Reality Z; Rocky; Run the world; Smart Consumer; Spoiler; Star Wars; Stitches; The Cars; The Christmas Show; The Fashion Book; The Final Countdown; The Hollywood Reporter; The Loop; The Mandalorian; The New York Times; The room to be; The Witcher; Thriller; Titanic; Toy Story; Trackers; Typical Spanish; Twin Peaks; Vicious Magazine; Washington Post; Wasp Network; West Side Story; Wheely; Wonder Woman; X-Men; You

ii. Names of Shops, Ships, Hotels, Companies and Enterprises (65)

Acuario Lifestyle Hotel; Air Europa; Altamar Hotels & Resorts; Amazon; Aqua & Sport Center; Arctic Trucks; Bajamar Express; beCordial Hotels & Resorts; Bioeasy Biotechnology; Black Watch; Boeing 737 Max; British Airways; Bull Hotels; Cabify; CaixaBank; Canarias Smart Grid; Canary Flash; Canary Fly; Coca-Cola European Partners; Customer Travel; Easyjet; Europa Press; Fairplay; Fox; Free Motion; Fund Grube; General Markets Food Iberica; Gloria Palace Royal Hotel; Hard Rock Hotel; HMK Holdings LP; Hotel Princess; Hotel Suites & Villas by Dunas; Iberia Express; Idea Market; Lemonkey; JET2; Just Eat; Language Campus; London School; Lopesan Hotel Group; Microsoft; Mycarflix; Norwegian; Oliva Beach; Oneport; Playitas Resort; Paraguas Events; Queen Victoria; Reciclown; Robinson Club Jandía; Room Mate; Ryanair; Sabina Beauty & Fashion; Santa Catalina Royal Hideaway Hotel; Secrets (Lanzarote Resort & Spa); Spanair; Spar; Thomas Cook; Toca Sport de Costa Teguise; Topcar; Transcoma Shipping; Universal Music; Viking Sky; Vueling; Winnipeg

iii. Names of Organizations, Institutions, Celebrations, Campaigns, Challenges and Prizes (57)

Alan Turing; Astro Pi 'Mission Space Lab'; Atlantic Schools; Beartalent; Black Friday; Blue Monday; Bols Around the World 2019; Charter 100; copa EHF Challenge; #ChairChallenge; Chefs For Spain; Clean Ocean Project; Club Camping y Caravaning; Doodle de Google; Drag Queen del Carnaval de LPGC; Drag Queen Maspamoon; EuroShop Retail Design Award; FITUR Gay; Flex Challenge; Gold List 2019; Grammy; Gran Canaria Blue; Greenpeace; Guiness; Halloween; Harvard Medical School; Hollywood Film Awards; International School Anita Conrad; London School of Economics; Maspamoon; 40 Music Awards; Masterchef Celebrity; Miss International Spain 2019; National Geographic; Nursing Now; Operación Market; Oscar; Photocall; Playitas Nature; Pulitzer; Queen Victoria; Rainbow Fun Run; Save the Children; Spain for Sure; Stormtroopers Santa-Cruz; The Animal Academy; The Best; The British English Olympics; The Fountain of Praise; Top 10; Top 10 Re Think; concurso RE Think Hotel; TUI Holly; Scotland Yard; Wall Street; Winter is not coming; World Central Kitchen

iv. Names of Sports, Sport Teams, Gyms, Events and Tournaments (46)

ACB Kids; ACB Kids Basket Cup; Atlantic Games; Baifo Extreme; Basket Tara; Boxing Team Formento; Campeonato del Mundo de la World Mountain Running Association; Clinic Baby Basket; Club Voley Playa Net 7 Gran Canaria; EHF Cup; el City; EPIC Gran Canaria Riu Hotels & Resorts (vuelta ciclista); Escuela de Basket TEA del CB7P; Europa League; Final Four de la Euroliga; Final Four de la NCAA; Fitness Macrofit; Football Project; Garmin Titan Desert; Gran Canaria BeachCamp 2020; Gran Canaria Historic Rally; IV Grand Pink Run;

Haría Extreme Lanzarote; Harlem Globetrotters; Herbalife GC; Ironman Lanzarote; la Champions; La Isleta Bike; Liga Canaria de Esports HiperDino; Los Angeles Lakers; LPA Night Run; Macrofit; Manchester City; Ocean Bay; X Open Canarias de Bridge; V Open Fotosub; RETAbet Bilbao Basket; Sporting; The Best; The Market Puerto Rico; Trofeo Carranza eSports; Trofeo César Manrique Optimist; Trooping the Colour; United; Volcano Triatlón; Wimbledon

v. Names of Social/Musical Events, Fairs and Exhibitions (41)

Agaete Chillout; B-Travel; Blue Generation; Canarias Cinema; Canari-on; Deep Sea; Farra World; Fashion Week; Fashion Weekend; Fluor Moon Diabetes; Freedom Festival Maspalomas; Gran Canaria Sum Festival; Jameos Music Festival; Jornada Bankia Forward; Gala Drag Queen; I Love Music Festival; Life Pro Nutrition; LPA Beer & Music Festival; LPA Motown; Maspalomas Costa Canaria Soul Festival; Maspalomas Pride; Mojo Music Festival; Monopol Music Festival; 'Nibiru World Tour 2020'; Nissan Tech Days; Oasis Market; Oil & Gas Meeting Day; Organic Meeting Point; Pre-drag; Primavera Sound 2019; Santa Catalina Wedding Day; Starlite; Sun & Stars Festival de Gran Canaria; The Market Puerto Rico; The Very Best of Dire Straits; Triana Happy Market; Welcome Cruceros!; Welcome Her; WOMAD del Charlton Park; World Travel Market; Worldwide Vegan Chalking Night

vi. Names of Characters, Singers or Musical Groups (38)

Animal Roots; Backstreet Boys; Billo's Caracas Boys; Bocinegro Downhome; Boy Devil; Brass Connection; Brothers in Band; Cat Noir; Cry Baby; Daddy Yankee; Dire Straits; Drag Chuchi; Drag Sethlas; Europe; Film Symphony Orchestra; Gran Canaria Big Band; Juicy M.; Kitt; Ladybug; Lady Gaga; New York Voices; Paris Monster; Perry Mason; Peter Pan; Picaretas Reggae; Rainbow Gospel Choir; Red Beard; Rolling Stones; Second; los Simpson; Snow; Strawberry DJ; Sugar Hill Band; Superman; Sweet California; Swingstar; The Limboos; The Prodigy

vii. Names of Apps, Social Networks, Videogames, Platforms, Forums, Digital Items (29)

Canarias7 Experience; e-Crossminton; Endpoint Security; Eurohoops; Facebook; Fitbit; For sale; Gastronomika Live; Google; Google Arts & Culture; Gran Canaria Wellness; Instagram; Matlab; Netflix; Netflix Party; Netwalker; Panther-Grifols; Shorts; Spotify; Thebrightside.travel; Think 2BU; Tik Tok; Twitter; Unfold; web Down Detector; WhatsApp; WikiLeaks; YouTube; Zoom

viii. Acronyms (27)

Regata ARC (Atlantic Rally for Cruisers); BATW (Bols around the World); BBC (British Broadcasting Corporation); BREXIT (Britain Exit); CEO (Chief Executive Officer);

COVID (Corona Virus Disease); COVID-19 (Corona Virus Disease 2019); DUP (Democratic Unionist Party); EHF (European Handball Federation); FBI (Federal Bureau of Investigation); FFP2 (Filtering Face Pieces); IAAF **(International Association of Athletics Federations);** IHF (International Handball Federation); ISS (International Space Station); Jr (Junior); MET (Metropolitan Museum); Mr (Míster); NBA (National Basket Association); NCAA (National Collegiate Athletic Association); OK[6] ("Oll Korrect" instead of "All Correct"; PCR (Polymerase Change Reaction); SMS (Short Message Service); UEFA **(Union of European Football Association);** USB (Universal Serial Bus); WMRA (World Mountain Running Association); WNBA (Women's National **Basketball** Association); WOMAD (World of Music, Arts & Dance)

ix. Toponyms and Names of Leisure Places (23)
Burger King; Catalina Park; Central Park; Disneyland; el Royal; Experience Center del Centro Comercial y de Ocio 7 Palmas; Food Market; Gastro Gallery; Guinate Park; Hard Rock de Playa del Inglés; Holiday World Maspalomas Center; McDonald's; Mogán Mall; Oasis Park; Oasis Wildlife; Old Trafford; Salobre Golf; Siam Park; Sitycleta; Staples Center; The Paper Club; Tropic; WiZink Center

x. Commercial Brands, Names of Natural Species and Diseases (17)
aby Paco; Baby Pelón; Barbie; Captur e-tech Plug-in; Clipper; Coca Cola; Clío e-Tech; Down; Hello Kitty; Metoo; MINI Sidewalk Cabrio; Off-Roader AT32; Parkinson; Pepsi; Rolls Royce; Satisfyer; Thermomix

xi. Names Related to Politics (4)
Albagate; BREXIT; impeachment; Watergate

References

Andersen, Gilse (2014): "Pragmatic borrowing." In: *Journal of Pragmatics* 67, 17–33.
Andersen, Gilse (2015): "Pseudo–borrowings as cases of pragmatic borrowing: Focus on Anglicisms in Norwegian." In Cristiano Furiassi/Hendrik Gottlieb (Eds.): *Pseudo English. Studies on False Anglicisms in Europe:* Berlin/Boston: Mouton de Gruyter, 123–144.
Andersen, Gilse (2017): "A corpus study of pragmatic adaptation: The case of the Anglicism [jobb] in Norwegian." In: *Journal of Pragmatics* 113, 127–143.

---

6 The form OK occurred for the first time in 1839 as a sort of joke in a satirical article published in the *Boston Morning Post, which became very popular.* Cf. https://www.smithsonianmag.com/smart-news/how-word-ok-was-invented-175-years-ago-180953258/

Andersen, Gilse/Furiassi, Cristiano/Ilic, Biljana Misic (2017): "The pragmatic turn in studies of linguistic borrowing." In: *Journal of Pragmatics* 113, 71–76.

Balteiro, Isabel (2014): "The influence of English on Spanish fashion terminology: –ing forms." In: *ESP Today* 2, 156–173.

Bolaños–Medina, Alicia/Luján–García, Carmen (2010): "Análisis de los anglicismos informáticos crudos del léxico disponible de los estudiantes universitarios de traducción." In: *Lexis* 34, 241–274.

Brito–Pérez, Fayna (2002): Los anglicismos en la prensa canaria: Un estudio sincrónico. In *Estudios de Filología Moderna y Traducción en los Inicios del Nuevo Milenio* Coord. Sonia Bravo Utrera. Las Palmas de Gran Canaria: Universidad de Las Palmas de Gran Canaria, 449–485.

Chapelle, Carol (2013): "Introduction to Encyclopedia of Applied Linguistics." *Encyclopedia of English Linguistics*. English Book 3. Oxford: Wiley and Sons Inc.

Crespo–Fernández, Eliezer/Luján–García, Carmen (2018): *Anglicismos sexuales en español. El inglés como recurso eufemístico y disfemístico en la comunicación virtual*. Granada: Editorial Comares.

Crystal, David (1987): *The Cambridge Encyclopaedia of Language*. Cambridge: Cambridge University Press.

Crystal, David/Davy, Derek (1969): *Investigating English Style*. New York: Longman.

Delgado Álvarez, Alberto (2005): "Los anglicismos en la prensa escrita costarricense." In: *Káñina. Revista de Artes y Letras* 29, 89–99.

Develotte, Christine/Rechniewski, Elizabeth (2001): "Discourse analysis of newspaper headlines: A methodological framework for research into national representations." In: *Web Journal of French Media Studies* 4, halshs–01510703.

Dor, Daniel (2003): "On newspaper headlines as relevance optimizers." In: *Journal of Pragmatics* 35, 695–721.

Drange, Eli–Marie Danbolt (2009): *Anglicismos en el lenguaje juvenil chileno y noruego. Un análisis comparativo*. Bergen: University of Bergen dissertation.

Erling, Elizabeth J./Walton, Alan (2007): "English at work in Berlin." In: *English Today* 23, 32–39.

Estornell–Pons, María (2012): "Préstamos del inglés en revistas femeninas: Entre la necesidad denominativa y la estrategia pragmática." In: *Pragmalingüística* 20, 61–91.

Fairclough, Norman/Wodak, Ruth (1997): "Critical discourse analysis." In: Van Dijk (Ed.): *Discourse as Social Interaction*. London: Sage, 258–284.

Fasold, Ralph W. (1990): *The sociolinguistics of Language*. Cambridge, MA: Basil Blackwell.

Fiedler, Sabine (2017): "Phraseological borrowing from English into German: Cultural and pragmatic implications." In: *Journal of Pragmatics* 113, 89–102.

Finardi, Kyria (2016): "English in Brazil: Insights from the analysis of language policies, internationalization programs and the CLIL approach." In: *Education and Linguistics Research* 2, 54–68.

Fowler, Roger (1991): *Language in the News. Discourse and Ideology in the Press*. London: Routledge.

Furiassi, Cristiano/Pulcini, Victoria/Rodríguez–González, Félix (Eds.) (2012): *The Anglicization of European Lexis*. Amsterdam/Philadelphia: John Benjamins.

Gani, Martin (2007): "Anglicizing Italian." In: *English Today* 23, 40–41.

García–Morales, Goretti/González–Cruz, María Isabel/Luján–García, Carmen/Rodríguez–Medina, María Jesús (2016): *La presencia del inglés en la publicidad televisiva española, 2013–2015*. Madrid: Síntesis.

Gómez–Capuz, Juan (2004): *Préstamos del español: lengua y sociedad. Cuadernos de lengua española*. Madrid: Arco Libros.

González–Cruz, María Isabel (1995): *La convivencia anglocanaria: Estudio sociocultural y lingüístico. 1880–1914*. Las Palmas de Gran Canaria: Cabildo Insular de Gran Canaria.

González–Cruz, María Isabel (2003): "Anglicismos innecesarios en el habla culta de Las Palmas de Gran Canaria." In: *EPOS. Revista de Filología. UNED* 19, 193–218.

González–Cruz, María Isabel (2012): "English in the Canaries: Past and present." In: *English Today. The International Review of the English Language* 109, 20–28.

González–Cruz, María Isabel (2015): "Anglicizing leisure: The multimodal presence of English in Spanish TV adverts." In: *Calidoscópio* 13, 339–352.

González–Cruz, María Isabel (2021): "Anglicismos en los titulares del periódico digital *Canarias 7*. Categorías, usos y funciones." In: Luján–García, Carmen (Ed.): *Anglicismos en los nuevos medios de comunicación. Tendencias actuales*. Granada: Editorial Comares, 73–96.

González–Cruz, María Isabel/Luján García, Carmen (2003): "On English loanwords in Canarian Spanish: Past and present." In: *Revista Canaria de Estudios Ingleses* 46, 199–219.

González–Cruz, María Isabel/Rodríguez–Medina, María Jesús (2011): "On the pragmatic function of Anglicisms in Spanish: A case study." In: *Revista Alicantina de Estudios Ingleses* 24, 257–273.

Görlach, Manfred (2001): *A Dictionary of European Anglicisms. A Usage Dictionary of Anglicisms in Sixteen European Languages*. Oxford: Oxford University Press.

Guerrero–Salazar, Susana (2007): *La creatividad en el lenguaje periodístico*. Madrid: Cátedra.

Hart, Geoff (2002): *The five w's of online help systems*. Online at: https://www.geoff–hart.com/articles/2002/fivew.html <04.12.2021>.

Ibáñez–Rosales, Ismael (2019): "Rewriting the news. The amphibious relationship between populist Podemos and print media in Spain." In: Encarnación Hidalgo–Tenorio/Miguel–Ángel Benítez–Castro/Francesca De Cesare (Eds.): *Populist Discourse. Critical Approaches to Contemporary Politics*. New York: Routledge, 51–64.

Khoutyz, Irina (2009): "Anglicisms as a means of pragmatic marker." In: *Scientific Bulletin of 'Politehnica' University of Timisoara* 8, 5–11.

Kortmann, Bernd (2010): "Foreword." In: *Discourse Behaviour and Digital Communication*. xxxii–xxxiv. Hershey and New York: Information Science Reference.

López–Zurita, Paloma (2005): "Economic Anglicisms: Adaptation to the Spanish linguistic system." In: *Ibérica* 10, 91–114.

Luján–García, Carmen (1998): "Anglicismos en los titulares de la prensa canaria actual: Un estudio comparativo." In: *Philologica Canariensia* 4, 129–146.

Luján–García, Carmen (2012): "The impact of English on Spanish daily life and some pedagogical implications." In: *Nordic Journal of English Studies* 11, 1–21.

Melchers, Gunnel/Shaw, Philip/Sundkvist, Peter (2019): *World Englishes*. London/New York: Routledge.

Misic Ilic, Biljana (2017): "Pragmatic borrowing from English into Serbian: Linguistic and sociocultural aspects." In: *Journal of Pragmatics* 113, 103–115.

Moreno–Ortiz, Antonio (2019): "Mi opinión cuenta: La expresión del sentimiento en la Red." In: Sara Robles–Ávila/Antonio Moreno–Ortiz (Eds.): *Comunicación mediada por ordenador. La lengua, el discurso y la imagen*. Madrid: Cátedra, 38–74.

Morín, Regina (2006): "Evidence in the Spanish language press of linguistic borrowings of computer and Internet–related terms." In: *Spanish in Context* 3, 161–179.

Nelson, Cécile L./Proshina, Zoya G./Davis, Daniel R. (2019): *The Handbook of World Englishes*. Wiley Online Library.

Nuñez–Nogueroles, Eugenia E. (2017): "An up–to–date review of the literature on Anglicisms in Spanish." In: *Diálogo de la lengua* 9, 1–54.

Nuñez–Nogueroles, Eugenia E. (2018): "A corpus–based study of Anglicims in the 21st century Spanish press." In: *Analecta Malacitana (AnMAL Electrónica)* 44, 1–37.

Núñez–Nogueroles, Eugenia E. (2019): "Anglicisms at the pragmatic level: A literature review." In: M. A. Martínez Cabeza/R. J. Pascual Hernández/B. Soria Clivillés/R. G. Sumillera (Eds.): *The Study of Style Essays in English Language and Literature in Honour of José Luis Martínez–Dueñas*. Granada: Editorial Universidad de Granada, 157–174.

Padilla Cruz, Manuel (2013): "Pragmatics and meaning." In: *The Encyclopedia of Applied Linguistics*. Oxford: John Wiley & Sons, 1–8.

Pano, Ana (2007): Los anglicismos en el lenguaje de la informática en español. El 'misterioso mundo del tecnicismo' a través de foros y glosarios en línea. Online at: http://amsacta. unibo.it/2370/1/Lenguaje_informa-tica_ceslic_PANO.pdf <15.11.2022>.

Partington, Alan/Taylor, Charlotte (2018): *The Language of Persuasion in Politics. An Introduction*. Oxon/New York: Routledge.

Peterson, Elizabeth (2017): "The nativization of pragmatic borrowing in remote language contact situations." In: *Journal of Pragmatics* 113, 116–126.

Planchon, Cécile (2014): "Anglicisms and online journalism: Frequency and patterns of usage." In: *Belas Infiéis* 3, 43–61.

Quintero–Ramírez, Sara (2019): "Metaphors of victory and defeat in sports headlines in English and Spanish." In: *Revista de Lingüística y Lenguas Aplicadas* 14, 141–151.

Rodríguez–González, Félix (1996): "Functions of Anglicisms in Contemporary Spanish." In: *Cahiers de lexicologie* 68, 107–128.

Rodríguez–González, Félix (2012): Anglicismos en el mundo del deporte: variación lingüística y sociolingüística. *BRAE tomo XCII cuaderno XXXVI*, 261–285.

Rodríguez–González, Félix (2017): *Gran diccionario de anglicismos*. Madrid: Arco/Libros S.L.

Rodríguez–Medina, María Jesús (2000): "El anglicismo en el español: Revisión crítica del estado de la cuestión." In: *Philologica Hispalensis* 14, 99–112.

Rogoyska, Agnieszka Czech/Zboch, Magdalena (2016): "Anglicisms in online German newspapers and magazines. A quantitative and qualitative analysis of articles in 'Die Welt', 'Der Spiegel', and 'Der Stern' in February 2016." In: *Social Communication* 2, 25–58.

Rosenhouse, Judith/Kowner, Rotem (Eds.) (2008): "Introduction." In: Judith Rosenhouse/ Rotem Kowner (Eds.): *Globally Speaking. Motives for Adopting English Vocabulary in Other Languages*. Clevedon/New York: Multilingual Matters, 1–3.

Salaverría, Ramón (2005): *Redacción periodística en Internet*. Pamplona: Ediciones Universidad de Navarra.

Sanou, Rosa María/Albiñana, Graciela/Galli, Graciella/Castañeda, Claudia (2017): *Anglicismos en San Juan. Usos y actitudes*. Editorial Facultad de Filosofía, Humanidades y Artes.

Shostack, Galina/Gillespie, David (2014): "Communicative tactics of creating headlines in British newspapers." In: *Procedia. Social and Behavioural Sciences* 154, 276–279.

Taimo, Rotimi (Ed.) (2010): *Discourse Behaviour and Digital Communication*. Hershey/
   New York: Information Science Reference.

Thomas, B. J. (1989): *Advanced Vocabulary and Idioms*. London: Edward Arnold.

Thomas, Jenny (1995): *Meaning in Interaction. An Introduction to Pragmatics*. London/
   New York: Longman.

Van Dijk, Teun A. (1998): "Opinions and ideologies in the press." In: Allan Bell/Peter Garrett
   (Eds.): *Approaches to Media Discourse*. Malden: Blackwell, 21–62.

Vázquez, María (2011): "El inicio del anglicismo en la prensa Mexicana: La Gazeta de México
   (1774–1809)." In: *Revista de Humanidades* 31/32, 155–177.

Yoko Iyeiri, Mariko Fukunaga

A Corpus-based Analysis of Negation in Selected 19th-century American Missionary Documents in Honolulu

Abstract: The present study discusses negation in the Hawaii Corpus, which our research team has compiled by using material left in Hawaii by members of the American Board of Commissioners for Foreign Missions in the 19th century. Since our project is still at the initial stage, some of the conclusions are inevitably tentative, but this study shows that the establishment of the auxiliary *do* in negation was still in progress in the Hawaii Corpus and perhaps more generally in 19th-century English. Although it was nearing the completion, there were still some verbs that stayed with *do*-less negation to a noticeable extent. These exceptional verbs include *have*, *know*, and *doubt*, of which lexical *have* merits particular attention. While lexical *have* occurs in *do* negation in contemporary American English, it illustrates *do*-less negation fairly extensively in the Hawaii Corpus, suggesting that the establishment of *do* negation with lexical *have* was not reached in 19th-century American English. This study also demonstrates that forms of negation differ in the writings by different authors. Clarissa Armstrong's English is worthy of particular notice in this context, as its relatively informal style is characterized by various aspects of negation, including the frequency of negation itself, the use of *do*, *not*, *no doubt*, and *neither . . . or* (instead of *neither . . . nor*).

1 Introduction

The Hawaiian Mission Children's Society Library (HMCS Library) in Honolulu holds an excellent collection of 19th-century journals, letters, and an autobiography written by members of the American Board of Commissioners for Foreign Missions (ABCFM), who migrated to Hawaii in the first half of the 19th century (cf. Forbes/Kam/Woods 2018: 1). By assembling selected writings from this collection, our research team has compiled the ABCFM Hawaii Corpus (hereafter simply Hawaii Corpus), which currently encompasses approximately 653,100 words. This is to provide material for research into 19th-century American English, and more specifically the language of the missionary community. In this case study, we will discuss variable aspects of negation in the data, with a special focus on the use of the auxiliary *do* in negation. While negative constructions are relatively stable in the 19th century, the use of *do* in negation was not yet consistent. After a brief description of the corpus, we will discuss to what extent the shift from *do* negation to *do*-less negation has been reached in it, moving thereafter to other aspects of negation in the corpus. Since the language of the writings by Clarissa Armstrong, one of the eight authors in the Hawaii Corpus, has turned out to deviate from the overall trend, the latter half of this study, where frequency of negation itself and negation with *not, no doubt,* and *neither* are discussed, pays much attention to her English.

In the remainder of this paper, we will begin with the description of the Hawaii Corpus (Section 2), as it forms the central part of our ongoing project. We will then shift to the discussion of negation as a case study based on this corpus, summarizing some relevant previous studies (Section 3), discussing the shift from *do*-less to *do* negation (Section 4), and exploring other aspects of negation with a particular focus on Clarissa's English (Section 5). These will be followed by the concluding section (Section 6).

2 The Hawaii Corpus

The eight authors we have chosen for the Hawaii Corpus were born between 1795 and 1805 in New England. They landed on the Hawaiian Islands in the first to fifth company or missionary group of the ABCFM, as shown in Tab. 1.[1] To give some biographical details of the members, Elisha Loomis was "responsible for the first printing in Hawaii" (Forbes/Kam/Woods 2018: 442), Levi Chamberlain became the Superintendent of the Secular Affairs of the Mission after arriving in Hawaii (170), Lorrin Andrews was a chief high school instructor at Lahainaluna (62), Peter Gulick was devoted to pastoral work (293), Dwight Baldwin was involved in missionary work and also in medical practice (92), and Richard Armstrong was "a minister, teacher, advisor, and doctor" (74). Levi Chamberlain and Maria Patton got married on 1 September 1828 in Hawaii, whereas Richard and Clarissa Armstrong were sent to Hawaii as a couple. Both Clarissa and Maria had worked as teachers before their marriages (78, 172–173).

---

1 For details of the companies, see Forbes/Kam/Woods (2018): members of the first company, for example, departed Boston, Massachusetts on 23 October 1819 on *Thaddeus*, which landed at Kailua on 4 April 1820, and those of the fifth company departed New Bedford, Massachusetts on 26 November 1831 on *Averick*, which arrived at Honolulu on 17 May 1832. For the biographical sketches of the authors, we rely on Forbes/Kam/Woods (2018).

In view of their educational or vocational backgrounds, it appears that they were well-educated as 19th-century standard English users. Apart from Peter Gulick's autobiography and Clarissa Armstrong's letters (1839–1889), all texts are journals written in the early 19th century as shown in Tab. 1.[2] Some journal entries of Clarissa's texts (1831–1838) show features characteristic of "letters" such as the use of "you": "I wish you would keep a journal, & often sketch things that you would not otherwise think worth mentioning" (Clarissa Armstrong, 1832).[3]

Tab. 1: Breakdown of the Hawaii Corpus (Version 1.2).

ABCFM Company	Writers	Gender	Born-Died (Texts)	No. of Words
1st	Elisha Loomis	male	1799–1836 (1824–26)	29,300
2nd	Levi Chamberlain	male	1792–1849 (1822–28)	228,500
3rd	Maria (Patton) Chamberlain	female	1803–1880 (1825–49)	69,500
3rd	Lorrin Andrews	male	1795–1868 (1827–28)	24,100
3rd	Peter Johnson Gulick	male	1796–1877 (1876–77)	55,800
4th	Dwight Baldwin	male	1798–1886 (1848–58)	139,900
5th	Richard Armstrong	male	1805–1860 (1831–34)	24,500
5th	Clarissa C. Armstrong	female	1805–1891 (1831–89)	81,500
			Total	653,100

3 Negation in 19th-century American English

Negation in 19th-century English is relatively stable, when viewed within the framework of its long history, in which some major changes took place. This is perhaps one of the reasons why relatively little attention has been paid to 19th-century negation to this day. However, the development of the auxiliary *do* was

---

2 We have selected transcribed texts on the website (*Digital Archives: HMCS Library Journal Collection*), but the first author visited the library twice to see the original material and investigate their reliability. The current project members include Akira Moriya as well as the authors of this paper, while we would also like to acknowledge the contribution by Tomonori Iso, who was formerly a member and involved in the compilation of the corpus.

3 Clarissa's entry for 28 March 1834 proves that some of her journals were actually sent to her friends: "Yesterday I sent a journal of 80 pages, together with some pictures to my friends – Capt. Basset took them & said he expected to see a Capt. at Tahaiti bound direct to America – so in haste I sent it, & forgot to send a letter I have ready for Mother & Elizabeth – ".

still underway. The major expansion of *do* took place in Early Modern English (El-legård 1953; Nurmi 1999, among others), but examples of *do*-less negation, as in *I know not*, are still observed to a noticeable extent in Late Modern English, especially until the 18th century (Tieken-Boon van Ostade 1987; Iyeiri 2004). This state of affairs is continuous in the 19th century, though to a much lesser extent (cf. Curry 1992).

In recent years, thanks to the increasing availability of large historical corpora, several studies focusing afresh on 19th-century English negation have appeared. Yadomi (2015), for example, explores the *Corpus of Historical American English* (COHA) with the result that *do*-less negation as in *I know not* is observed to a noticeable extent in 19th-century American English and remnant even in the 20th century, though to a minor extent. Hirota (2020) also delves into COHA. Although his central aim is to examine the development of *have to* in Late Modern English, he also notes the widespread use of *do*-less negation with lexical *have* in 19th-century American English, refuting Varela Pérez's (2007) comment that the shift from *do*-less to *do* negation was more or less complete with *have* in the 19th century. These studies show that *do* negation was not yet established in 19th-century American English, hinting at the availability of both *do*-less and *do* negation in the Hawaii Corpus. Hence, the shift from *do*-less to *do* negation is one of the main concerns in the remainder of this paper, though some other aspects of negation will also be explored, especially in relation to the discussion of Clarissa Armstrong's English.

4 *Do*-less vs. *Do* Negation in the Hawaii Corpus

4.1 Overall Trend with All Lexical Verbs

As mentioned in the previous section, *do*-less as well as *do* negation is expected to appear in the Hawaii Corpus, which comprises 19th-century texts in American English. There are indeed both types in the dataset, as in (1)–(4):

(1)   . . . but I *see not* how I can do it, especially as I am requested to address them again tomorrow. (Dwight Baldwin, 1857)

(2)   He left her at Lahaina and *did not see* her on the way. (Levi Chamberlain, 1827)

(3) . . . whether they are to join the church I *know not*. (Clarissa C. Armstrong, 1859)

(4) We *do not know* what they were taken for. (Clarissa C. Armstrong, 1832)

Before discussing different tendencies due to different verbs and different authors, it is appropriate to see the overall trend in the Hawaii Corpus. When all lexical verbs are considered, including lexical *have* and *need*, there are 1,010 relevant examples in the corpus, of which 199 (19.7%) illustrate *do*-less negation and 811 (80.3%) *do* negation.[4]

From these statistics, it is probably safe to state that the establishment of *do* negation is nearing completion.[5] Although *do*-less negation is not yet negligible, this is, to a large extent, due to the inclusion of all lexical verbs. It is well-known that some verbs display a clear and exceptional preference for *do*-less negation, which are therefore conventionally excluded from analysis. The first to note is lexical *have*, whose behaviour deviates from that of other lexical verbs even today: in British English at least, it still retains *do*-less negation, particularly when it is used in the stative sense, as in "We haven't any butter" (Quirk et al. 1985: 131).[6] It is, therefore, of no surprise if lexical *have* behaved differently from other verbs in the past. This is why it is almost customary to exclude it from analysis.

The inventory of additional verbs to be set aside is controversial: the list can be long or short. The minimum will be to exclude *know* and *doubt* only, both of which stayed with *do*-less negation until rather late and, like *have*, tended to be frequent enough to affect the overall statistics if included (cf. Tieken-Boon van Ostade 1987), whereas the maximum could be anything like Söderlind's (1951) list of verbs that occur only in *do*-less negation in John Dryden's prose, namely *believe,*

---

4 *Need* and *dare* are known to be often ambiguous as to whether they are an auxiliary verb or a lexical one, but in the Hawaii Corpus this ambiguity does not arise. First of all, it does not yield any examples of *dare* of the non-auxiliary use. As for *need*, the dataset yields four examples of the non-auxiliary use, none of which are ambiguous: they are followed either by *to*-infinitives or noun phrases, as in: [. . .] *he did not need to be referred to places in the Bible* (Levi Chamberlain, 1823); and *Man does not need a master in practical religion* (Dwight Baldwin, 1857).

5 Cf. the scale of language change presented by Nevalainen/Raumolin-Brunberg (2003: 54–55): incipient (below 15%), new and vigorous (15–35%), mid-range (36–65%), nearing completion (66–85%), and completed (over 85%).

6 Quirk et al. (1985) note in addition the third alternative *have got* for the stative meaning. See also Trudgill/Nevalainen/Wischer (2002) for the stative and dynamic uses of *have* in British and American English.

care, change, deny, derive, desire, die, do, fear, give, go, insist, leave, mistake, perform, plead, pretend, proceed, prove, stand, stay, suffer, and *value.* Visser's (1969: 1534) list of *wot, know, trow, care, doubt,* and *mistake* and Ellegård's (1953: 199) list of *know, boot, trow, care, doubt, mistake, fear, skill,* and *list* are also often used for deciding on the verbs to exclude or at least to treat separately in previous studies (cf. Nurmi 1999).[7] This study opts for the shortest, namely a separate treatment of *have, know,* and *doubt,* which would affect the data when mixed with the other verbs. They will be discussed, but separately in this study.[8] The following two sections will deal with the further refining of the data of *do*-less and *do* negation.

4.2 *Have* in the Lexical Use

Negation of *have* in the lexical use merits special attention. It is almost conventionally excluded from the analysis of *do* negation, but this immediate exclusion has curtailed our chance to know about *do*-less and *do* negation of this verb. As mentioned in the introduction, contradicting remarks are available on *have* in the lexical use: Hirota (2020) shows that the rate of *do* negation of the lexical verb *have* is just above 20% even in the 1900s, refuting Varela Pérez's (2007) remark that the shift to *do* negation of lexical *have* was more or less complete in 19th-century American English. It is, therefore, worth examining to what extent lexical *have* retains *do*-less negation in our dataset.

The Hawaii Corpus finds both *do*-less and *do* negation with lexical *have*:

(5)   The day *had not* the least appearance of a Sabbath. (Lorrin Andrews, 1827)

(6)   I *did not have* much time to read. (Dwight Baldwin, 1857)

As expected, the distribution of the two constructions of lexical *have* differs significantly from the overall trend discussed in the previous section: the eight

---

7 Although Ellegård's list is often used in studies on the auxiliary *do,* it may need updating when viewed retrospectively from the computer age. The first author wonders, for example, if it is necessary to have *boot* in the list of this kind.

8 *Mistake* is another verb often mentioned in this context – it is shared by the lists of Söderlind (1951: 215–216), Ellegård (1953: 199), and Visser (1969: 1534) –, but seems to be rarer than *know* and *doubt.* The Hawaii Corpus does not provide any relevant examples of this verb.

authors in the Hawaii Corpus provide a total of 60 relevant examples, of which as many as 56 (93.3%) illustrate *do*-less negation (e.g., *have not*) and only four *do* negation (e.g., *do not have*).[9] Dwight Baldwin and Clarissa Armstrong give two examples each of *do* negation side by side with a much larger number of *do*-less negation, while all the other authors constantly use *do*-less negation when lexical *have* is involved.

Hence, *have not* is predominant in the entire dataset, irrespective of whether *have* is dynamic or stative in meaning. In other words, the result shows that lexical *have* was among the exceptionally conservative verbs that stayed essentially with *do*-less negation in the 19th century even in American English, corroborating Hirota (2020). Therefore, in the discussion of *do*-less and *do* negation in the following sections, lexical *have* will be set aside from statistics. For the sake of consistency, the policy hereafter is to exclude *need* and *dare* in addition, which, like *have*, display the double functions as an auxiliary and a lexical verb, though in practice their inclusion or exclusion hardly affects any results, since there are only four examples of *need* in the lexical use (one example of *do*-less negation and three of *do* negation) and there are no examples of *dare* in the lexical use in the Hawaii Corpus.[10]

4.3 *Do*-less and *Do* Negation Once Again

Apart from lexical *have*, we have decided, as mentioned above, to discuss *know* and *doubt* separately, both of which are explicitly more conservative than the overall trend. In the Hawaii Corpus, the behaviours of *know* and *doubt* indeed deviate from the overall trend. See Fig. 1, which shows the raw frequencies of *do*-less and *do* negation of these verbs as against the other relevant verbs. It justifies the separate analysis of *know* and *doubt* from the other verbs. *Doubt* is not as frequent as *know*, but it clearly favours *do*-less negation, contrary to the near establishment of *do* negation in the Hawaii Corpus in general. The verb *know* fluctuates between *do*-less and *do* negation, but its behaviour differs significantly from the remaining verbs, with which the use of *do* negation reaches 90.8% (739/75+739). All in all, Fig. 1 reconfirms with further confidence that the shift to *do* negation is nearing its completion in the language of the Hawaii Corpus, though there are some minor exceptions. Hereafter, we will exclude *know* and *doubt* in addition to *have* and *need* in the lexical use, when *do* negation is discussed.

---

9 *Have to* is not counted in these statistics.
10 See Note 4 above.

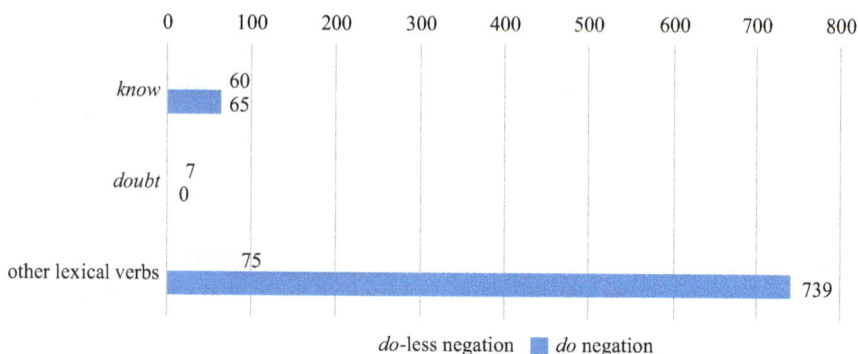

Fig. 1: Raw frequencies of *do*-less and *do* negation of *know*, *doubt*, and other lexical verbs (excluding *know* and *doubt* as well as *have* and *need*) in the Hawaii Corpus.

These are the only verbs to be excluded in the analysis of *do*, since our policy is to limit such exclusions to the minimum. Still, it is probably appropriate to state that there are more potential candidates to be considered in this relation. They remain included in the statistics for the sake of simplicity and consistency, but are worth mentioning. The first are biblical expressions, the existence of which is a characteristic feature of our dataset:

(7)   Woe is me if I *preach not* the Gospel. (Dwight Baldwin, 1857)

(8)   I am found of them that *asked not* for me. (Levi Chamberlain, 1824)

Considering the missionary nature of the corpus, it is of no surprise that reference to the Bible is on occasion incorporated into the text. Due to the biblical tone of the discourse in general, it is not always easy to extract relevant passages only, but one can identify 30 plus examples at least that are citations from the Bible, spreading among different authors with some concentration on Levi and Maria Chamberlain. As in (7) and (8), they usually illustrate *do*-less negation. They could also have been excluded from analysis, but this would have only strengthened our argument that *do* negation is fairly well established in the Hawaii Corpus, highlighting even further the exceptional behaviours of *know* and *doubt*.[11]

The last to be noted, though included in the statistics, is *let*. At first sight, it may look like a verb to be immediately separated, since it takes the *do*-less

---

11 Two examples of biblical translations have been excluded for a different reason, i.e., their use of lexical *have*.

forms *let us not* and *let's not* in contemporary English, suggesting that it has always been exceptional in the history of English. On the other hand, it is not always mentioned as an exceptional verb in previous studies of *do* negation (cf. 4.1. above), probably because its exceptional behaviour applies only to hortative *let us not* or *let's not*, which may not be so frequent in written English. In the Hawaii Corpus there are 16 examples of *let* used with *not*, of which only two, both fairly biblical, are relevant:

(9)   *Let* us *not* be weary in well doing (Dwight Baldwin, 1857)

(10) O Lord, *let* us *not* be slack in doing the parents' duties! (Dwight Baldwin, 1848)

As expected, both (9) and (10) illustrate *do*-less negation, but this does not mean that *let us not* and *let's not* have always been in these forms. Referring to Visser (1963–1973), Denison (1998) gives examples of *don't let's* and *let's don't*, together with the comment that negation of *let's* has three possible forms "*let's not V* and *don't let's V*, both recorded from the seventeenth century, and AmE *let's don't V*, from 1918" (p. 253). There is, therefore, reason to treat *let* when the contrast between *do*-less and *do* negation is considered. *Do* negation is existent in the history of hortative *let*.

When all usages of *let* are considered, it is still a verb that favours *do*-less negation. Of the remaining 14 examples of *let*, only two are in *do* negation, both in similar contexts and by the same author:

(11) It is high time for me to be in bed now as baby *did not let* me sleep till two last night & it is now almost eleven o'clock. (Maria Chamberlain, 1840)

(12) My baby was very restless last night. *Did not let* me sleep till 3 o'clock. (Maria Chamberlain, 1840)

The rest are in the imperative, illustrating *do*-less negation, as in:

(13) *Let* them *not* say we are tabu: . . . (Levi Chamberlain, 1828)

While the construction here may look ambiguous as to whether *not* modifies *let* or the infinitive verb *say*, it is perhaps appropriate to consider (13) as an illustrative case of *do*-less negation, since examples like (14), where *not* is located immediately after *let*, are also encountered repeatedly in the corpus:

(14) Lord *let not* me thus invert the order of things; *let not* this curse hang over
my head, let me not deceive myself; . . . (Maria Chamberlain, 1825)

This example suggests that *let not me* and *let me not* are mere alternatives.

In view of the fairly strong tendency for *let* to occur in *do*-less negation, it
could also have been excluded from analysis, though its inclusion does not affect
the overall trend as it is infrequent. The exclusion would again only strengthen
the trend revealed above: the shift from *do*-less to *do* negation is nearing its completion except with some specific verbs.[12]

4.4 *Do*-less vs. *do* Negation in the Writings of the Eight Authors

We have hitherto made a fairly extensive analysis of *do*-less and *do* negation, dealing with the corpus as a whole. This helps to see the overall trend in the corpus,
but there are, in fact, eight authors involved, whose different tendencies are also
of interest. Figure 2 exhibits the rates of *do*-less and *do* negation in their writings.
As in the previous section, the statistics exclude *know, doubt*, as well as *have* and
need. The graph shows that the predominance of *do* negation is a shared feature
across the board. This is of no surprise, since the eight members are all from the
same area in the United States, belonging to the same generation. They stayed in
the same community in Hawaii, with a shared aim. Still, some authors appear to
merit attention: Elisha Loomis and Maria Chamberlain are inclined to preserve *do*-
less negation to a larger extent than others, whereas Dwight Baldwin and Clarissa
Armstrong are progressive, showing an almost consistent use of *do* negation.[13]

Some of the documents by Dwight and Clarissa are dated late, extending to
the second half of the 19th century. While this may be relevant to the relatively
larger proportions of *do* negation in their writings, one also needs to be aware that
do negation has been established to a lesser extent in Peter Gulick's *Autobiography*,
which was also written in the late 19th century. The difference in genres may be

---

12 While this section has dealt with biblical examples and the verb *let* as two separate issues,
some examples belong to both categories. Hence, the examples that need attention are not so
numerous in the end.

13 It also deserves attention that Dwight and Clarissa are progressive in the use of lexical
have as well, which has not been included in the statistics here. The four exceptional examples
of *do* negation of lexical *have* are shared by Dwight and Clarissa (two examples each), though
one of the examples of *have* in Clarissa's writings is causative. As discussed above, *do*-less negation is essentially the norm with lexical *have* in our corpus.

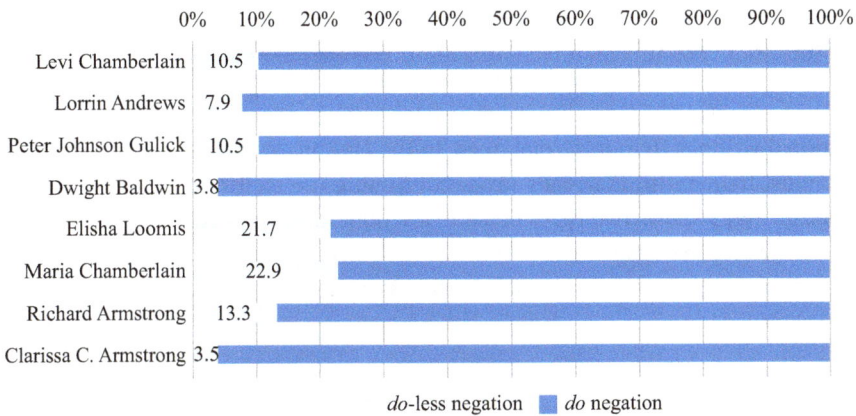

| | 0% | 10% | 20% | 30% | 40% | 50% | 60% | 70% | 80% | 90% | 100% |

Levi Chamberlain | 10.5
Lorrin Andrews | 7.9
Peter Johnson Gulick | 10.5
Dwight Baldwin | 3.8
Elisha Loomis | 21.7
Maria Chamberlain | 22.9
Richard Armstrong | 13.3
Clarissa C. Armstrong | 3.5

do-less negation   ■ *do* negation

Fig. 2: The rates of *do*-less and *do* negation in the writings of the eight authors.

relevant to this: the readership of autobiographies is generally wider than that of journals, in that they are more public. To fully explicate the stylistic differences among the eight authors' writings, however, further extensive research is necessary, including not only negation but other linguistic aspects.

At the present stage of our project, we are at least confident that the style of Clarissa's writings is relatively less formal, when compared with other texts in the corpus. This applies not only to her letters, which are clearly private, but also to her journals, which are often written in relatively informal style like letters, sometimes even with an addressee (cf. Section 2). The extensive use of *do* negation in her writings, therefore, probably corroborates the alleged view that the expansion of *do* is a change from below (cf. Tieken-Boon van Ostade 1990; Blake 1996). In the remaining sections, where we investigate some additional features of negation, we will highlight the relatively informal style of Clarissa's English.

5 Additional Aspects of Negation with a Particular Focus on Clarissa's English

5.1 Frequency of Negation

The present section explores other aspects of negation than *do*, with a particular focus on Clarissa's English, which is allegedly relatively informal. The first to consider is the frequency of negation itself. It is known about Present-day English that negation is attested more commonly in spoken than in written English

(Tottie 1981). Although the contrast between spoken and written English may be difficult to confirm in historical data, Iyeiri's (2018) analysis of Benjamin Franklin's English in the 18th century demonstrates that a comparable result is obtainable on the scale of formality: negation tends to be more frequent in relatively informal writings than in formal ones. In the Hawaii Corpus, negation is indeed the most frequent in Clarissa's texts, confirming the stylistic inclination of her English. Fig. 3 shows two types of statistics, both to see how frequent negation is in her writings as against the entirety of the Hawaii Corpus: the normalized frequencies of negative items (including the cases of partial negation) and of negative clauses:[14]

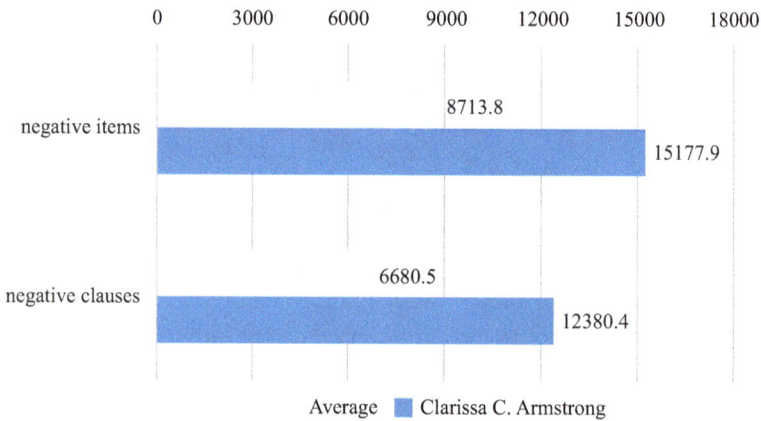

Fig. 3: Negation in Clarissa Armstrong's writings as against the trend in the entire dataset of the Hawaii Corpus (per million words (hereafter pmw)).

Clarissa's negation is almost twice as frequent as the average in the entire dataset both in terms of negative items and of negative clauses, suggesting the relative informality of her style. Obviously, there are other authors that also yield clearly larger figures than the average – Lorrin Andrews, for example, uses negation fairly commonly (14,190.9 for negative items and 9,419.1 for negative clauses) –, but Clarissa's figures are the largest.

---

14 Negative items in this study are so-called *n*-words only, namely words beginning with *n* such as *not, never, no, nothing*, etc. Hence, negatively-coloured items such as *scarcely* and *barely* are not considered. Likewise, negative clauses are clauses with negative items thus defined. Partial negation is excluded from the latter.

5.2 Negative Clauses with *Not*

The second feature to be investigated is whether negation is expressed by the simple negative adverb *not*, as in (15), or other negative items such as *never* and *nothing*, as in (16):

(15) I would *not* desire to change my course. (Clarissa Armstrong, 1832)

(16) Mr. Stewart's departure casts a cloud over the station which *nothing* will dispel until another as good as he joins it. (Levi Chamberlain, 1825)

The common use of *not* instead of other negative items such as *never*, *nothing*, etc. is considered to characterize relatively informal style, and this has been confirmed both in contemporary and historical data (cf. Iyeiri/Yaguchi/Baba 2015; Iyeiri 2018). This is similar to, though not exactly the same as, Tottie's (1988) distinction between *not*-negation and *no*-negation, of which the former increases when the style becomes less formal.[15] The proportion of negative clauses with *not* to the total of all negative clauses in Clarissa's writings counts 74.1%, whereas the corresponding rate in the entire dataset of the Hawaii Corpus is 68.9%. Again, there are obviously other authors whose corresponding proportions are above the average, e.g., Levi Chamberlain (72.6%) and Dwight Baldwin (72.7%), but Clarissa gives the largest rate among the eight authors. This again confirms the relative informality of Clarissa's writings.

5.3 *No Doubt*

Thirdly, the relatively fixed form *no doubt* is to be examined.[16] It can occur normally as a clausal constituent as in (17) or as a disjunctive adverbial in a parenthetical way as in (18):

---

15 Tottie's concept of *not*-negation is more complex than the simple use of *not*: it has to be accompanied by non-assertive forms such as *any* and *ever* to make a perfect contrast to *no* and *never* in *no*-negation. The stylistic direction is, however, the same whichever scale is used, though of course the comparison of detailed figures between the two different scales is not recommended. In the historical data in which non-assertive forms themselves develop as time passes, it may in some cases be easier or even desirable to go for the simpler scale.

16 One of the anonymous reviewers has pointed out that *no doubt* does not convey negative sense. This is a reasonable comment indeed, but we would still like to examine its use in this section, as it contains the negative item *no*, an *n*-word defined under Note 14. The discussion

(17) That he did this, there can be *no doubt*. (Elisha Loomis, 1824)

(18) The author as well as his uncles, & aunts, was *no doubt*, a polished scholar; [. . .] (Peter Johnson Gulick, 1877)

In some cases, *I have no doubt* as a whole is disjunctive or parenthetical, qualifying the entire clause:

(19) The surface has now become hard, and *I have no doubt* would have supported my weight could I have descended to it. (Elisha Loomis, 1824)

As these disjunctive uses convey a comment of the author to the whole clause, they are known to be attested commonly in involved style, which is a characteristic feature of spoken English generally (cf. Quirk et al. 1985; Biber et al. 1999). Supposing that the contrast between spoken and written English is comparable to the scale of informal and formal styles, they are probably more frequent in texts written in relatively informal style in the Hawaii Corpus. In other words, *no doubt*, at least as far as its disjunctive use is concerned, is expected to be comparatively frequent in Clarissa's texts.

Indeed, *no doubt* is the most frequent in Clarissa's writings as Tab. 2 shows, and that by a long margin. More relevant is the fact that ten of the eleven examples of *no doubt* in her texts are of the disjunctive or parenthetical type Table 2 gives a total of 20 examples of disjunctive *no doubt* – seventeen *no doubt* alone and three *I have no doubt* –, of which as many as ten are found in Clarissa's documents. Obviously, the text length matters in statistics of this kind, but Tab. 2 indicates that the normalized frequency of *no doubt* is also the highest in Clarissa's texts. Her examples of disjunctive *no doubt* are attested initially, medially, and finally, showing that the use is fully established in her English:[17]

---

in this section predicts that the present research is extendable in various other directions, including disjunctive adverbials in general in our future studies.

17 Biber et al. (1999: 872–874) investigate the three positions of "stance adverbials" including *no doubt*—"stance adverbials" correspond to disjunctive adverbials in the present paper—and demonstrate that medial position is on the whole the most common. They also show that initial position is more favoured in written texts than in conversation while final position is more favoured in conversation. This is certainly an interesting finding from the stylistic perspective, though relevant examples in the Hawaii Corpus are not numerous enough to allow this analysis.

Tab. 2: The raw frequencies of *no doubt* in the writings of the eight authors.

Authors	Disjunctive uses		Other uses	Totals (pmw)	
	no doubt	I doubt not			
Levi Chamberlain	1	0	3	4	(17.5)
Lorrin Andrews	0	0	0	0	
Peter Johnson Gulick	3	1	0	4	(71.7)
Dwight Baldwin	2	0	1	3	(21.4)
Elisha Loomis	0	1	1	2	(68.3)
Maria Chamberlain	2	0	1	3	(43.2)
Richard Armstrong	0	0	0	0	
Clarissa C. Armstrong	9	1	1	11	(135.0)
Totals	17	3	7	27	(41.3)

(20) *No doubt*, my health would have been much better (Clarissa Armstrong, 1836)

(21) You have *no doubt* heard of the religious interest at Punahou (Clarissa Armstrong, 1859)

(22) They do not all see the importance of it, but will by & by, *no doubt*. (Clarissa Armstrong, 1835)

A total of 27 examples of *no doubt* may not necessarily form a strong piece of evidence, but the possibility of Clarissa's English being relatively informal has been largely supported, especially when combined with other features of negation also showing the relative informality of her text.

5.4 Neither . . . Or

Finally, the coordinate construction *neither . . . or* deserves a brief comment. As in Present-day English, it is customary to use *nor* instead of *or* in this structure in the Hawaii Corpus, as illustrated by:

(23) but Providentially, *neither* he *nor* I was injured by the accident. (Peter Johnson Gulick, 1829)

On the other hand, the corpus provides six examples of *neither . . . or*, of which four are encountered in Clarissa's English.[18] For example:

(24) Strange as it may seem, yet true, I have *neither* time *or* place to pray. (Clarissa Armstrong, 1836)

As her text is relatively voluminous, it will probably be fairer to state that her English gives four examples of *neither . . . or* as opposed to one example of *neither . . . nor*, still confirming that *neither . . . or* characterizes her English.

This is once again relevant to the style of English: it is known that *neither . . . or* was one of the linguistic forms ruled out by normative grammarians in the 18th century (Nevalainen 2014). Although the construction has a long history in English (cf. Iyeiri 2001), it was presumably indicative of relative informality within the context of the Late Modern English period. Thus, this is another feature that highlights Clarissa's relatively informal style.

Incidentally, the remaining two examples of *neither . . . or* are found in the writings by Levi Chamberlain and Richard Armstrong, of which the example given by the former is worth mentioning in passing:

(25) Mr. Goodrich states that Koahou *neither* gives attention to the palapala *or* the pule himself *nor* enjoins attention to it upon his people: but on the contrary violates the Sabbath & encourages his people to do the same. (Levi Chamberlain, 1825)

In (25), *neither* is followed by *or*, but subsequently by *nor* when the new clause with *enjoys* is introduced. This may be due to the stretched distance from *neither*.

6 Conclusion

We have hitherto discussed various aspects of negation in the Hawaii Corpus, with some focus on *do*-less and *do* negation. In accordance with the general trend in 19th-century American English, *do* negation is fairly well-established in the Hawaii Corpus, though there still remain some verbs that lagged behind

---

18 The following example, where the second conjunction *or* appears in the subordinate clause, is not counted: *I can neither pray that he may live or die, for I know not what is best for him or me – only let the will of the Lord be done* (Clarissa Armstrong, 1834).

in this development. Lexical *have*, for example, still abides with *do*-less negation to a noticeable extent in the data. This is among the most important findings in this study, since *have* is often and immediately eliminated from analysis in studies on the development of *do*. Other verbs that deviate from the overall trend are *doubt* and *know*, both staying with *do*-less negation to a larger extent than other verbs. Although this is generally a shared feature among the eight authors involved, the analysis based on different authors has revealed that Baldwin and Clarissa are slightly more progressive in the use of *do*.

The second part of the analysis dealt with other aspects of negation, particularly those that highlight the difference of Clarissa's style from the general tendency in the Hawaii Corpus. Not only the use of *do* negation but also other features of negation indicate that her English, at least in the documents included in the Hawaii Corpus, is relatively informal. The use of negation itself is the most frequent in her English and it tends to rely on the use of *not*. She also employs *no doubt* fairly commonly, particularly in disjunctive ways. Her use of *neither . . . or* instead of *neither . . . nor* is also noticeable. The eight authors in the corpus were well-educated, and all belonged to the same generation and to the same community with shared missionary aims. Hence, individual deviations from the average tend to be quite subtle. Still, Clarissa's deviation from the average has turned out to be always marked and consistent. For the confirmation of the possible factors behind this, e.g., gender, the dates of her documents, or genres, further research is necessary. This is probably an area where corpora of a compact size like the Hawaii Corpus can make an interesting contribution, though of course this is possible only within the framework of the general trend of the history of English, for whose exploration the use of larger and perhaps more representative corpora would be desirable.

References

Biber, Douglas/Johansson, Stig/Leech, Geoffrey/Conrad, Susan/Finegan, Edward (1999): *Longman Grammar of Spoken and Written English*. Harlow: Pearson Education.
Blake, Norman F. (1996): *A History of the English Language*. Basingstoke: Macmillan.
Curry, Mary Jane (1992): "The *do* variant field in questions and negatives: Jane Austen's complete letters and *Mansfield Park*." In: Matti Rissanen/Ossi Ihalainen/Terttu Nevalainen/Irma Taavitsainen (Eds.): *History of Englishes. New Methods and Interpretations in Historical Linguistics*. Berlin: Mouton de Gruyter, 705–719.
Davies, Mark (2010–): *The Corpus of Historical American English*. Online at: https://www.en glish-corpora.org/coha/ <14.04.2022>.
Denison, David (1998): "Syntax." In: Suzanne Romaine (Ed.): *The Cambridge History of the English Language,* vol. IV: 1776–1997. Cambridge: Cambridge University Press, 292–329.

COHA= *Corpus of Historical American English*. [See Davies (2010–).]

Ellegård, Alvar (1953): *The Auxiliary* do. *The Establishment and Regulation of its use in English*. Stockholm: Almqvist & Wiksell.

Forbes, David W./Kam, Ralph Thomas/Woods, Thomas A. (2018): *A Biographical Encyclopedia of American Protestant Missionaries in Hawai'i and their Hawaiian and Tahitian Colleagues, 1820–1900*. Honolulu: Hawaiian Mission Children's Society.

Hawaiian Mission Houses. *Digital Archives: HMCS Library Journal Collection*. Online at: http://hmha.missionhouses.org/collections/show/3 <14.04.2022>.

Hirota, Tomoharu (2020): "Diffusion of *do*: The acquisition of *do* negation by *have (to)*." In: Merja Kytö/Erik Smitterberg (Eds.): *Late Modern English. Novel Encounters*. Amsterdam: John Benjamins, 117–142.

Iyeiri, Yoko (2001): *Negative Constructions in Middle English*. Fukuoka: Kyushu University Press.

Iyeiri, Yoko (2004): "The use of the auxiliary *do* in negation in *Tom Jones* and some other literary works of the contemporary period." In: Isabel Moskowich–Spiegel Fandiño/ Begoña Crespo García (Eds.): *New Trends in English Historical Linguistics. An Atlantic View*. La Coruña: Universidade da Coruña, 223–240.

Iyeiri, Yoko (2018): "Negation in Benjamin Franklin's writings: A stylistic analysis of his autobiography and letters." In: Yukio Tono/Hitoshi Ishihara (Eds.): *Proceedings of the 4th Asia Pacific Corpus Linguistics Conference (APCLC 2018), Takamatsu, Japan, September 17–19*, 178–183.

Iyeiri, Yoko/Yaguchi, Michiko/Baba, Yasumasa (2015): "Negation and speech style in professional American English." In: *Memoirs of the Faculty of Letters, Kyoto University* 54, 181–204.

Nevalainen, Terttu (2014): "Variation in negative correlative conjunctions in 18th–century English." In: Ken Nakagawa/Shigenobu Fuami/Osamu Imahayashi/Kazuhisa Ishikawa/ Yasuaki Ishizaki/Tomohiro Kawabata/Keisuke Koguchi/Yuka Makita/Fuminori Matsubara/Satoshi Ohta/Hisao Osaki/Mayumi Sawada/Mitsumi Uchida/Kyoko Wakimoto/Tomohiro Yanagi/Eiko Yoshida (Eds.): *Studies in Modern English. The Thirtieth Anniversary Publication of the Modern English Association*. Tokyo: Eihosha, 21–36.

Nevalainen, Terttu/Raumolin–Brunberg, Helena (2003): *Historical Sociolinguistics. Language Change in Tudor and Stuart England*. Harlow: Pearson Education.

Nurmi, Arja (1999): *A Social History of Periphrastic* do. Helsinki: Société Néophilologique.

Quirk, Randolph/Greenbaum, Sydney/Leech, Geoffrey/Svartvik, Jan (1985): *Comprehensive Grammar of the English Language*. London: Longman.

Söderlind, Johannes (1951): *Verb Syntax in John Dryden's Prose*. Vol. 1. Uppsala: A.–B. Lundequistska.

Tieken–Boon van Ostade, Ingrid (1987): *The Auxiliary* do *in Eighteenth–Century English. A Sociohistorical–Linguistic Approach*. Dordrecht: Foris.

Tieken–Boon van Ostade, Ingrid (1990): "The origin and development of periphrastic auxiliary *do*: A case of destigmatisation." In: *NOWELE* 16, 3–52.

Tottie, Gunnel (1981): "Negation and discourse strategy in spoken and written English." In: David Sankoff/Henrietta Cedergren (Eds.): *Variation Omnibus*. Carbondale, Illinois: Linguistic Research, 271–284.

Tottie, Gunnel (1988): "*No*–negation and *not*–negation in spoken and written English." In: Merja Kytö/Ossi Ihalainen/Matti Rissanen (Eds.): *Corpus Linguistics, Hard and Soft*.

Proceedings of the Eighth International Conference on English Language Research on Computerized Corpora. Amsterdam: Rodopi, 245–265.

Trudgill, Peter/Nevalainen, Terttu/Wischer, Ilse (2002): "Dynamic *have* in North American and British Isles English." In: *English Language and Linguistics* 6, 1–5.

Varela Pérez, José Ramón (2007): "Negation of main verb *have*: Evidence of a change in progress in spoken and written British English." In: *Neuphilologische Mitteilungen* 108, 223–246.

Visser, Frederik T. (1963–1973): *An Historical Syntax of the English Language* 4 Vols. Leiden: E. J. Brill.

Yadomi, Hiroshi (2015): "The regulation of the auxiliary *do*: *Do*-less negative declarative sentences in American English from 1800 to the Present Day." In: *Zephyr* 27, 44–70.

Gerold Schneider

Do Non-native Speakers Read Differently? Predicting Reading Times with Surprisal and Language Models of Native and Non-native Eye Tracking Data

Abstract: Theories of entrenchment and usage-based models have revolutionized cognitive linguistics and are also spearheading the paradigm shift in linguistics from theory-driven to empirical research. Entrenched, formulaic sequences are easier to process for native speakers, but more difficult to learn for L2 learners. We investigate the correlation between reading times as manifested in eye tracking corpora and text-derived measures of formulaicity, e.g., surprisal, word frequency, and a discourse-related pragmatic feature, predict reading times of L1 and L2 readers, and assess the differences. We use freely available corpora, such as GECO, which contains eye tracking based reading times by several native and non-native speakers.

We address the following RQs:
1) Which features correlate to and are predictive of reading times?
2) Are the features and their weights similar for L1 and L2 readers?
3) What is the role of individual variation?
4) Can L2 reading times be predicted as well as L1 times?
5) Does a comparison of L1 and L2 reading times reveal to us which constructions are particularly taxing for L2 readers?

We establish a ranking of features and show that surprisal is a less important feature for language learners, supporting recent findings that they can profit less form context due to less exposure and lack of routinization. Individual variation is strong and unsystematic, and learners can be predicted less well, partly also because slower readers (among them many L2) have lower model fit and can be seen as less efficient at the reading task. We finally zoom in on zones that are particularly taxing for learners, and observe that they find unusual word order, rare words and constructions and idioms harder to process. Our predicted reading times are quite accurate, the error is smaller than individual variation. This means that our models are suitable for cognitive and didactive purposes.

https://doi.org/10.1515/9783111017433-008

1 Introduction

This study quantitatively assesses reading times, aims to gauge the relative importance of the factors involved in a linear regression model, and it describes differences between reading times and factors when comparing native speakers (L1) and language learners (L2). Particularly, the influence of surprisal and of discourse-related factors are assessed, and where the ranking of features differs between L1 and L2 readers. The predictions of our model are quite accurate, on average the prediction error is much smaller than individual variation.

Quantitative methods and statistical models have revolutionized linguistics and especially cognitive linguistics (Glynn/Fischer 2010; Newman/Rice 2010; Janda 2013; Divjak/Levshina/Klavan 2016). Correlations between frequencies or frequency-derived measures and mental processing have been reported in numerous studies. For example, Ellis/Frey/Jalkanen (2009) show that there are strong correlations between collocation strength and word recognition. Wulff (2008) discusses that for the detection of collocations a frequency-based approach performs better than a similarity-based approach, indicating that frequency and semantics are intricately related. The Firthian hypothesis which says that a word is largely defined by the frequency of its context has given rise to models of distributional semantics (Sahlgren 2006).

Frequency and expectation can be used as a measure of what is easier to process and what is more expected. Rayner/Duffy (1986) have shown that the probability of words has an influence on the recognition of words if they are in isolation. The probability of words in their context is also related to recognition speed. Concerning frequent word sequences, which often grow into formulaic sequences, Conklin/Schmitt (2012) confirm:

> Virtually every study, using a variety of research methodologies, shows that formulaic language holds a processing advantage over nonformulaic language for native speakers. [. . .] The crucial role of frequency in processing clearly applies not only to individual words but also to formulaic sequences. It appears that frequency of exposure is a key aspect of learning formulaic sequences. (56)

If frequency and frequency-derived measures such as expectations (Shannon 1951) are predictive of human processing load, then models using these factors should be able to predict them. Reaction times have been widely accepted as measures of processing time (Grön 1996; MacWhinney 2001; Norman/Shah/Turkstra 2019). The reaction time in language reception in the form of reading texts is reading time (RT). RT is a psycholinguistic reaction time for integrating the read material. Smith/Levy (2013) show that the probability of a word in its context, so-called surprisal, closely correlates with reading time, and Schneider (in press) predicts reading time using cognitive measures like surprisal. Frank (in press) summarizes the approach of predicting reading times with surprisal as follows:

> if linguistic prediction is probabilistic (i.e., statistical), it can be formalized and quantified using concepts from information theory. The most successful of these information-theoretic measures is surprisal – the negative logarithm of word's occurrence probability given the (linguistic) context. (3)

Simple, parsimonious, but reliable language models for native speakers can be built in this way.

Conklin/Schmitt (2012) also refer to language learning. Entrenched, formulaic sequences are more difficult to learn for L2 learners (Schneider/Gilquin 2016). Frequency of exposure plays a key role in language learning. But in L2 (second language) research, the question of how much reading times correlate with, or can be predicted by, language models have been less well investigated. While Pawley/Syder (1983) point out that language learners, due to their lack of exposure, have serious restrictions of building up nativelike routinization and thus intuition, Gries/Wulff (2005) show that language learners, too, are aware of the constructions in the language that they learn. Language learners partly base their knowledge of L2 on the constructions of their L1 (first language) and adapt them to make a choice on what to utter. The arising transfer can both be a help or a source of error and increased processing time, as the research tradition of second-language acquisition (SLA) has well documented (e.g., Saville-Troike/Barto 2016).

Frequency of exposure also plays a major role in grammaticalization and language change. "Frequency is not just a result of grammaticisation, it is also a primary contributor to the process" (Bybee 2007: 337). This insight is on the one hand the cornerstone of construction grammar (Goldberg 2006; Hilpert 2019). On the other hand, the lower frequency with which language learners have been exposed to constructions and sequences also leads to the expectation that rare constructions and idiomatic sequences may be harder to process for learners, both in language production and reception.

The choices which speakers, listeners and readers have to make, involve complex mental processes (Larsen-Freeman 1997; Larsen-Freeman/Cameron 2008). Well-studied instances of speaker decisions are alternations such as the dative shift (Bresnan et al. 2007; Bresnan/Nikitina 2009), for which logistic regression models can predict the outcome with high accuracy. But alternations are only one of the many choices that people have to make when they use language, and they mainly relate to language production. Decisions are required at every word, both to utter and to integrate it during reading, or at least every word sequence, due to routinization. In unexpected contexts, decisions are harder and take more time. In the context of SLA, the few well-studied areas include e.g., Verb-Argument Constructions (Gries/Wulff 2005; Ellis 2013). A model of the interacting complex phenomena and the discourse is still largely absent, however. Ellis (2013) summarizes this lack of research on the topic as follows:

> Research to date has tended to look at each hypothesis by hypothesis, variable by variable, one at a time. But they interact. And what is really needed is a model of usage and its effects upon acquisition. We can measure these factors individually. But such counts are vague indicators of how the demands of human interaction affect the content and ongoing coadaptation of discourse. (8)

For language learners, more contexts and more words are unexpected, and as they are less skilled in routinization (Pawley/Syder 1983) – a general increase in reading time can be expected. Segalowitz/Segalowitz (1993) report longer reaction times and more variability in L2 than in L1 speakers, using a lexical decision task. Despite this early experiment, there is still relatively little research on L2: "there are as yet very few applications of reaction time methodologies in applied linguistics" (Racine 2014: 4).

In this study, we aim to contribute to these lacunae by using context-aware language models. In particular we use surprisal, and other context-based measures. An important pragmatic factor is recency in discourse: has an entity been introduced before, when was it mentioned last? Recent mentions are more present and more quickly accessible in speakers' and listeners' minds. An important syntactic measure is punctuation – explicit markers of clause and sentence boundaries also mark boundaries of processing units. A trivial but important factor to consider is word length – longer words take more time to read. We use the factors to predict reading times in psycholinguistic experiments obtained by measuring eye tracking (e.g., Conklin/Pellicer–Sánchez/Carrol 2018), and we compare L1 and L2 readers. The correlation between surprisal (Levy/Jaeger 2007) and reading times is generally accepted, but it is unclear how much it correlates with other factors, and what differences between native speakers and language learners are, and also the role of individual differences has not been studied sufficiently.

Specifically, we address the following research questions:

1) Which features correlate to and are predictive of reading times?
2) Are the features and their weights similar for L1 and L2 readers?
3) What is the role of individual variation? This question needs to be addressed because possible differences between L1 and L2 could be overshadowed by individual differences.
4) Can L2 reading times be predicted as well as L1 times?
5) Does a comparison of L1 and L2 reading times reveal to us which constructions are particularly taxing for L2 readers?

Our paper is structured as follows. We present a brief overview of previous re-search in comparison to our study in section 2, and data and methods in section 3. We present quantitative results in section 4, where we first assess correlations of reading times to our investigated features, and then use linear regression to pre-dict reading times. In section 5, we present a qualitative study. Particularly, we discuss which linguistic phenomena are taxing for L2 readers, i.e., phenomena for which require considerably longer processing times.

2 Related Approaches

Eye Tracking data can be used as models of mental load and processing time to researchers. In this section, we give a brief review of related approaches.

2.1 Correlations between Reading Times, Surprisal and Other Factors

The correlation between surprisal (Levy/Jaeger 2007) and reading times has been confirmed by several studies in eye tracking experiments (Frank et al. 2013). Eye movement experiments have shown that surprisal correlates to reading times (Demberg/Keller 2008), but it is unclear how much it correlates with other fac-tors. We first give a brief impression of the data compiled by Frank et al. (2013). This corpus contains individual sentences in isolation, a controlled setting in which discourse factors and semantics should not play a major role, so that only the local context influences processing. Surprisal can thus be expected to be par-ticularly important. We measure the size of the correlation of surprisal, and com-pare it to other factors. Correlation strength is intuitive to interpret.

For the first 7724 words of the Frank Corpus (Frank et al. 2013), which in-cludes 1931 words by four readers, Schneider (in press) observes a Pearson cor-relation of 0.25 between bigram surprisal and reaction time (RT) expressed in the variable RT Go-Past, which gives the total gaze time in milliseconds for each token, i.e., the milliseconds spent until finally leaving to further right). A correlation of about 0.25 may seem low; but when considering which other fac-tors correlate, most correlate less strongly. Tab. 1, adapted from Schneider (in press) lists a selection of further variables.

The only factor with a similarly high correlation that Schneider (in press) found in the Frank corpus is word length in characters – longer words take lon-ger to read.

Tab. 1: A selection of correlating factors of four reader in Frank et al. (2013).

RTrightbound correlated to:	Pearson Correlation	My Comments
Length of word in letters	0.256	Highly correlating factor
Bigram Surprisal	0.256	Equally high
Observed / Expected Collocation	0.012	Very low
Position of word in sentence	0.129	Longer sentences take longer to read
Sentence number	−0.071	No slowdown during reading progress

The influence of word frequency on RT has been investigated in many studies (e.g., Rayner/Duffy 1986). While psycholinguistic studies more typically obtain predictability by presenting sentence fragments to subjects (cloze tasks), we use surprisal calculated from large corpora, like Demberg/Keller (2008) and Shain (2019), in order to address the criticism by Ellis (2013) that interactions between variables and decisions of speakers or readers need to be considered. For the sake of parsimony, we use a simple surprisal model, and only those features which are most significant, as reported in previous research. According to Schneider (in press) the most significant features for L1 readers are: word length, presence of punctuation, distance to last previous occurrence of the same word, and surprisal. We use these four features for predicting RT of L2 readers in the current study.

2.2 Reading Times of Language Learners

Racine (2014) states that reaction-time research in applied linguistics is generally still rare. Also, in the area of L2 eye tracking, there are only few studies comparing reading times of L1 and L2 speakers, in particular Underwood/Schmitt/Galpin (2004), Siyanova–Chanturia/Conklin/Schmitt (2011), and Schilk (2017).

Underwood/Schmitt/Galpin (2004) focus on the processing of formulaic sequences. They report mean fixation times of 201 ms (at a standard deviation of 26 ms) for L1 readers, and 228 ms (at a standard deviation of 29 ms) for relatively advanced L2 readers. They conclude that the final word of formulaic sequences are fixated significantly less long by native speakers, indicating their routinization advantage and suggesting that they are more likely to store entire formulaic sequences as single units in the mental lexicon.

Siyanova–Chanturia/Conklin/Schmitt (2011) measure differences in the processing of idioms with figurative meanings. They conclude that idioms are read significantly faster by L1 readers, irrespective of whether they have compositional (literal) or non-compositional (figurative) meaning.

Schilk (2017) compares reading times of selected verb-object and adjective-noun collocations based on frequent learner errors (Nesselhauf 2005). He compares less advanced L2 speakers to more advanced L2 speakers and concludes that the less advanced speakers show significantly longer fixation times for both verb-object and adjective-noun combinations than the more advanced speakers.

While these three studies provide valuable insights and confirm the hypothesis that L2 readers process the selected phenomena more slowly, they cannot offer the broad overview considering all phenomena in their interrelated nature as Ellis (2013) proposes. In order to model this interrelated nature, natural language models can be used. We predict reading times with linear regression based on a variety of features including surprisal. Frank (in press) suggests to use recursive neural networks trained on reading times form L1, L2 or both types of readers. Our approach uses regression modelling instead, which is typically slightly less accurate but more parsimonious, as regression models easily allow us to asses factor weights, measure model fit and explain areas of prediction inaccuracy. Frank's proposal bears enormous promise, but currently "research on bilingual comprehension by neural networks is clearly still in its infancy" (in press: 14).

3 Related Approaches

In this section, we introduce our data and methods.

3.1 Data

There are several corpora that are annotated for reading time using eye tracking data. For our study, we have considered the following four sources:

1. **Reading times for model evaluation** (Frank et al. 2013). It contains 205 simple domain-independent sentences read by 43 participants. The motivation for the compilation was that "understanding newspaper or narrative texts requires vast amounts of extra-linguistic knowledge to which the models have no access . . . a more appropriate data set for model evaluation would consist of independent sentences that can be understood out of context" (Frank et al. 2013: 1185). The corpus also contains ten L2 readers.

2. **Ghent Eye tracking Corpus** (GECO; Cop et al. 2017). This is knowledge-dependent corpus, which entails that extra-linguistic knowledge influences reading time, but also offers the change to include discourse features. An

entire Agatha Christie novel is read out by a dozen of L1 and L2 speakers. The motivation for the collection of the corpus was: "this corpus has the potential to evaluate the generalizability of monolingual and bilingual language theories and models to the reading of long texts and narratives" (Cop et al. 2017: 602).

3. **Dundee Corpus** (Kennedy/Hill/Pynte 2003; Kennedy et al. 2013): 10 native English and 10 native French speakers read a text of 56,000 words. The corpus is not freely available.

4. **Provo Corpus** (Luke/Christianson 2018): 55 paragraphs, containing 2,800 words are read out by 84 native speakers of English. The corpus is available for free, but it has no L2 readers and was thus not suitable for our study.

Based on this comparison, we decided to use the Ghent Eye tracking Corpus (GECO; Cop et al. 2017) as our main corpus. Additionally, we also measure reading times in Reading Times for Model Evaluation (Frank et al. 2013). We restricted our investigation to the 12 L1 readers whose data is complete (some others have e.g., not read the entire novel), and to the 7 L2 readers who had less than 50% daily exposure to English. While discarding some L2 readers increases data sparseness, concentrating on the least exposed readers allows us to concentrate on prototypical L2 readers. According to Cop et al. (2017) readers with more than 50% daily exposure (Bilinguals L2) show no significant differences compared to native English speakers in terms of the performance in the tests which all participants had to take (Cop et al. 2017: 607, Tab. 1, last column) while the differences to speaker with less than 50 daily exposures are highly significant (Cop et al. 2017: 607, Tab. 1, second last column). These tests included the LexTALE test, spelling score, and lexical decision accuracy. There was no significant difference in text understanding between L2 and native English speakers, which indicates that both groups read the novel similarly carefully.

All L2 speakers in this study are native speakers of Dutch, which has the advantage that they are comparable in terms of L1 influence, but adds the serious limitation that just one L1 background is reflected in the data. It will not be possible to discern which areas of slowdown point to general learner-specific processing, and which are typically difficult for L1 Dutch speakers, due to inference or due the language-specific differences. Typologically, Dutch is a Germanic language like English, and the enormous influence of French on English should also not add major difficulties to Dutch speakers, who typically have a working knowledge of French.

3.2 Methods

We correlate reading times (RT) and to relevant factors, and then predict RT with these factors. We always use the total reading times, i.e., the total gaze duration, sometimes involving more than one gaze if the reader backtracks. As correlation measure, we use Pearson correlation. For the prediction of reading times, we use linear regression. In what follows, we list the predictors used in the model. These are surprisal, distance, word length and punctuation.

Surprisal (Levy/Jaeger 2007), our first feature, is generally defined as the probability of a word in its context, or p(word|context) in Bayesian terms. It is usually expressed as a logarithm to give an information-theoretic value, the surprise in bits for seeing a new word in the given context.[1] The detailed definitions can vary, we are using a simple operationalization: the probability of a word linearly combined with the probability of transition from the previous word: "the forward transitional probability $P(w_k|w_{k-1})$ is a simple form of surprisal" (Demberg/Keller 2008).

Our definition is thus:

$$bigram\ surprisal = log\frac{1}{p(w_k)} + log\frac{1}{p(w_k|w_{k-1})}$$

We have learned the probabilities from the British National Corpus (Aston/Burnard 1998). The probability of a word is simply its frequency divided by the corpus size. An example of a sentence with bigram surprisal is given in Fig. 1. We can see areas of low surprisal, for instance the pronoun *I*, which is generally frequent, and even more so at the beginning of a sentence, which explains why surprisal for *I* is lower in its first occurrence than after *when* later in the sentence. A further example is the word *to*, which is frequent and also in a common context in both occurrences here. The context *trying to make* is slightly less common than *what to do*, which leads to a slightly higher surprisal, an expectation that is also mirrored by a slightly higher reading time of *to* in *trying to make*. Surprisal is highest for the name *John Cavendish* – even the frequent name *John* is so infrequent that it cannot be predicted from the previous words, unless we have discourse-specific knowledge.

Surprisal allows us to measure chunking (Altenberg 1998) and the competition between the idiom and syntax principle (Sinclair 1991). Linguistic contexts dominated by the idiom principle have low surprisal, many chunks, are easy to

---

[1] We cannot provide an introduction to Information Theory here, but let us look at a simple example: in order to express 8 equally likely words, 3 bits are needed, as 2^3 equals 8.

process, but contain little information. Linguistic contexts which make maximal use of syntactic creativity can compress a lot of information into few words, but this makes it very hard for readers or listeners to follow: surprisal is very high, the continuation of the utterance is hard to predict. Shannon's (1951) noisy channel easily breaks down when redundancy is too low. In spoken language this can lead to misunderstanding and uncertainty, while in written language it typically leads to longer reading times and backtracking. According to Levy/Jaeger (2007), successful communication needs to strike a balance between the two: surprisal should stay approximately constant. This is the principle of uniform information density (UID). "UID can be seen as minimizing comprehension difficulty" (Levy/Jaeger 2007: 850).

UID holds quite well in spoken language, while some compressed written genres (Biber/Conrad 2009), particularly the scientific genre, exhibit frequent areas of high surprisal (Schneider/Grigonyte 2018).

ID	Word	Reading Time (ms)	Surprisal	
115	I	512		11.263337
116	was	279		16.195808
117	trying	225		12.843803
118	to	231		11.66212
119	make	184		15.584163
120	up	470		17.04785
121	my	0		15.787277
122	mind	277		19.215173
123	what	214		15.162532
124	to	130		11.381907
125	do	0		17.664406
126	when	468		13.040814
127	I	0		17.910504
128	ran	0		19.851737
129	across	3723		24.424627
130	John	555		26
131	Cavendish	717		26

Fig. 1: An example sentence from GECO with bigram surprisal.

Word probability is correlated to word recognition speed (Rayner/Duffy 1986), both in isolation and in context. Predictability of the context in psycholinguistics is often obtained by presenting sentence fragments to subjects. We use surprisal instead, which allows us to address all phenomena in their complexity and interaction (Ellis 2013). Eye movement experiments have shown that surprisal correlates to reading times (Demberg/Keller 2008). Correlations to EEG activity has also been investigated (Frank et al. 2013). Shain (2019) shows that word frequency and predictability from the context are hard to separate and that predictability by means of surprisal is a better predictor. We thus do not include frequency separately.

Smith/Levy (2013) show that the effect of word predictability on reading time is logarithmic, across 6 orders of magnitude, from very rare to very frequent words. The logarithmic correlations entail that the modelling of surprisal as an information-theoretic value using a logarithmic scale is cognitively adequate.

Surprisal gives us a language model, albeit a simplified one. It is surface-oriented, in the sense that it uses extremely small amounts of context. In a real-world discourse, previously seen words are expected and are thus read fast. We address this shortcoming by measuring the distance to the most recent occurrence of the current word. This feature, **distance**, is our second feature. RT depends on word frequency, but this effect largely disappears after three repetitions (Rayner/Raney/Pollatsek 1995) in the discourse. Church (2000) observes that the probability for seeing a content word twice in a text is closer to (p(word) /2) than p(word) * p(word) which would be expected under the independence assumptions. Particularly the GECO material, where an entire novel is read, needs an integration of discourse-related features. The correlation in GECO between the logarithm of the distance and RT is 0.46 for L1 and 0.38 for L2 readers, values that are so high that we decided to include them. For previously unseen words, a default value of distance=10000 is given.

The third feature to be included is **word length**. This feature is trivially related to RT – longer words take longer to read. We measured a correlation between the logarithm of word length and RT is 0.64 for L1, and 0.55 for L2 readers. We expect this feature to dominate the feature weights.

As punctuation symbols are too small to measure fixations, and as they are often never fixed on, the slowdown caused by punctuation is not directly accessible in GECO. The full wordform in the data simply includes punctuation symbols. We have removed them and instead introduce a binary feature **punctuation**, which we set whenever a word is followed by a punctuation symbol. We do not distinguish between commas, full stops or other punctuation symbols.

3.3 Linear Regression and Step-wise Regression

Linear regression techniques and mixed models are frequently used in linguistics (see e.g., Winter 2013; Gries 2015; Speelman/Heylen/Geeraerts 2018; or Schneider/Lauber 2019). We are predicting the observed reading times (RT) for each word in the corpus.

We use multivariate models as many factors are involved. They comprise surprisal, distance to the last previous occurrence of the word, length of the word, presence of punctuation. They were the most significant features for predicting the reading time of L1 speakers in GECO in Schneider (in press). These factors in combination partly explain the observed reading times. A frequently used measure of the percentage of the data that is explained by the model is the R^2 metric. Molnar (2020) summarizes its function as follows:

> R-squared tells you how much of your variance can be explained by the linear model. R-squared ranges between 0 for models where the model does not explain the data at all and 1 for models that explain all of the variance in your data.

We also report the adjusted R^2, a version of R^2 which takes the number of factors used into consideration. This is important as a higher number of factors increases the likelihood of overfitting, and reduces the parsimony of the model. This adjustment is an operationalization of Occam's razor, a principle which states that if several theories explain a fact equally well the simpler explanation should be given preference.

The complex multifactorial nature of language in general, and reading time in particular, involves correlations between the many features. We employ model selection with stepwise regression in the form of step-down methods for ranking the weights of features. The step-down method for feature ranking, leave-one-out, (function drop1), is part of the R base package. Rodríguez (2020) describes stepwise regression as follows:

> The basic idea of the procedure is to start from a given model . . . and take a series of steps, by either deleting a term already in the model, or adding a term from a list of candidates for inclusion.

Stepwise regression leads to more reliable results than using the model with all significant features because interactions between the features are taken into account. An assessment of feature weights based on full models also has the problem that the standard regression function aov() in R uses the F-measure in such a way that it depends on the order of the tested features in the entered formula. A further standard function for linear regression models (function lm in R) report each factor level separately, which makes it difficult to assess the overall importance of a feature.

4 Quantitative Results

In this section, we present our quantitative results. In the next section, we then take a qualitative perspective.

First (section 4.1), we focus on individual differences. The differences are so big that we suggest to pool participants. In particular, we will use mean reading times. Schneider (in press) discusses the motivation for using means or also modes in more detail. For our current purpose, we intend to model typical L1 and L2 readers, abstracting away from individual differences. Then (section 4.2), we predict reading times with linear regression models.

4.1 Differences between Individuals and L1 vs L2

The individual differences between the participants are very pronounced. The first four readers in the Frank corpus (all L1) have a mean reading time of between 150 ms and 274 ms per word. In GECO, the differences are similar: the fastest L1 reader has a mean of 124 ms, the slowest 253 ms. The L1 mean in GECO is 199 ms, and the standard deviation is 43 ms. L2 readers are generally slower – their mean is 266 ms, at 34 ms standard deviation. The densities of reading speed are plotted in Fig. 2, with the means as dashed lines.

Schneider (in press) reports a Pearson correlation of 0.25 for RT and surprisal for the Reading Times for Model Evaluation corpus (Frank et al. 2013). We found considerably lower correlation in GECO: for L1, the correlation has a mean of 0.159, and for L2, the mean is 0.128. The difference between the Frank corpus and GECO partly stems from the fact that L2 readers have lower correlations, and partly from the fact that GECO is a coherent discourse so that other factors play an important role. It can also be observed that fast readers generally exhibit a stronger correlation, which may indicate that they manage better to concentrate on the important subtasks, such as predicting likely continuations. The same explanation can also be adduced for language learners, which have had much less exposure to language material (Pawley/Syder 1983). The density curve for the correlations of individuals to surprisal, split by L1 and L2, is given in Fig. 3, with the means of all readers added as a dashed line.

The correlation between RT and the correlation (between RT and surprisal) is −0.449 for L1, and −0.401 for L2 readers. The fact that there is such a meta-correlation means that fast readers correlate more strongly to surprisal. Efficient readers match the surprisal model considerably better, they probably manage to profit better from the context.

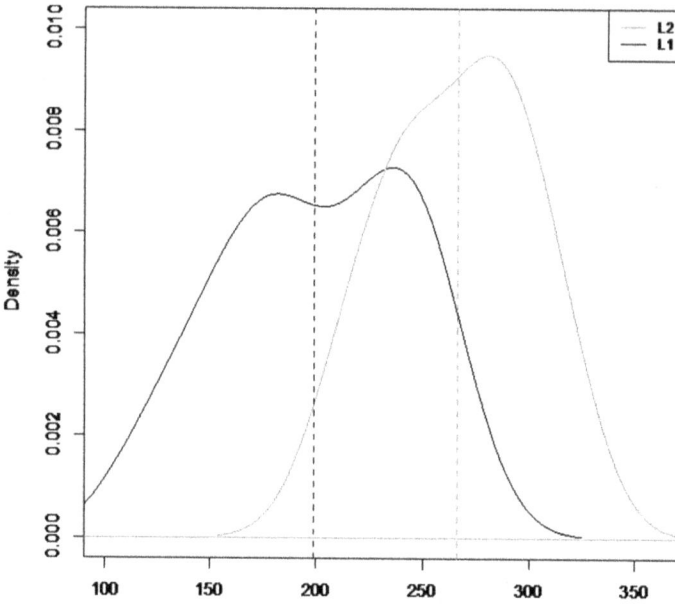

Fig. 2: Density curves of per-word reading time means per participants, split by L1 and L2.

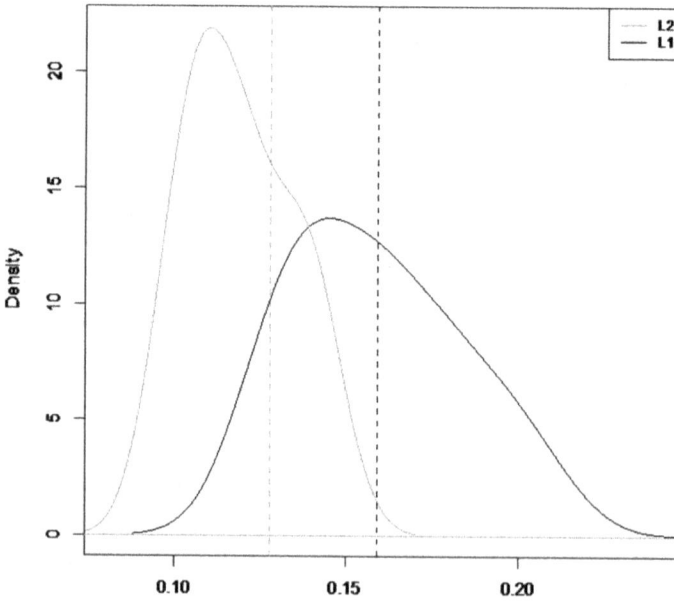

Fig. 3: Correlations between reading time and surprisal, by L1 and L2 individuals.

The very strong individual variation means that individual reading times are also not very strongly correlated: the reading time of a different reader is as good a predictor as surprisal – the mean of the RT correlations between the L1 readers in GECO is 0.150. As individual variation is so strong, we use the mean of the reading times of L1 and L2 as a smoother variable, henceforth RT means. The correlation of the RT means to surprisal is considerably higher: 0.35 for L1, and 0.25 for L2. RT means plotted against reading times, with trend lines for L1 and L2, are given in Fig. 4. The fact that the trend line is less steep for L2 also shows that L2 readers have lower correlation to surprisal, suggesting that they manage less to profit from the context.

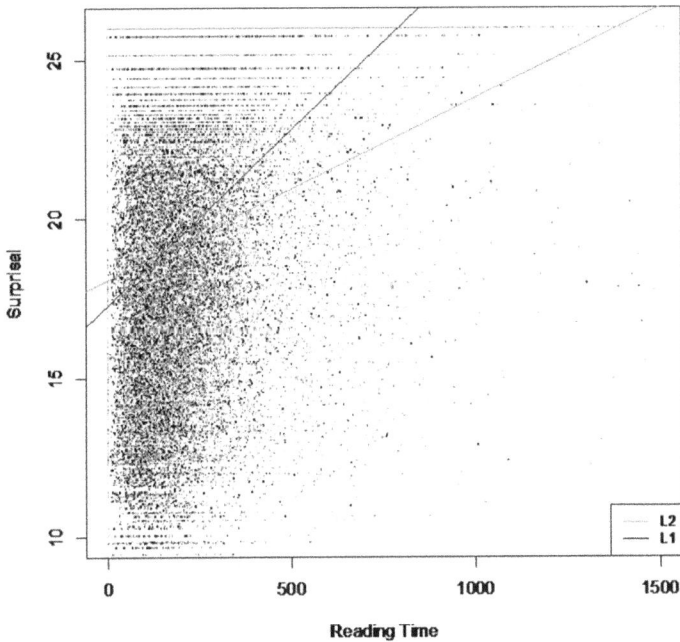

Fig. 4: Plot of surprisal against reading time, with trend lines for L1 and L2.

4.2 Predicting Reading Times with Regression Models

In order to assess the weights of the various factors, we use linear regression models to predict the reading times of L1 and L2 readers.

4.2.1 Individual Variation

In a first pilot model (trained on the Frank corpus), the individual readers (four L1 readers) are kept as a factor in order to assess the weight of the factor individuality. The factor weights are given in Fig. 5.

	Df	Sum Sq	Mean Sq	F value	Pr(>F)	
SURPRISAL	1	13818343	13818343	602.734	< 2e-16	***
LENGTH	1	15508232	15508232	676.445	< 2e-16	***
tags	38	4479610	117884	5.142	< 2e-16	***
subj_nr.f	3	9748779	3249593	141.742	< 2e-16	***
word_pos	1	48112	48112	2.099	0.14748	
sent_nr	1	1284480	1284480	56.027	7.94e-14	***
prob	1	180147	180147	7.858	0.00507	**
SURPRISAL:LENGTH	1	30	30	0.001	0.97126	
Residuals	7676	175980675	22926			

Fig. 5: R output for L1 factor weights in Frank's corpus.

As can be seen in the Fig. when considering the F-score values in the second last column, word length (LENGTH) is the most important factor, surprisal (SURPRISAL) emerges as almost equally important, followed by the individual reader (subj_nr.f) and POS tag (tags). Further significant factors are the tagger confidence (prob), and the sentence number. We did not include these factors in our current study, though. The position of the word in the sentence (word_pos) is not a significant factor. The fact that tagger confidence is significant is an interesting psycholinguistic observation, which we will not pursue further as it is not an argument of the current paper, but words that are ambiguous for the tagger have longer RT, i.e., they need more processing effort.

The strong individual variation observed thus far could prompt one to use a mixed model approach in which the subject is a random effect. We used a mixed model with the lme4 package of R, which reported only a very small systematic effect by the reader: standard deviation of the random effect of the individual was 42.2, more than 7 times smaller than the residual (311.7). We thus decided to predict the much smoother RT means rather than individual reading times.

4.2.2 Prediction of L1 RT

We now present a model predicting L1 RT means, and then a different one for L2 RT means in Section 4.3.3 below. Both models are trained on GECO. The L1 model is given in Fig. 6.

```
> fitL1 = lm(ppMean1 ~ LENGTH + SURPRISAL + log(distance) +
PUNCTUATION, data=eyegecomBOTH)
> summary(fitL1)

Call:
lm(formula = ppMean1 ~ LENGTH + SURPRISAL + log(distance) +
PUNCTUATION,
    data = eyegecomBOTH)

Residuals:
    Min      1Q  Median      3Q     Max
-245.40  -54.82  -12.90   37.82 1335.31

Coefficients:
                Estimate Std. Error t value Pr(>|t|)
(Intercept)       5.2164     3.5401   1.474    0.141
LENGTH           27.5095     0.4238  64.907  < 2e-16 ***
SURPRISAL         1.4293     0.1915   7.465 8.95e-14 ***
log(distance)     4.0678     0.4128   9.854  < 2e-16 ***
PUNCTUATIONyes   40.0453     2.3420  17.099  < 2e-16 ***
---
Signif. codes:  0 '***' 0.001 '**' 0.01 '*' 0.05 '.' 0.1 ' ' 1

Residual standard error: 87.45 on 11513 degrees of freedom
Multiple R-squared:  0.4753,     Adjusted R-squared:  0.4751
F-statistic:  2608 on 4 and 11513 DF,  p-value: < 2.2e-16
```

Fig. 6: R output for factor weights for L1 on GECO.

The quality of the model can be assessed in several ways. Fig. 6 shows that R^2 of the model is 0.475 (and adjusted R^2 is very similar as we have a simple model), which means that the model explains 47.5% of the variation in the data. The predictions of the model are 61.6 ms off on average (second column), which is 34% of the RT mean of 199 ms (last column). The average error is modelled on the calculation of the standard error: the squared difference between observed RT mean (O) and the model prediction (E) is calculated, which indicates the variance, and the square root of this expression delivers the standard deviation. The Z-score mean, i.e., standard deviation of our prediction divided by standard deviation of individual reading times, is 0.54, which means that our predictions are typically off by 54% of the standard deviation. The Z-scores mean is below 1, which indicates that individual variation is much larger, we can conclude that this model makes a reasonably accurate prediction of reading time. The Z-score of the best model is 0.51, which means that our predictions is off by 51% of the individual variation. In other words, our predicted RT is well within the expected individual variation, which means that the predictions of the model can be used fairly reliably for applications that aim to predict RT of a typical reader, the reader that our model predicts would be a totally unobtrusive test person.

The performance of this model is compared to simpler models, using step-wise regression and feature ablation, in Tab. 2. The dominant factor of word length (line 1) already makes linear predictions that are only off by about 35%. The best model (last line) is one percent better. Surprisal on its own is 45% off, word length and surprisal in combination is off by 34.6%. The increase in accuracy generally mirrors the ranking of factor weights.

Tab. 2: Prediction accuracy of linear regression models on L1.

QUALITY OFPREDICTION	√(O-E)^2=typical error in ms	mean(Z-score)= typical error/sd	relative offness=typical error/mean
Length (L)	63.30	0.5244	34.92%
Surprisal (S)	82.14	0.6805	45.32%
L+S	62.69	0.5194	34.59%
L+S+punctuation	62.13	0.5148	34.28%
L+S+punctuation+distance	61.65	0.5108	34.02%

4.2.3 Predictions of L2 RT

We now turn to the prediction of L2 RT. We use the same factors as in the last line of Tab. 2 (i.e., length + surprisal + punctuation + distance) to predict the reading times of the L2 readers in GECO. The L2 model is given in Fig. 7.

We can see that the model fit is much lower. R^2 is only 0.332. The lower model fit also explains why the T values are generally lower. The order of the factor weights is similar, but surprisal is slightly less significant.

The lower model fit also means that L2 readers are less systematic. Also, the accuracy of predicting L2 RT means is lower than the one for L1 RT means. Tab. 3 compares the quality of predictions. The typical error increase from 62 to 91 ms, the Z-score increases from 0.51 to 0.56. This is still below 1, which means that we also predict an unobtrusive L2 reader, but it is harder to predict RT of language learners.

In addition, word recognition seems to be more difficult for L2 readers than for L1 readers, possibly because more words are unknown or unfamiliar to L2 readers. The mechanical and trivial correlation between word length and reading time is 0.667 for L1, but 0.570 for L2 readers. As longer words are typically rarer and harder to learn (Graën/Alfter/Schneider 2020) a lower correlation between word length and RT is not necessarily expected.

```
> fitL2 = lm(ppMean2 ~ LENGTH + SURPRISAL + log(distance) +
PUNCTUATION, data=eyegecomBOTH)
> summary(fitL2)

Call:
lm(formula = ppMean2 ~ LENGTH + SURPRISAL + log(distance) +
PUNCTUATION,
    data = eyegecomBOTH)

Residuals:
    Min      1Q  Median      3Q     Max
-373.46  -80.55  -20.75   54.13 2029.28

Coefficients:
              Estimate Std. Error t value Pr(>|t|)
(Intercept)    46.1320     5.3545   8.616  < 2e-16 ***
LENGTH         33.1838     0.6411  51.764  < 2e-16 ***
SURPRISAL       0.9737     0.2896   3.362 0.000776 ***
log(distance)   4.1487     0.6244   6.645 3.18e-11 ***
PUNCTUATIONyes 23.1290     3.5424   6.529 6.89e-11 ***
---
Signif. codes:  0 '***' 0.001 '**' 0.01 '*' 0.05 '.' 0.1 ' ' 1

Residual standard error: 132.3 on 11513 degrees of freedom
Multiple R-squared:  0.3324,     Adjusted R-squared:  0.3322
F-statistic:  1433 on 4 and 11513 DF,  p-value: < 2.2e-16
```

Fig. 7: Factor weights for L2 on GECO.

Tab. 3: Prediction accuracy of linear regression models on L2 compared to L1.

QUALITY OF PREDICTION	$\sqrt{(O-E)^2}$=typical error in ms	mean(Z-score)= typical error/sd	relative offness=typical error/mean
L1 : L+S+punctuation+distance	62.13	0.5148	34.02%
L2 : L+S+punctuation+distance	91.21	0.5635	38.84%

4.2.4 Model Analysis and Feature Order

In order to interpret the L1 and L2 models psycholinguistically, we assessed their feature weights. A model with so many features, particularly when dealing with a highly redundant system like Natural Language (MacWhinney/Bates 1989; Shannon 1951) leads to a range of strong interactions. While the feature significance p(|t|), and the t-value delivered by lm() in R, and also the F-measure from aov() provide useful hints for model selection and interpretation, they partly depend on the order in which the features appear in the equation. The leave-one-out method drop1 is a step-wise regression approach and gives a more reliable impression of relative feature weights. The R output for this is given in Fig. 8. The model for L1 is given at the top of the Fig., the one for L2 at the bottom.

```
> drop1(fitL1, test = "F")
Single term deletions

Model:
ppMean1 ~ LENGTH + SURPRISAL + log(distance) + PUNCTUATION
              Df Sum of Sq        RSS    AIC  F value     Pr(>F)
<none>                      88041895 103000
LENGTH         1 32217059 120258954 106590 4212.938 < 2.2e-16 ***
SURPRISAL      1   426115  88468011 103054   55.722 8.95e-14 ***
log(distance)  1   742605  88784500 103095   97.108 < 2.2e-16 ***
PUNCTUATION    1  2235771  90277666 103287  292.366 < 2.2e-16 ***
---
Signif. codes:  0 '***' 0.001 '**' 0.01 '*' 0.05 '.' 0.1 ' ' 1

> drop1(fitL2, test = "F")
Single term deletions

Model:
ppMean2 ~ LENGTH + SURPRISAL + log(distance) + PUNCTUATION
              Df Sum of Sq         RSS    AIC  F value     Pr(>F)
<none>                      201419529 112532
LENGTH         1 46878434 248297964 114940 2679.539 < 2.2e-16 ***
SURPRISAL      1   197751 201617281 112541   11.303 0.0007762 ***
log(distance)  1   772440 202191969 112574   44.152 3.175e-11 ***
PUNCTUATION    1   745828 202165357 112573   42.631 6.888e-11 ***
---
Signif. codes:  0 '***' 0.001 '**' 0.01 '*' 0.05 '.' 0.1 ' ' 1
```

Fig. 8: Step-wise regression with leave-one-out on L1 and L2 model.

The order of features suggested by our regression experiments (Fig. 7) is confirmed by looking at the *F*-measures:

> Word length > punctuation ≥ distance to previous occurrence of same word > surprisal

In the comparison between L1 and L2 it can be observed that all F values of L2 are lower, as the model fit is much lower. L2 readers show much more variability and their reading times are harder to predict. In the comparison of the *F*-values we can observe that surprisal is indeed less important for L2 readers, again confirming the lack of routinization and expectation of the continuation of the text. L2 readers also seem to make less efficient use of punctuation symbols, which give clues to the syntactic structure. The discourse feature of the distance to the last previous occurrence of the same word, and the trivial feature of word length are also less important for L2 readers, but they keep more of their predictive power in comparison to other features.

4.2.5 Prediction of L2 RT by L1 RT

Finally, we consider a model in which we add L1 routinization experience and vocabulary knowledge to predict L2 reading time. We do so by adding L1 RT means as an independent variable. This model assesses how useful it is to know L1 RT to predict L2 RT, in comparison to other factors. If L1 and L2 readers had nearly identical reading behaviour, we would expect that L1 RT overshadows all other factors. The feature weights of the corresponding linear model are given in Fig. 9.

```
> fitb2 = lm(ppMean2 ~ LENGTH + log(distance) + ppMean1 + SURPRISAL
+ PUNCTUATION, data=eyegecomBOTH)

> drop1(fitb2, test="F")
Single term deletions

Model:
ppMean2 ~ LENGTH + log(distance) + ppMean1 + SURPRISAL + PUNCTUATION
               Df Sum of Sq       RSS    AIC   F value    Pr(>F)
<none>                      177940797 111107
LENGTH          1 11224825 189165622 111809  726.1976 < 2.2e-16 ***
log(distance)   1   186672 178127469 111117   12.0769 0.0005124 ***
ppMean1         1 23478732 201419529 112532 1518.9724 < 2.2e-16 ***
SURPRISAL       1    11521 177952318 111105    0.7453 0.3879729
PUNCTUATION     1     8157 177948954 111105    0.5277 0.4675837
---
Signif. codes:  0 '***' 0.001 '**' 0.01 '*' 0.05 '.' 0.1 ' ' 1
```

Fig. 9: Feature weights of a model predicting L2 reading times with L1 reading time as predicting variable.

RT means of the L1 readers (ppMean1) is the strongest predictor as its F-value is highest, but word length has almost equally strong weight. We can conclude that L2 readers read texts differently, but L1 reading times are still marginally the best predictor.

5 Qualitative Results

After we have seen that there are strong differences not only in the reading speed but also in the way L1 and L2 readers read a text, we will investigate which linguistic phenomena are treated differently by L1 and L2 readers, with the aim of finding out what L2 readers find particularly difficult. For this investigation, we have visualised the differences between the reading times using a heat map in MS Excel, and zoom in on areas of particularly strong differences. Strong differences are automatically marked by yellow to dark red highlighting. Words and zones with large differences between L1 and L2 readers stand out in strong colours.

In order to relate L2 RT means to L1 RT means we employ the overuse measure O/E or *Observed divided by Expected*. The expected value is the mean of L1 and L2. O/E(L2) is then:

$$O/E(L2) = \frac{O(L2)*2}{O(L1) + O(L2)}$$

In order to group the O/E value around 0 we display O/E-1 in the second column of the following visualisations. A value of 0 expresses equal reading time for L1 and L12, +1 means that L2 readers take longer than L1 (which happens if all L1 readers have no fixation and thus RT of 0 on a word), a negative number means that L2 readers are faster than L1. As we wanted to spot zones of reading difficulty for L2 readers in addition to individual words, we also calculate the mean over 5 words. This value is given in column 3 and can serve as an indication of relative reading difficulty. In the last column we list the total RT of the last 5 words, i.e., the absolute reading difficulty. All values represent the means across the readers of the L1 and L2 class, respectively. As L1 readers use about 200 ms per word (see Fig. 2 in Section 4.1 above), values above 1000 ms for 5 words are also indicative of an area where L2 readers experience a slow-down.

By reading the entire heat-map-enriched corpus vertically, we were able to identify several linguistic phenomena that L2 readers spent a lot of time on. These are:

- Fronting, i.e., non-canonical word order
- Zero-relative pronouns
- Rare vocabulary items
- Nominalisations
- Long attachments
- Rare constructions
- Unusual word meanings
- Complex preposition and phrasal verb constructions
- Idioms
- Irregular and strong verbs

In the following, we present screenshots of the heat-maps and identify the zones in which the L2 readers slowed down. Examples of non-canonical word order due to fronting are given in Figs. 10 and 11. The fronted object *what* in the sentence *That's just what I want* in Fig. 10, and the auxiliary-subject inversion triggered by *never* in *Never have I seen such a ghastly look on any man's face* in Fig. 11 cause a considerable slowdown in L2 readers compared to L1 readers.

CHECK	O/E - 1	across 5 OI	across 5 RT
that	0.406	-0.270	1125.308
s	0.406	0.123	948.538
just	0.042	0.310	996.615
what	0.809	1.661	2997.692
I	0.509	2.171	2868.385
want	0.778	2.544	4610.846

Fig. 10: Heat-map for "That's just what I want".

CHECK	O/E - 1	across 5 OI	across 5 RT
Never	0.275	0.629	742.231
have	0.205	0.956	824.000
I	0.651	1.036	702.846
seen	0.215	1.688	905.923
such	0.711	2.057	1093.846
a	0.046	1.828	998.231
ghastly	0.140	1.764	1096.692
look	0.351	1.463	1241.154
on	-0.149	1.100	1147.385
any	0.192	0.580	888.538
man	0.527	1.061	943.154
s	0.527	1.447	817.923
face	0.108	1.204	839.923

Fig. 11: Heat-map for "Never have I seen such a ghastly look on any man's face".

The relative pronoun *what* in Fig. 10 already slows down L2 readers, but zero-relative pronouns are processed with even more difficulties.

CHECK	O/E - 1	across 5 OI	across 5 RT
It	-0.224	0.036	1113.077
was	0.700	0.860	1125.923
one	0.383	1.342	1316.923
of	-0.040	0.791	926.846
the	0.359	1.177	852.538
longest	0.067	1.469	953.846
and	1.000	1.770	889.846
blackest	0.144	1.530	985.923
I	0.637	2.207	967.231
have	0.469	2.317	1231.538
ever	-0.256	1.993	1140.000
seen	0.520	1.513	1251.923

Fig. 12: Heat-map for "It was one of the longest and blackest I have ever seen".

Fig. 12 shows the effect of such a zero-relative clause. The absence of the relative pronoun (*that I have ever seen*) seems to trigger a considerably longer processing time in non-native readers. The fact that personal pronouns in the nominative case are often a good indicator for being subjects of a subordinate relative clause may be better known to native readers than to language learners, who have less routine.

Rare vocabulary items are a difficulty that L2 readers often face – the probability that it is unknown or in the case of *pince-nez* in Fig. 13 may be retrieved via the other foreign language French creates a delay. Observe that this delay is much more local (across 5 OE drops to and even below 1 three words later) than the one seen in Fig. 12, where a large region of surrounding words is affected (across 5 OE stays above 1.5 until the end of the sentence).

CHECK	O/E - 1	across 5 OI	across 5 RT
He	0.392	1.761	935.154
wore	0.352	1.476	1300.308
gold-rimmed	0.283	1.291	1626.923
pince-nez	0.282	1.829	2523.308
and	0.057	1.367	2459.385
had	0.321	1.296	2617.615
a	-0.087	0.857	2237.385
curious	0.058	0.631	1986.846
impassivity	0.266	0.615	1512.385
of	-0.582	-0.024	1335.462
feature	-0.059	-0.404	1506.846

Fig. 13: Heat-map for "He wore gold-rimmed pince-nez and had a curious impassivity of feature".

Nominalisations, particularly if they occur in a very formal register, can challenge L2 readers. The old-fashioned formulation *in the main* can be seen in Fig. 14. The frequency of *in the main* reduces in the corpus of historical American English (COHA, Davies 2010) from 0.1 per 10000 words around the year 1900 to only 0.04 around the year 2000. L1 readers have typically had more exposition to rarer registers, literary genres, and retreating constructions.

CHECK	O/E - 1	across 5 OI	across 5 RT
Mrs	0.208	0.883	1468.538
Inglethorp	0.306	1.031	1439.615
kind	-0.190	0.528	1333.154
as	0.479	1.059	1380.385
she	0.488	1.291	1543.923
might	0.084	1.167	1456.308
be	0.772	1.633	1145.077
in	0.585	2.409	1155.077
the	0.493	2.422	1392.000
main	0.162	2.096	1179.000

Fig. 14: Heat-map for "Mrs Inglethorp, kind as she might be in the main".

Fig. 15 shows a heavy nominalisation, *neatness*, in combination with the rare and old-fashioned word *attire*. The zone ending at *attire* takes L2 readers more than twice as long to read.

CHECK	O/E - 1	across 5 O	across 5 RT
The	0.470	1.489	1095.154
neatness	0.331	1.588	1296.769
of	0.473	1.831	1161.077
his	0.440	1.962	1346.769
attire	0.384	2.098	1433.846
was	0.061	1.689	1304.385
almost	0.020	1.378	1112.769
incredible	0.074	0.979	1299.385

Fig. 15: Heat-map for "The neatness of his attire was almost incredible".

Long attachments, i.e., phrases that are quite far away from their governor, are also more difficult for L2 readers. Fig. 16 gives the example of the subordinate clause *to come* which only starts after two inserted prepositional phrases (*to him* and *over her shoulder*). The structure in Fig. 17 also contains a fronted element (*what*). Fronting has the effect that the distance between the object *what* and its governing verb *been* are quite long. Further, it is a complex phrasal verb, Phrasal verbs are a feature of spoken language, a register with which L2 readers may be less familiar than L1 readers. As a result, processing speed decreases considerably.

CHECK	O/E - 1	across 5 O	across 5 RT
Cynthia	0.112	0.695	1355.769
called	0.021	0.303	1051.154
to	-0.054	0.480	1029.385
him	0.128	0.326	827.077
over	0.503	0.709	1273.000
her	0.249	0.846	1242.077
shoulder	0.420	1.246	1388.538
to	0.605	1.905	1612.077
come	0.628	2.406	1810.000
and	0.128	2.031	1334.154
join	0.267	2.049	1249.000
us	0.004	1.633	980.615

Fig. 16: Heat-map for "Cynthia called to him over her shoulder to come and join us".

CHECK	O/E - 1	across 5 OI	across 5 RT
Have	-0.128	-1.650	359.538
some	0.547	-0.738	681.692
coffee	0.098	-0.878	806.846
and	0.270	0.391	965.077
tell	0.190	0.976	1203.000
us	0.799	1.904	1159.769
what	0.319	1.675	1077.000
you	0.634	2.212	1048.231
have	-0.109	1.833	986.308
been	0.252	1.895	941.923
up	0.910	2.006	978.308
to	0.108	1.795	896.923

Fig. 17: Heat-map for "Have some coffee and tell us what you have been up to".

Infrequent constructions are generally difficult. This is illustrated in Fig. 18, which gives the example of a participial, *having been occupied*.

CHECK	O/E - 1	across 5 OI	across 5 RT
and	0.678	1.043	1094.923
that	0.309	1.000	1027.923
there	0.547	1.497	1215.538
was	0.201	1.623	1031.154
no	0.321	2.057	1103.385
sign	0.272	1.651	1090.385
of	0.345	1.687	1069.769
the	0.820	1.960	1153.000
room	0.252	2.011	1398.769
having	0.321	2.011	1573.692
been	-0.079	1.660	1445.692
occupied	0.107	1.421	1501.615

Fig. 18: Heat-map for " . . . and that there was no sign of the room having been occupied".

Unusual and archaic word meanings are also difficult. The word *gay* with the meaning *joyful* seems to be less familiar to L2 readers, as shown in Fig. 19.

CHECK	O/E - 1	across 5 OI	across 5 RT
But	0.504	0.781	961.846
they	0.569	1.226	1299.231
were	0.202	1.437	1366.923
both	0.752	2.267	2415.769
gay	0.257	2.284	2414.846
enough	0.253	2.033	2861.615
this	0.120	1.584	2735.923
afternoon	0.288	1.670	3158.154

Fig. 19: Heat-map for "But they were both gay enough this afternoon".

Complex preposition and phrasal verb constructions, as we have already seen in Fig. 16, can lead to slower processing by L2 readers. In Fig. 20, we can see a sequence of four PPs that all attach to the main verb *went*.

CHECK	O/E - 1	across 5 OI	across 5 RT
and	0.334	0.249	982.538
went	0.330	0.587	1095.769
rapidly	0.588	1.114	1612.692
past	0.192	1.149	1605.846
me	0.259	1.703	1661.615
down	0.350	1.720	1875.308
the	0.780	2.169	1791.385
stairs	0.214	1.795	1434.846
across	0.318	1.921	1500.077
the	0.192	1.855	1290.769
hall	0.393	1.897	1187.077
to	0.151	1.269	1006.385
the	0.218	1.273	858.769
boudoir	-0.189	0.765	761.692

Fig. 20: Heat-map for ". . . and went rapidly past me down the stairs across the hall to the boudoir".

Next, as Siyanova–Chanturia/Conklin/Schmitt (2011) have shown, idioms are often more difficult to process for L2 readers than for L1 readers, as Fig. 21 illustrates on the basis of *wit's end for money*. The meaning of this idiom is to be puzzled, and not knowing what to do.

CHECK	O/E - 1	across 5 OI	across 5 RT
I	1.000	0.443	620.462
don	0.183	0.633	474.038
t	0.183	1.063	486.615
mind	0.579	1.731	737.000
telling	0.180	2.126	766.769
you	-0.037	1.089	834.385
that	0.422	1.328	927.962
I	0.351	1.496	908.923
m	0.351	1.267	710.462
at	0.406	1.493	756.923
my	0.165	1.695	768.923
wit	0.519	1.791	818.962
s	0.519	1.959	981.615
end	0.547	2.155	1319.769
for	0.506	2.256	1360.615
money	0.101	2.192	1467.462

Fig. 21: Heat-map for "I don't mind telling you that I'm at my wit's end for money".

Finally, we turn to an example from morphology. The irregular verb *fling* causes a local slowdown for many L2 readers, see Fig. 22.

CHECK	O/E - 1	across 5 Ol	across 5 RT
John	0.155	1.111	1560.538
flung	0.428	1.351	1769.692
the	0.335	1.576	1741.000
match	-0.058	0.912	1436.769
into	-0.027	0.833	1277.923
an	0.046	0.725	1175.923
adjacent	0.093	0.390	1119.154
flower	-0.151	-0.096	957.000
bed	-0.311	-0.349	881.000

Fig. 22: Heat-map for "John flung the match into an adjacent flower bed".

6 Discussion and Conclusion

We have used language models such as surprisal and regression as a cognitive model in order to predict RT of native speakers (L1) and language learners (L2) with a linear regression method using eye tracking data, especially the GECO corpus. Our goal is both application-driven, aiming to accurately predict reading behaviour of L1 and L2 readers, and also cognitive, aiming to assess the most important factors, and the differences between L1 and L2 readers. Let us revisit our research questions from the introduction again.

In addition, we have seen that individual variation between the readers is very strong. Fast readers exhibit a better model fit, potentially because they can concentrate better on the task. L1 readers are faster than L2 readers, and L1 readers exhibit a better model fit, they are more efficient readers both in terms of speed and model fit. RT predictions are off by 34–40% in our linear regression. Our prediction errors are considerably below individual variation, which means that our models predict a plausible reader.

We have also seen some evidence on which constructions are harder for L2 in the qualitative results section. Let us revisit our research questions from the Introduction.

1) Which features correlate to reading times?
We have seen that all four features that we selected (word length, presence of punctuation, distance to previous occurrence of same word, surprisal) are highly correlated to RT and are significant predictors in a regression model. There are strong correlations between reading times and surprisal, but there are also other

factors. In particular, for predicting reading times, we have seen the following order of features:

Word length > punctuation ≥ distance to previous occurrence of same word
> surprisal.

Word length is a trivial predictor, longer words simply take longer to read. Presence of punctuation, mostly commas and full stops, lead to significantly slower RT, because the meaning of the clause is processed by the reader. The discourse-related feature of the distance to the previous last occurrence of the same word shows how much knowledge of the semantic background of the individual discourse, here a novel, helps readers to integrate new information, and how much introduced entities are salient on the readers' mind, expecting their re-appearance (Church 2000). To be able to assess the impact of discourse was a motivation for collecting the GECO corpus, with the aim "to evaluate the generalizability of . . . language theories and models to the reading of long texts and narratives" (Cop et al. 2017: 602). We could profit from this potential in our study.

Surprisal, although a highly significant feature, turns out be less important than the discourse feature of last occurrence of the same word. While the strong influence of surprisal is well known (Demberg/Keller 2008; Smith/Levy 2013) we could place it more precisely in the hierarchy of significant factors. The ranking that we obtained by linear regression was also confirmed by stepwise regression (section 4.2.4) and by feature ablation experiments (section 4.2.2).

2) Are the features and their weights similar for L1 and L2 readers?
The order of feature weights is similar, but there are two notable differences: first, surprisal is less significant for L2 readers than for L1 readers. This result is in line with Underwood/Schmitt/Galpin (2004), Siyanova–Chanturia/Conklin/Schmitt (2011), and Schilk (2017), in which L2 readers found idioms and formulaic word sequences more difficult to process, even if considering retrieval time for individual words. In other words, the lower level of routinization of L2 readers is apparent, as already anticipated by Pawley/Syder (1983). Second, the presence of punctuation symbols (mostly these are commas and full stops) is a less important feature for L2 readers than for L1 readers. In terms of F-value, punctuation is three times stronger than the distance to the previous occurrence of the same word, while for L2 readers, these two features are similarly important. It seems that native speakers manage better to read clauses as a single unit. This observation also supports the view that idiomatic units are processed faster and as single units by L1 readers, and that they exhibit a less linear reading behaviour, pausing at semantic boundaries rather than at difficult words or constructions, as we have qualitatively assessed in section 5.

3) Is the individual variation between the readers bigger or smaller than the difference between L1 and L2?

The difference between L1 and L2 RT has a mean of 67 ms. As the standard deviation of RTs is 43 ms for L1 and 34 ms for L2, the between-group differences are only slightly bigger. In other words, individual variation is very strong in L1 and in L2. The very strong individual variation means that individual reading times are not very strongly correlated: the reading time of a different reader is as good a predictor as surprisal. At the same time, individual variation is too unsystematic to serve as a useful random effect in a mixed model. This is why we decided to pool the readers as and predict RT means across the individuals.

Pooling participants is less common than using a mixed-effects model, in which the individual is a random effect. Experiments with mixed models on GECO (Schneider accepted) revealed, however, that individual variation is not systematic. The standard deviation of the random effect of the individuals is more than seven times smaller than the residual. We thus use pooling participants as a noise reduction method. While the method of predicting average reading time can be seen as a shortcoming, it also offers a number of attractive characteristics. First, it allows us to keep a simpler, parsimonious model. Second, for the task of predicting typical reading times, irrespective of individual behaviour, for instance as a proxy to reading difficulty, it is an appropriate and simple smoothing technique. Third, it leads to better performance in downstream applications aiming to model typical readers (Hollenstein 2020; Klerke/Plank 2019). Hollenstein (2020) states that for the aim of predicting typical readers, averaging is a good option: "The eye movement measurements were averaged over all native-speaking readers of each dataset to obtain more robust estimates." (41). Fourth, averaging greatly reduces the number of skipped words, for which the data set gives reading times of 0 ms, about 39% of all words are skipped, be that due to parafoveal reading (Rayner 1998) or a low sampling rate of the eye tracker (Andersson/Nyström/Holmqvist 2010). When using readers' means for each word, less than 1% of all words have RT of 0 ms in the GECO corpus. The fact that there are very few words that are skipped by all readers is a further indication that individual variation may be viewed as noise (unsystematic variation) rather than a signal (systematic variation).

4) Can L2 reading times be predicted similarly well as L1 times?

Both model fit and prediction accuracy of L2 readers is much lower than of L1 readers. R^2 for the prediction of L1 RT is 0.475, but only 0.332 for L2. L2 readers show more variability, less systematicity, and are harder to predict. This is also related to the observation that slower readers generally have lower correlation to surprisal, indicating that they are less efficient not only in the task of reading but probably also in knowing word sequences, idioms, and how a sentence is likely to continue.

5) Do increased reading times of L2 readers reveal to us which constructions are particularly taxing for L2 readers?
In the qualitative analysis in Section 5 above, we presented a selection of phenomena that stood out in the heat-map visualisation, and gave our interpretation. Salient phenomena that take L2 readers longer to process include fronting (non-canonical word order), zero constituents, rare words and constructions, nominalisations, long attachments, unusual word meanings, complex preposition and phrasal verbs, idioms, and irregular morphology. WE could detect these differences between L1 and L2 readers in a data-driven fashion, without selecting candidate phenomena beforehand.

Our study has several limitations. First, the list of features that we have selected, following Demberg/Keller (2008), Smith/Levy (2013), and Schneider (in press) is unlikely to be complete. We spent considerable time on testing further features, but some strong predictors may have escaped us, and we have also excluded two significant features, POS tag and tagger confidence, which we would like to include in future studies. Second, the fact that the L2 data contains native speakers of Dutch and no other language may add a bias. Particularly as Dutch is typologically related to English, our observations cannot be generalized to very different L1 languages. It would be interesting to include Readers with native languages from non-Indo-European backgrounds, for instance Finnish or Basque. Also, languages with considerably freer word order and stronger inflectional systems (e.g., Russian or German) or head-final languages like Japanese would be a desideratum.

We envisage many applications of our research, ranging from cognition to stylistics, automatic style checking and essay grading, understanding learner language, and language simplification.

Future research should include the significant feature of POS tag (section 4.2.1), more syntactic features, and further language models like BERT or neural networks. In cognitive linguistics, we would like to further distinguish pragmatic effects of world knowledge, for instance by including word embedding, discourse knowledge (our feature of the last occurrence of the same word, but also adding anaphora resolution), language sequence and idioms (surprisal) and syntactic features. For a language learning application, one can focus on phenomena and words that L2 readers find particularly hard, both generally, or from specific L1 backgrounds. Also on the individual level, eye tracking or self-paced reading reveals weaknesses and important study areas to which a given student should give particular focus.

References

Andersson, Richard/Nyström, Marcus/Holmqvist, Kenneth (2010): "Sampling frequency and eye–tracking measures: How speed affects durations, latencies, and more." In: *Journal of Eye Movement Research* 3, 1–12.

Altenberg, Bengt (1998): "On the phraseology of spoken English: The evidence of recurrent word combinations." In: A. P. Cowie (Ed.): *Phraseology. Theory, Analysis, and Applications*. Oxford: Oxford University Press.

Aston, Guy/Burnard, Lou (1998): *The BNC Handbook. Exploring the British National Corpus with SARA*. Edinburgh: Edinburgh University Press.

Biber, Douglas/Conrad, Susan (2009): *Register, Genre, and Style*. Cambridge: Cambridge University Press.

Bresnan, Joan/Cueni, Anna/Nikitina, Tatiana/Baayen, Harald (2007): "Predicting the dative alternation." In: Gerlof Bouma/Joost Zwarts/Irene Krämer (Eds.): *Cognitive Foundations of Interpretation*. Amsterdam: Royal Netherlands Academy of Science, 69–94.

Bresnan, Joan/Nikitina, Tatiana (2009): "The gradience of the dative alternation." In: Linda Uyechi/Lian Hee Wee (Eds.): *Reality Exploration and Discovery. Pattern Interaction in Language and Life*. Stanford: CSLI Publications, 161–184.

Bybee, Joan (2007): *Frequency of Use and the Organization of Language*. Oxford: Oxford University Press.

Conklin, Kathy/Schmitt, Norbert (2012): "The processing of formulaic language." In: *Annual Review of Applied Linguistics* 32, 45–61.

Conklin, Kathy/Pellicer-Sánchez, Ana/Carrol, Gareth (2018): *Eye–Tracking. A Guide for Applied Linguistics Research*. Cambridge: Cambridge University Press.

Church, Kenneth (2000): "Empirical estimates of adaptation: The chance of two noriegas is closer to p/2 than p^2." In: *Proceedings of the 17th conference on Computational linguistics*, 180–186.

Cop, Uschi/Dirix, Nicolas/Drieghe, Denis/Duyck, Wouter (2017): "Presenting GECO: An eye tracking corpus of monolingual and bilingual sentence reading." In: *Behavior Research Methods* 49, 602–615.

Davies, Mark (2010–): *The Corpus of Historical American English (COHA)*. Online at: https://www.english–corpora.org/coha/ <14.04.2022>.

Demberg, Vera/Keller, Frank (2008): "Data from eye–tracking corpora as evidence for theories of syntactic processing complexity." In: *Cognition* 109, 193–210.

Divjak, Dagmar/Levshina, Natalia/Klavan, Jane (2016): "Cognitive linguistics: Looking back, looking forward." In: *Cognitive Linguistics* 27, 447–463.

Ellis, Nick C. (2013): "Construction grammar and second language acquisition." In: Thomas Hoffmann/Graeme Trousdale (Eds.): *The Oxford Handbook of Construction Grammar*. Oxford: Oxford University Press, 365–378.

Ellis, Nick/Frey, Eric/Jalkanen, Isaac (2009): "The psycholinguistic reality of collocation and semantic prosody (1): Lexical access." In: Rainer Schulze/Ute Römer (Eds.): *Exploring the Lexis–Grammar Interface*. Studies in Corpus Linguistics. Amsterdam: John Benjamins, 89–114.

Frank, Stefan L./Monsalve, Irene F./Thompson, Robin L./Vigliocco, Gabriella (2013): "Reading–time data for evaluating broad–coverage models of English sentence processing." In: *Behavior Research Methods* 45, 1182–1190.

Frank, Stefan L. (in press): "Towards computational models of multilingual sentence processing." *Language Learning* (special issue *What is special about multilingualism?*).

Glynn, Dylan/Fischer, Kerstin (2010): *Quantitative Methods in Cognitive Semantics. Corpus–Driven Approaches*. Berlin/New York: Mouton de Gruyter.

Grön, Gerbrand J. (1996): "Cognitive slowing in patients with acquired brain damage: An experimental approach." In: *Journal of Clinical Experimental Neuropsychology* 18, 406–415.

Goldberg, Adele E. (2006): *Constructions at Work. The Nature of Generalization in Language*. Oxford: Oxford University Press.

Graën, Johannes/Alfter, David/Schneider, Gerold (2020): "Using multilingual resources to evaluate CEFRLex for learner applications." *Proceedings of the 12th Language Resources and Evaluation Conference*, 346–355. Online at: https://www.aclweb.org/anthology/2020.lrec-1.43.pdf <14.11.2022>.

Gries, Stefan (2015): "The most under–used statistical method in corpus linguistics: Multi–level (and mixed–effects) models." In: *Corpora* 10, 95–125.

Gries, Stefan Th./Wulff, Stefanie (2005): "Do foreign language learners also have constructions? Evidence from priming, sorting, and corpora." In: *Annual Review of Cognitive Linguistics* 3, 182–200.

Hilpert, Martin (2019): "Constructional approaches." In: Bas Aarts/Jill Bowie/Gergana Popova (Eds.): *The Oxford Handbook of English Grammar*. Oxford: Oxford University Press, 106–123.

Hollenstein, Nora (2020): *Leveraging cognitive processing signals for natural language understanding*. Zurich: ETH Zurich dissertation.

Janda, Laura A. (2013): *Cognitive Linguistics. The Quantitative Turn*. Berlin: Mouton de Gruyter.

Kennedy, Alan/Hill, Robin/Pynte, Joël (2003): *The Dundee Corpus*. Paper presented at the 12th European Conference on Eye Movement, Dundee, Scotland.

Kennedy, Alan/Pynte, Joël/Murray, Waine/Paul, Shiley–Anne (2013): "Frequency and predictability effects in the Dundee Corpus: An eye movement analysis." In: *Quarterly Journal of Experimental Psychology* 66, 601–618.

Klerke, Sigrid/Plank, Barbara (2019): "At a glance: The impact of gaze aggregation views on syntactic tagging." In: *Proceedings of the Beyond Vision and LANguage. inTEgrating Real–world kNowledge (LANTERN)*, 51–61.

Larsen-Freeman, Diane (1997): "Chaos/complexity science and second language acquisition." In: *Applied Linguistics* 18, 141–65.

Larsen–Freeman, Diane/Cameron, Lynne (2008): *Complex Systems and Applied Linguistics*. Oxford: Oxford University Press.

Levy, Roger/Jaeger, T. Florian (2007): "Speakers optimize information density through syntactic reduction." In: *Proceedings of the Twentieth Annual Conference on Neural Information Processing Systems*.

Luke, Steven G./Christianson, Kiel (2018): "The Provo Corpus: A large eye–tracking corpus with predictability norms." In: *Behaviour Research Methods* 50, 826–833.

MacWhinney, Brian J. (2001): "Psycholinguistics: Overview." In: Neil J. Smelser/Paul B. Baltes (Eds.): *International Encyclopedia of the Social & Behavioral Sciences*. Pergamon, 12343–12349.

MacWhinney, Brian/Bates, Elisabeth (Eds.) (1989): *The Crosslinguistic Study of Sentence Processing*. New York: Cambridge University Press.

Molnar, Christoph (2020): *Interpretable. Machine learning: A guide for making black box models explainable.* Unpublished manuscript. Online at: https://christophm.github.io/in terpretable-ml-book/ <01.10.2021>.

Nesselhauf, Nadja (2005): *Collocations in a Learner Corpus.* Amsterdam: John Benjamins.

Newman, John/Rice, Sally (2010): *Experimental and Empirical Approaches in the Study of Conceptual Structure, Discourse, and Language.* Stanford: CSLI Publications.

Norman, Rocío S./Shah, Manish N./Turkstra, Lyn, S. (2019): "Reaction time and cognitive-linguistic performance in adults with mild traumatic brain injury." In: *Brain Injury* 33, 1173–1183,

Pawley, Andrew/Syder, Frances Hodgetts (1983): "Two puzzles for linguistic theory: Native-like selection and native-like fluency." In: *Language and Communication* 191–226.

Racine, John P. (2014): "Reaction time methodologies and lexical access in applied linguistics." In: *Vocabulary Learning and Instruction* 3, 66–70.

Rayner, Keith (1998): "Eye movements in reading and information processing: 20 years of research." In: *Psychological Bulletin* 124, 372–422.

Rayner, Keith/Duffy, Susan A. (1986): "Lexical complexity and fixation times in reading: Effects of word frequency, verb complexity, and lexical ambiguity." In: *Memory and Cognition* 14, 191-201.

Rayner, Keith/Raney, Gary E./Pollatsek, Alexander (1995): "Eye movements and discourse processing." In: Robert F. Lorch Jr./Edward. J. O'Brien/Robert F. Lorch (Eds.): *Sources of Coherence in Reading*. Hillsdale, NJ: Lawrence Erlbaum Associates, 9–36.

Rodríguez, Germán (2020): *Introducing R.* Unpublished manuscript, Princeton University. Online at: https://data.princeton.edu/R <01.10.2021>.

Sahlgren, Magnus (2006): *The Word-Space Model: Using distributional Analysis to represent syntagmatic and paradigmatic relations between words in high-dimensional vector spaces.* Stockholm: Stockholm University dissertation.

Saville-Troike, Muriel/Barto, Karen (2016): *Introducing Second Language Acquisition.* 3rd edn. Cambridge: Cambridge University Press.

Segalowitz, Norman S./Segalowitz, Sidney J. (1993): "Skilled performance, practice, and the differentiation of speed-up from automatization effects: Evidence from second language word recognition." In: *Applied Psycholinguistics* 14, 369–385.

Schilk, Marco (2017): *Language processing in advanced learners of English: A multi-method approach to collocation based on corpus linguistic and experimental data.* Hildesheim: Universität Hildesheim Habilitation Thesis.

Schneider, Gerold (in press): "Correlations between reading times, collocation and surprisal." In: Manfred Krug/Ole Schützler/Fabian Vetter/Valentin Werner (Eds.): *Perspectives on Contemporary English*. Peter Lang: Series Bamberg Studies in English Linguistics.

Schneider, Gerold/Gaëtanelle, Gilquin (2016): "Detecting innovations in a parsed corpus of learner English." In: *International Journal of Learner Corpus Research* 2, 177–204.

Schneider, Gerold/Grigonyte, Gintare (2018): "From lexical bundles to surprisal and language models: Measuring the idiom principle on native and learner language." In: *Patterns in text: Corpus-driven methods and applications*. Studies in Corpus Linguistics Series. John Benjamins.

Schneider, Gerold/Lauber, Max (2019): *Statistics for Linguists.* Zürich: Pressbooks.

Shain, Cory (2019): "A large-scale study of the effects of word frequency and predictability in naturalistic reading." In: *Proceedings of the 2019 Conference of the North American*

Chapter of the Association for Computational Linguistics: Human Language Technologies. Vol 1. 4086–4094.

Shannon, Claude E. (1951): "Prediction and entropy of printed English." In: *The Bell System Technical Journal* 30, 50–64.

Sinclair, John (1991): *Corpus, Concordance, Collocation.* Oxford: Oxford University Press.

Smith, Nathaniel/Levy, Roger (2013): "The effect of word predictability on reading time is logarithmic." In: *Cognition* 128, 302–319.

Siyanova–Chanturia, Anna/Conklin, Kathy/Schmitt, Norbert (2011): "Adding more fuel to the fire: an eye–tracking study of idiom processing by native and non–native speakers." In: *Second Language Research* 27, 251–272.

Speelman, Dirk/Heylen, Kris/Geeraerts, Dirk (Eds.) (2018): *Mixed–Effects Regression Models in Linguistics.* New York: Springer.

Underwood, Geoffrey/Schmitt, Norbert/Galpin, Adam (2004): "The eyes have it: An eye movement study into the processing of formulaic sequences." In: Norbert Schmitt (Ed.): *Formulaic Sequences. Acquisition, Processing and Use.* Amsterdam: John Benjamins, 153–172.

Winter, Bodo (2013): *Linear Models and Linear Mixed Effects Models in R with linguistic applications.* Online at: https://arxiv.org/pdf/1308.5499.pdf <01.10.2021>.

Wulff, Stefanie (2008): *Rethinking Idiomaticity.* London: Continuum.

Index